IMAGES
of America

AUSTIN'S
ROSEWOOD NEIGHBORHOOD

ON THE COVER: Rosewood is a historically African American neighborhood on the east side of Austin, Texas. It takes its name from Rosewood Avenue, which runs through the middle of the area. Rosewood was first settled by Europeans in the late 19th century, but beginning around the 1910s, the City of Austin adopted as official policy the goal of segregating African Americans in East Austin. The cover shows a classroom at Anderson High School, the school designated for African Americans beginning in the 19th century. The photograph illustrates that vocational classes played a critical role at Anderson, and that education played a critical role in Rosewood. (Courtesy of AHC, CO2689.)

IMAGES
of America

AUSTIN'S
ROSEWOOD NEIGHBORHOOD

Jane H. Rivera, PhD, and Gilberto C. Rivera

ARCADIA
PUBLISHING

ISBN 978-0-7385-9597-9

Published by Arcadia Publishing
Charleston, South Carolina

Printed in the United States of America

Library of Congress Control Number: 2012938755

For all general information, please contact Arcadia Publishing:
Telephone 843-853-2070
Fax 843-853-0044
E-mail sales@arcadiapublishing.com
For customer service and orders:
Toll-Free 1-888-313-2665

Visit us on the Internet at www.arcadiapublishing.com

This book is dedicated to our parents, who taught us to love and respect our neighbors.

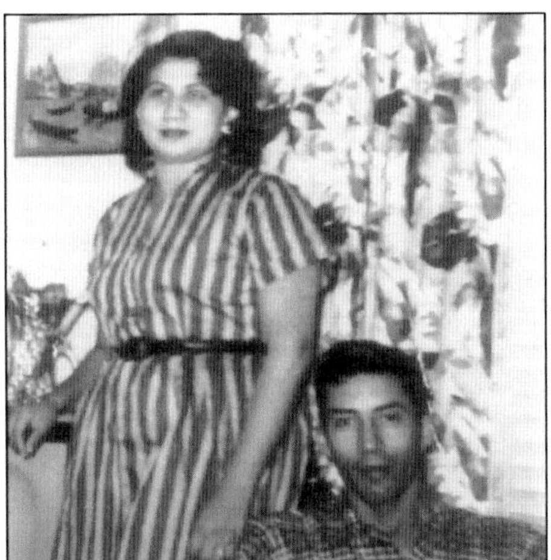

Ramon Garcia Rivera and Olivia Cortez Rivera, pictured in a 1950s photograph, are the parents of author Gilberto Cortez Rivera, who was born at home in Rosewood, in a house located where Conley-Guerrero Senior Center now sits. The midwife buried his umbilical cord in the backyard, and Ms. Rivera always said the cord tied him to the area, which is why he remains in Rosewood to this day. (Courtesy of Gilberto Cortez Rivera.)

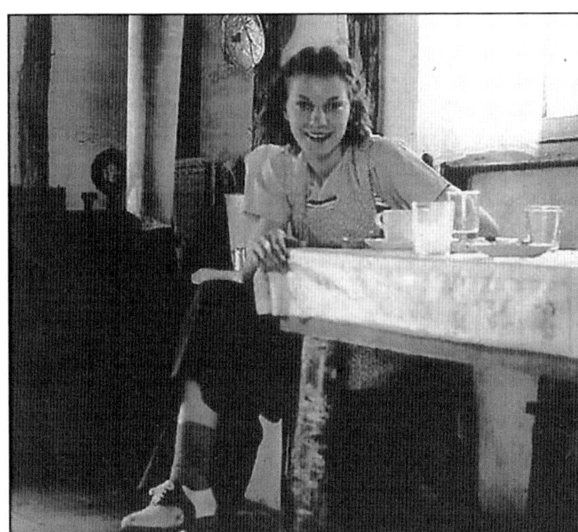

Vivian Josephine Bushong, mother of author Jane H. Rivera, is pictured at age 17, when she had just become a bride. Bushong's mother died when she was an infant, so during the Great Depression, she traveled widely with her father while he worked on road-building and other construction crews. (Courtesy of Jane H. Rivera.)

Contents

ACKNOWLEDGMENTS

We want to thank, first, all of our friends and neighbors who graciously contributed to this book and look forward to seeing their stories in print. We sincerely appreciate the guidance we received from Ora Houston and Rev. Dusty McCormick. We are also grateful for the assistance of the staff of the Austin History Center, the Booker T. Washington housing project, the Conley-Guerrero Senior Activity Center, the George Washington Carver Museum and Cultural Center, Huston-Tillotson University, and the Lyndon Baines Johnson Library and Museum for their assistance in identifying photographs that document Rosewood history and permitting us to use them in this book. Unless otherwise credited, all images in this book are from author Gilberto Rivera's personal collection. We also wish to thank our editors and mentors at Arcadia Publishing—Kristie Kelly, Lauren Hummer, and Laura Bruns—for their encouragement and guidance throughout the development process.

INTRODUCTION

Texas was one of the Southern states in which slavery was permitted. During Reconstruction, the period immediately following the defeat of the Confederacy in the Civil War, full rights were extended to former slaves. However, the news was slow in coming to Texas. Maj. George Granger arrived in Galveston on June 19, 1865, and issued General Order 3, which formally applied emancipation to Texas, two years after the fact. Emancipation Day, or Juneteenth, which celebrates the freeing of the slaves, was celebrated in Austin as early as 1900.

Austin passed an ordinance in 1906 requiring African Americans to enter public streetcars through the back door and sit in the rear. The African American community was outraged, and, when the city ignored their request to revoke the ordinance, began a boycott. Just like the bus boycott many years later in Montgomery, Alabama, African American owners of transportation gathered to offer rides to those who had depended on the streetcars. However, the institutionalization of segregation in Austin continued to escalate.

By 1928, the city council hired a Dallas firm to create the City of Austin Master Plan, which formally established East Austin as the residential area for African Americans. In the master plan, the authors noted that African Americans lived in all parts of the city, but east of East Avenue (present-day IH-35), the population was totally African American. The master plan recommended facilities and conveniences for African Americans be limited to the east side of the city, close to "the negro high school," acting as an incentive to draw them to the area. The plan stated, "This will eliminate the necessity of duplication of white and black schools, white and black parks, and other duplicate facilities for this area."

Local schools have been key institutions within Rosewood. The Austin Independent School District was founded in 1881, creating the Austin Colored High School eight years later. This school was moved and renamed Anderson High School in 1907 and moved twice more in 1913 and 1953, all within or very close to Rosewood. In 1971, seven years after the Civil Rights Act of 1964, US district judge Jack Roberts ordered the district to close all the African American schools and to integrate the African American students into other schools.

In the area of higher education, Huston-Tillotson University is a historically all-black college located near Rosewood that began as two separate colleges founded in the late 19th century to serve the African American population.

From the beginning, churches have been important to Rosewood's way of life, providing social and spiritual support to the area. David Chapel Missionary Baptist Church has been close to Rosewood since 1926 and in its current location since 1959; Mt. Zion Baptist Church moved to its current location in 1948; and Ebenezer Baptist Church moved to its current location in 1950. In the 1930s, the Austin Catholic Diocese moved the Mexican American parish—Our Lady of Guadalupe—near Rosewood, and parishioners followed their church. Holy Cross Catholic Church was founded in 1936 for African American Catholics in Rosewood and other East Austin neighborhoods.

One critical feature of early Rosewood was a vibrant African American business community. There were major business corridors on East Eleventh and Twelfth Streets and Rosewood Avenue. Local businesses included an array of neighborhood-serving establishments, including restaurants and barber and beauty shops. There was a very active nightlife at a number of locally owned clubs that featured live music, both local artists and famous African American entertainers from throughout the country. The business community benefited from a streetcar line operated by the Austin Rapid Transit Railway Company, chartered in 1890, which ended at the corner of Twelfth and Chicon Streets. By 1940, buses had replaced the trolley line.

In the late 1930s, African American homes near the railroad tracks in what is now the Homewood Heights area were condemned to make way for a new city incinerator. The incinerator burned trash, including hospital and slaughterhouse wastes, for the next 20 years. In 1957, the official Austin Development Plan recommended that, since most industrial development located within the city limits was in East Austin, any additional industrial development should also be in that part of the city. Such industrial development included manufacturing or processing such as slaughterhouses, utilities such as recycling plants or garbage dumps, wholesaling and warehousing, including gasoline storage tanks, and transportation such as railroads and railroad yards. Industrial zoning was overlaid on East Austin as a whole. As a result, private residences were also zoned industrial, which prevented homeowners from obtaining home improvement loans.

In 1933, paving began on East Avenue, a thoroughfare that ran north and south between then downtown and East Austin. At that time, the pavement extended north past the Eleventh and Twelfth Street corridors just west of Rosewood. In 1950, East Avenue was widened, and an overpass was constructed at Nineteenth Street (later renamed Martin Luther King Jr. Boulevard). East Avenue was being converted into a modern highway that was intended to connect to the national interstate highway system. By 1957, the interstate construction continued and East Avenue had become transformed into Interstate Highway 35. This major highway effectively divided East and West Austin.

In 1960, the school district opened Albert Sidney Johnston High School, east of Rosewood, to serve the white and Mexican American youth of East Austin. Johnston's student body was predominantly Mexican American, and it became a community center for Mexican Americans, just as Anderson was for African Americans.

The US Census of 1970 recorded that Austin was more segregated than at any other time in its history. Then University of Texas history major John Henneberger, now codirector of the Texas Low Income Information Service, was quoted in the *Daily Texan* on June 17, 1977, as saying, "Ninety-three percent of the black population would have to move into all-white neighborhoods to integrate the city." By the time of the Austin Housing Patterns Study, it was found that, "In the private sector, racial restrictions on property prohibited Blacks, and in some cases Mexican Americans, from buying or renting houses in most neighborhoods outside East Austin." In addition, the Housing Patterns Study noted that lending institutions had "red-lined" East Austin so that property owners were unable to obtain adequate loans to repair or expand their homes or businesses, since they were zoned industrial rather than being zoned in accordance with their use.

In 1975, the City of Austin applied for the first year of Community Development Block Grant (CDBG) funding from the US Department of Housing and Urban Development (HUD) to "eliminate blight" in Rosewood. In 1982, a city-funded development corporation built nine single-family homes just east of Rosewood on Oak Springs Drive—the first new single-family residence project in the area in over 20 years. The city then built five more such homes on Glen Oaks Drive in 1984, and 10 more on Glen Oaks Court in 1985 through CDBG grants to private builders. More individual homes were built by local residents, but there were no new single-family home subdivisions built in Rosewood until Green Doors, a private nonprofit, built six homes in Rosewood–Glen Oaks in 2007.

Current city policies encourage and even provide financial incentives to developers to construct buildings that include multi-family, high-density residential units mixed with retail units in central Austin, especially in less-developed areas such as East Austin. Numerous large private homes as well as dramatically large multi-family and multi-use structures were built throughout East Austin, including Rosewood, in the 2000s. As a result, the 2010 census documented a dramatic demographic shift in historic East Austin's population, including in Rosewood. From 2000 to 2010, there was a 27-percent decrease in African Americans, a 9.3-percent decrease in Hispanics, and a 40-percent increase in whites living in central East Austin.

In 2000, Austin Community College (ACC) opened the Eastview Campus on Webberville Road just east of Rosewood. The campus replaced the temporary ACC campus that had been located in the buildings of the former Anderson High School.

Rosewood has always been home to many active, outspoken people who worked to improve their community while maintaining its distinctiveness. At the Victory Grill dedication in 2010, Harold McMillan of Diverse Arts, an African American business, stated, "Jim Crow had a positive impact, in that it created strong and vital African American communities." This book will introduce some of the members of the strong and vital Rosewood community.

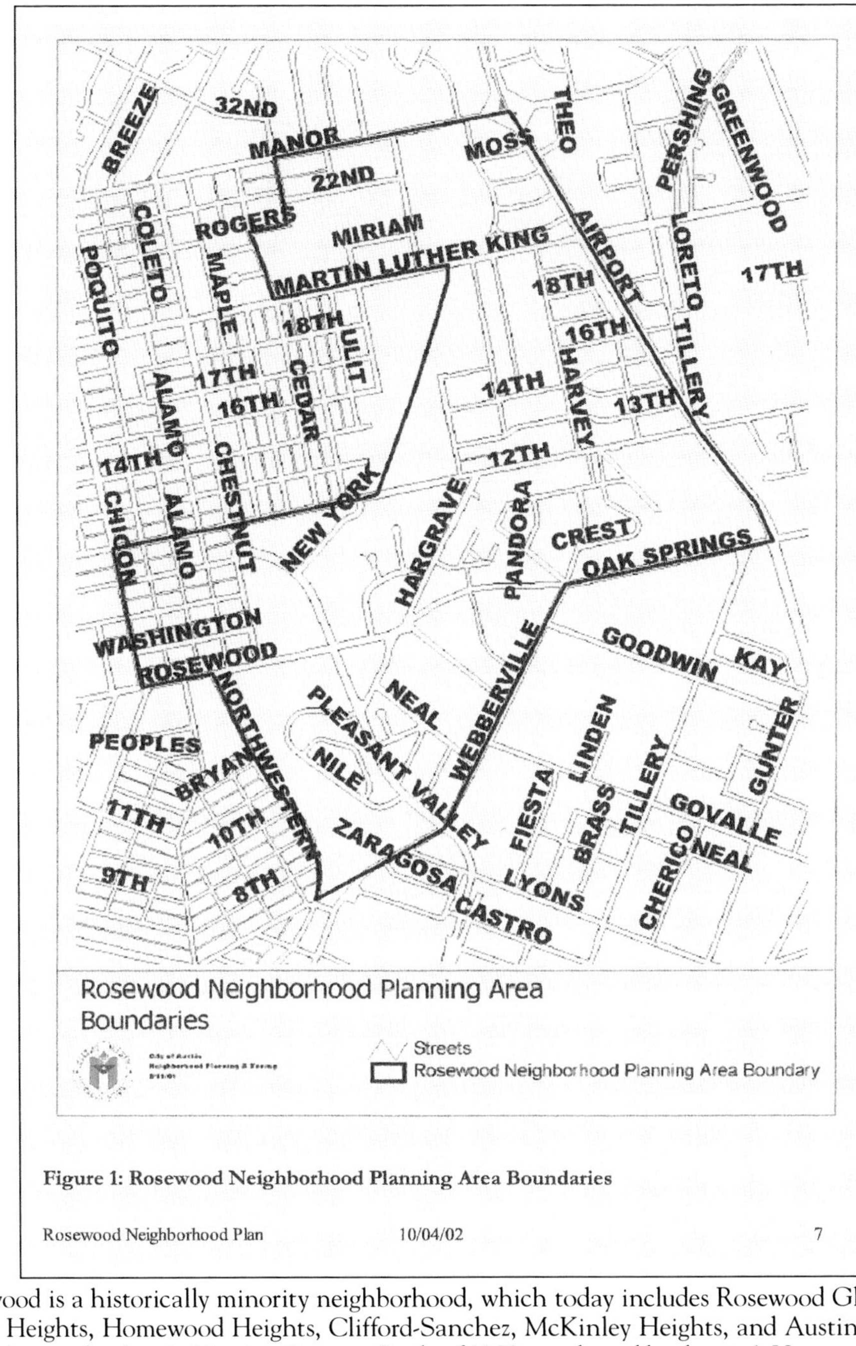

Rosewood is a historically minority neighborhood, which today includes Rosewood Glen Oaks, Foster Heights, Homewood Heights, Clifford-Sanchez, McKinley Heights, and Austin Heights. According to the Austin Housing Patterns Study of 1980, conducted by the city's Human Relations Commission, "Between 1910 and 1940, the City of Austin adopted as official policy the goal of segregating Black households in East Austin." This policy is critical to understanding the events that have shaped Rosewood and its proud residents. The current boundaries of the neighborhood were established by the City of Austin for its neighborhood planning effort in 1999, as shown in this map. This book includes people and events that affected Rosewood as well as residents and businesspeople of Rosewood itself. (Courtesy of City of Austin.)

One

Beginnings

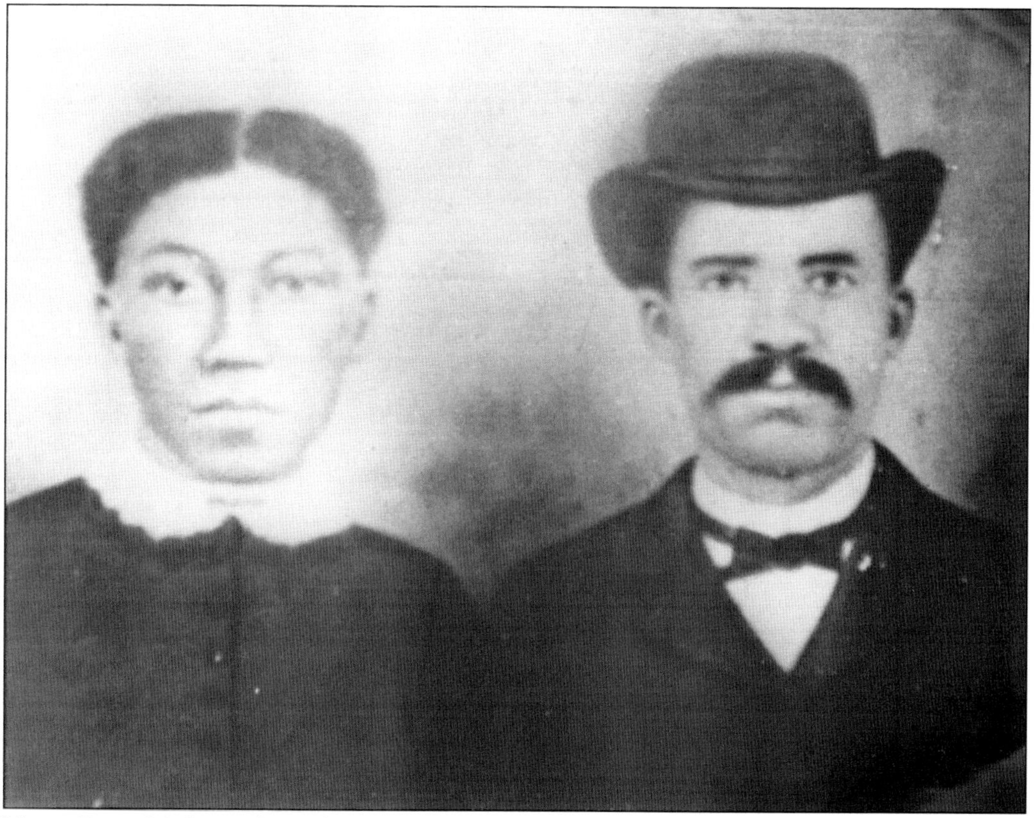

Henry Green Madison, shown here with his wife, Louise, was the first African American appointed to the governing body of Austin. He was tapped by Gov. E.J. Davis in 1871, during Reconstruction. William G. Wilson, Austin's second African American alderman, was also elected from a ward or district. (Courtesy of the AHC, PICB 09565.)

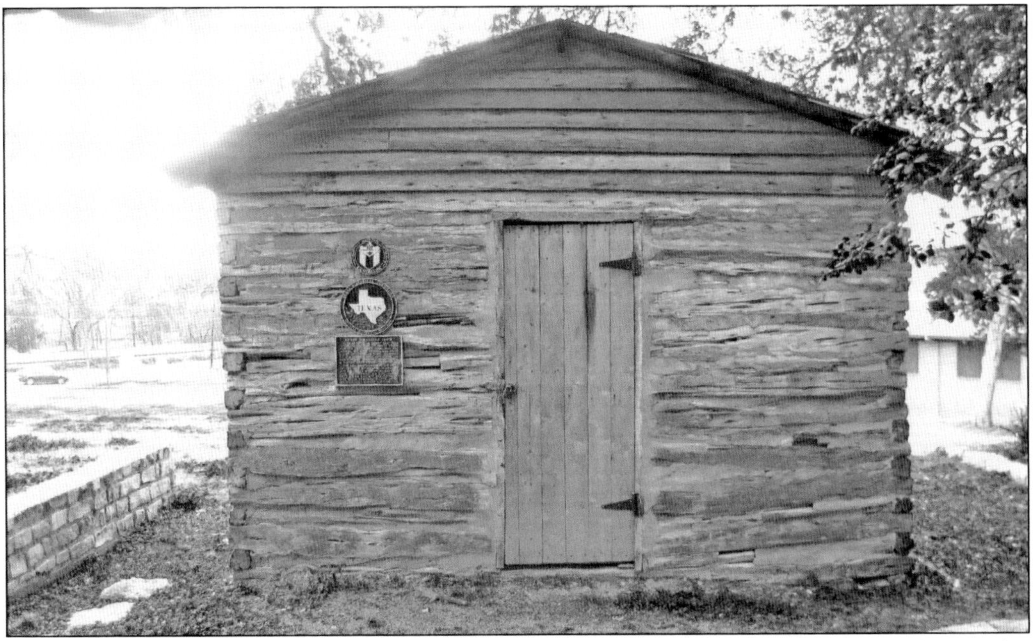

The Henry G. Madison Cabin was built around 1863 on East Eleventh Street. According to the historical plaque on the building, it was the ". . . homestead of Henry Green Madison (1843–1912), policeman and farmer, his wife Louise, and their eight children." The plaque does not note Mr. Madison's time on the city council. In 1886, Madison built a frame house enclosing the cabin, which kept it hidden until a razing crew found it in 1968. The log structure was donated to the City of Austin that year, dismantled, and reassembled on its current site in 1973 as an exhibit dedicated to the city's African American heritage.

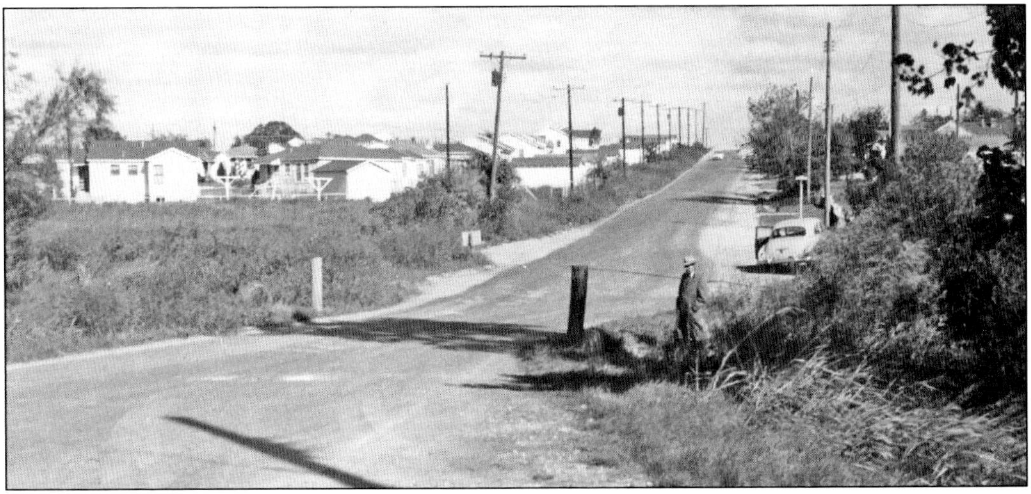

This is Martin Luther King Jr. Boulevard (then Nineteenth Street) in the 1930s. In 1903, the Austin City Directory listed streets for the first time, and in 1905, it listed streets in alphabetical order. The following Rosewood streets were listed in the 1905 directory: Alamo (with one family), New York (12 families), Pennsylvania (14 families), Poquita (now Poquito), Rosewood Avenue, and Washington (24 families). Although the numbered streets Twelfth through Nineteenth appeared in the 1905 directory, they extended only to the city limits just east of the area. (Courtesy of AHC, PICA 18079.)

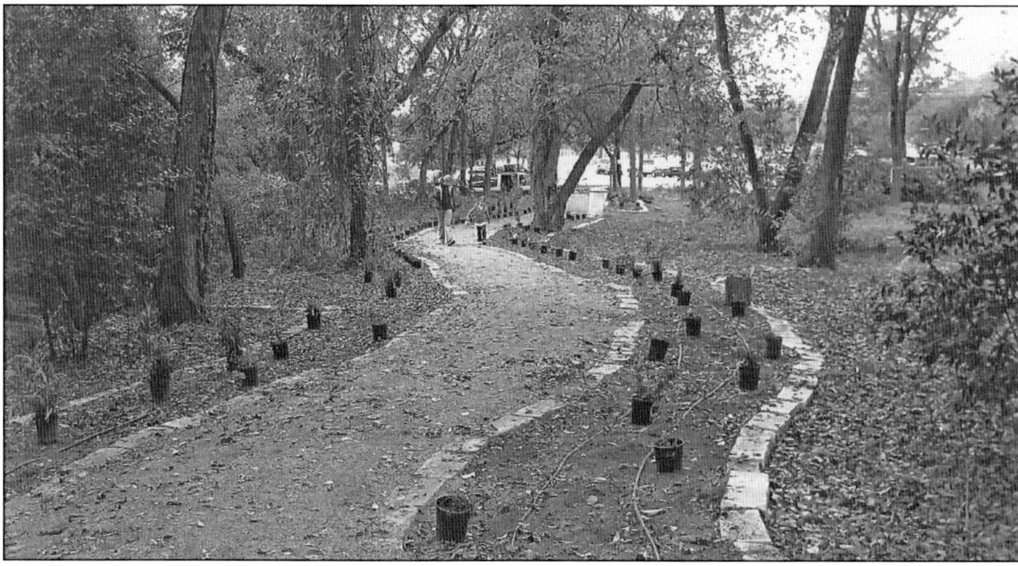

Webberville Road does not appear in the Austin City Directory until 1929. Author Gilberto Rivera recalls that Webberville was a dirt farm road even in the 1950s, when farmers used to drive wagons full of vegetables up the road. They took the vegetables to the artesian well, located at the current corner of Airport Boulevard and Oak Springs Drive, to wash them before sale. The well was capped by the city in the late 1950s or early 1960s.

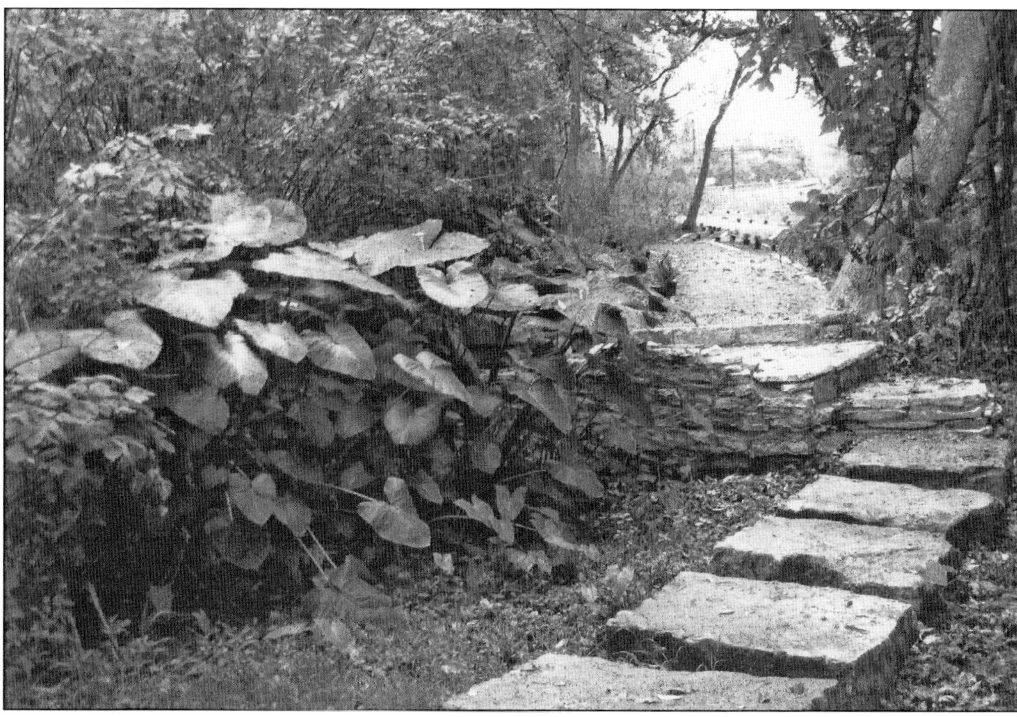

This photograph shows what the area looks like in 2009, following successful efforts by People Organized in Defense of Earth and Her Resources (PODER) and local neighbors to encourage the City of Austin to purchase the site and preserve it as a watershed. The photograph was taken following a major cleanup effort by volunteers organized by PODER and neighbors.

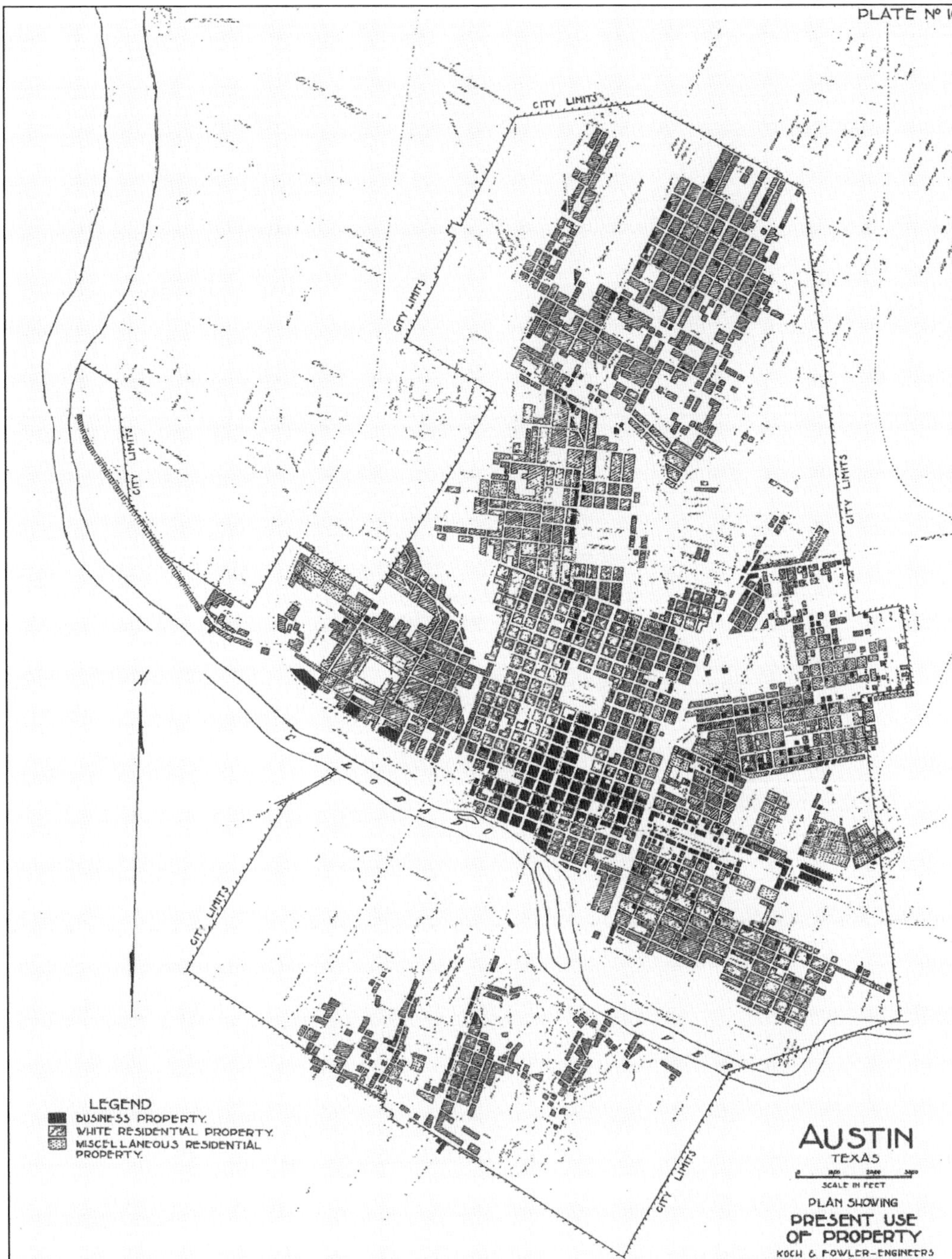

The City of Austin Master Plan of 1928 established a "Negro District," including Rosewood, east of what is now IH-35. The map shows residential segregation in Austin in 1927. The plan stated on page 377, "It is our recommendation that the nearest approach to the solution of the race segregation problem will be the recommendation of this district as a negro district; and that all facilities and conveniences be provided the negroes in this district as an incentive to draw the negro population to this area." (Courtesy of the City of Austin.)

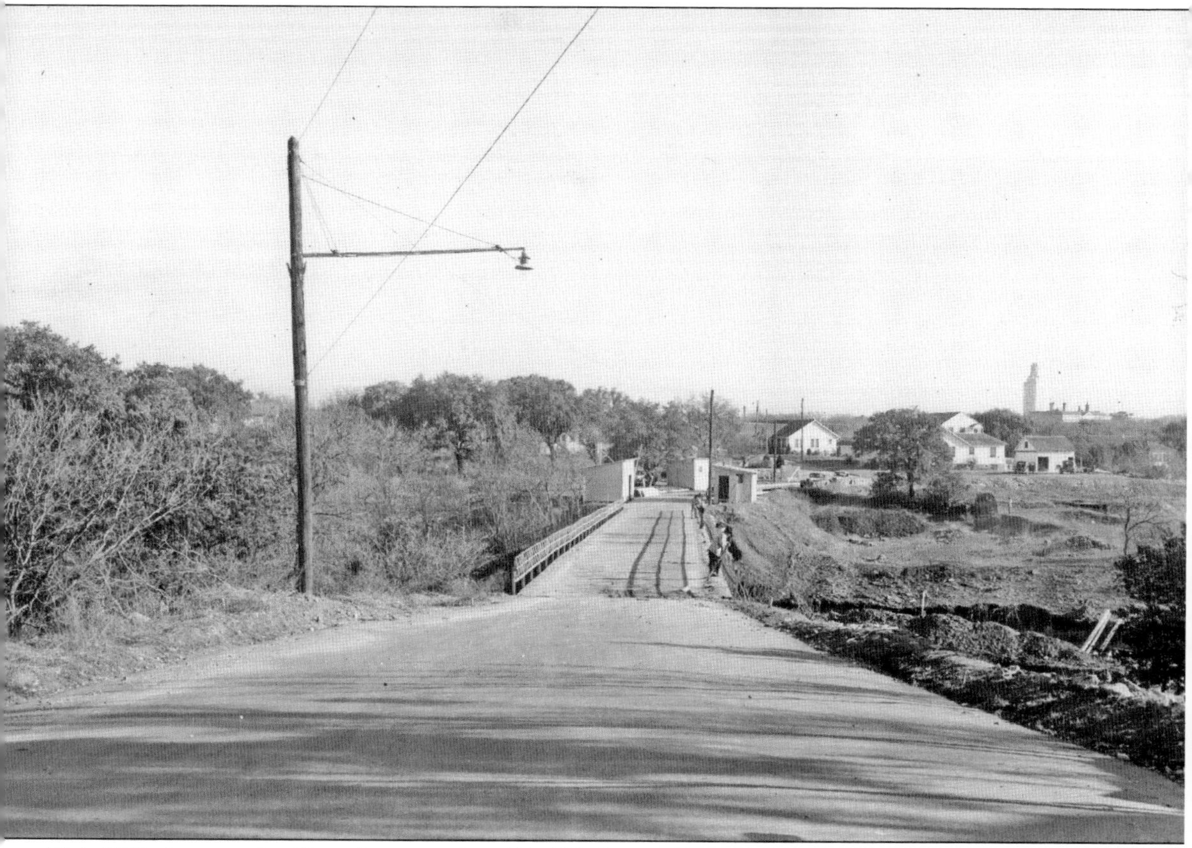

This 1930 photograph of East Avenue at East Twelfth Street shows what was to become Interregional Highway 35, or IH-35. Longtime East Austin residents call it the "Inter-racial Highway." The authors recall that when they were raising their children in Rosewood, no pizza delivery was available in all of East Austin. To order a pizza, one had to place an order by telephone and arrange delivery to the closest gas station on the west side of IH-35, then meet the delivery person to pick up the pizza. (Courtesy of AHC, CO2070.)

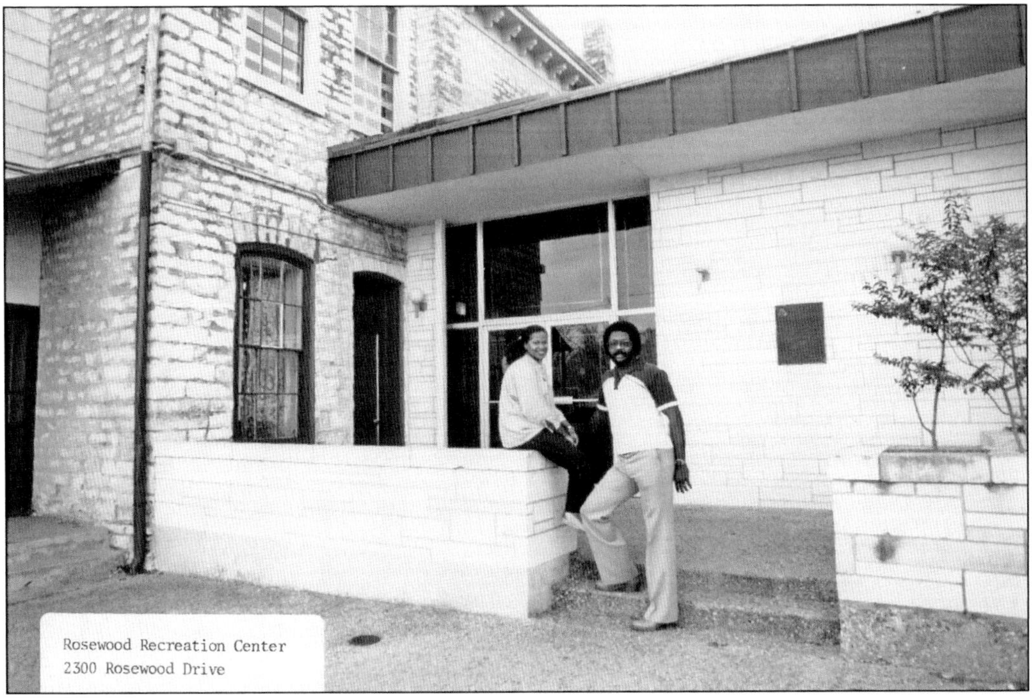

Rosewood Recreation Center was originally the home of Rudolph Bertram and his family and was later modified to serve as the recreation center. A year after the adoption of the 1928 Master Plan, the city dedicated the Rosewood Recreation Center and further developed it during the 1930s. The purpose of the recreation center was to provide a facility and recreational opportunities for the African American population. (Courtesy of AHC, PICA 18783.)

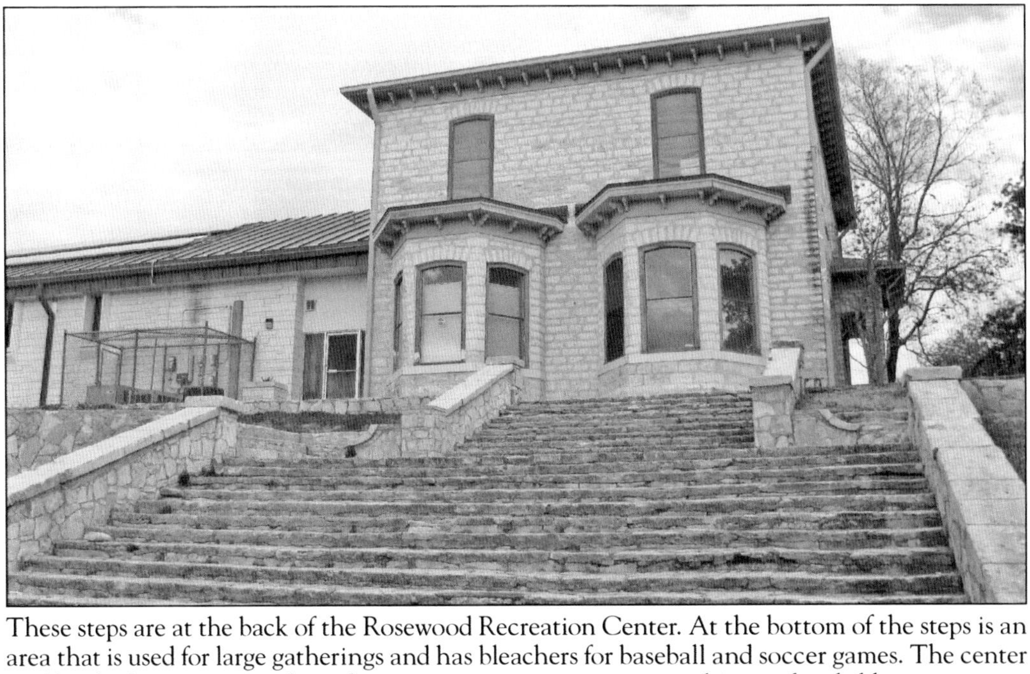

These steps are at the back of the Rosewood Recreation Center. At the bottom of the steps is an area that is used for large gatherings and has bleachers for baseball and soccer games. The center itself is the home to everything from senior activities to organized sports for children.

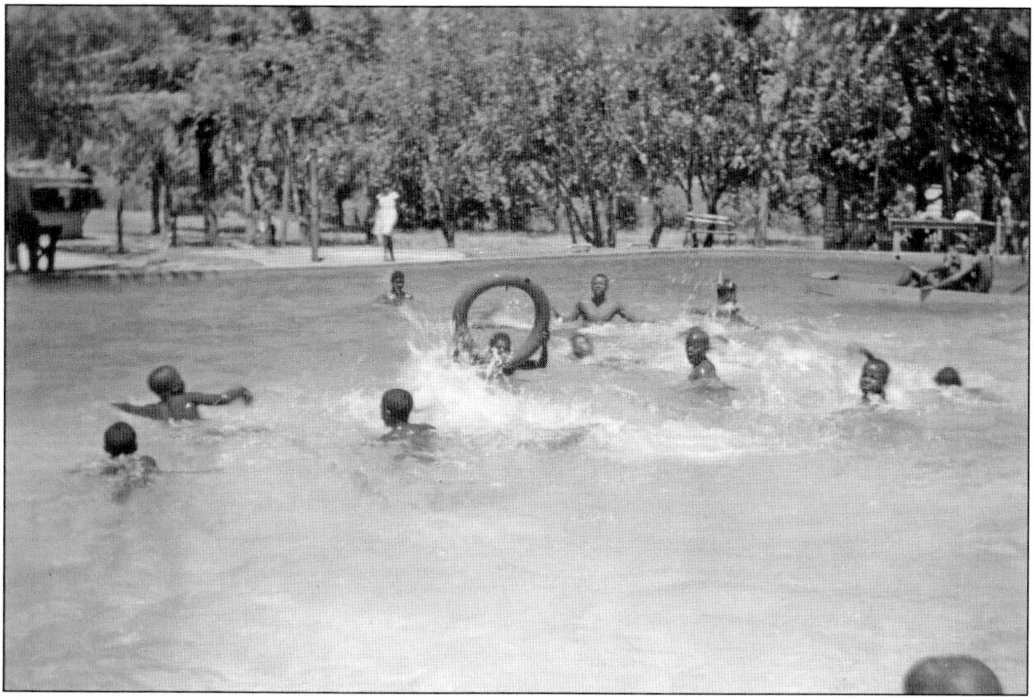

The notation on this photograph, taken on August 19, 1938, reads, "Austin Texas—Rosewood Park for Negroes. Intensive use of Swimming pool and other facilities demonstrates success of this recreation center." (Courtesy of AHC, PICA 24215.)

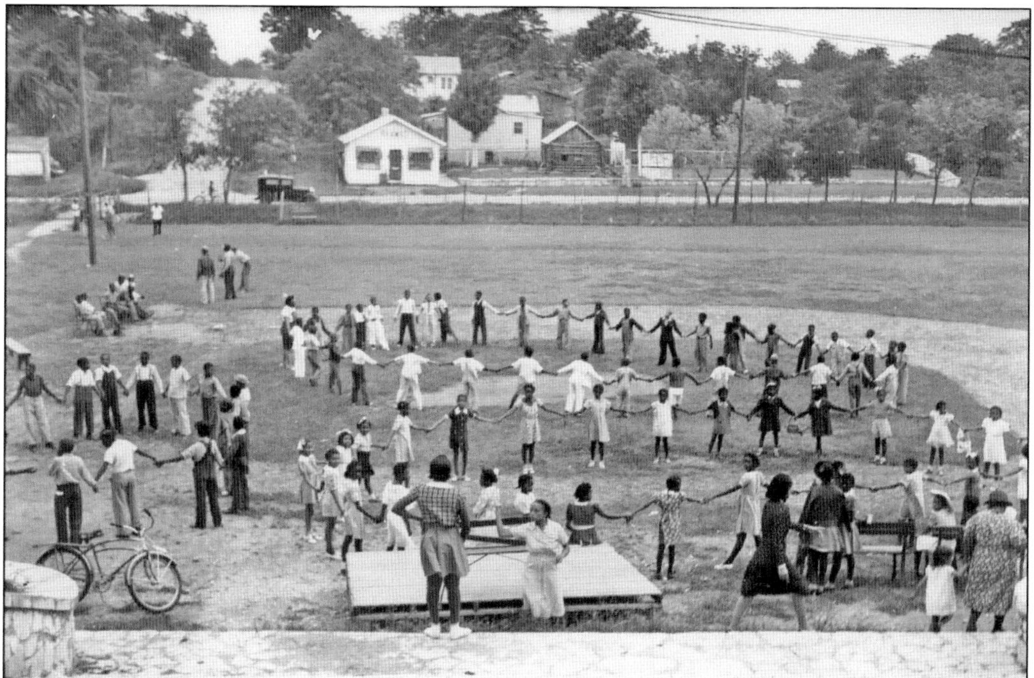

This photograph shows one of the organized children's activities at Rosewood Park. (Courtesy of AHC, PICA 24201.)

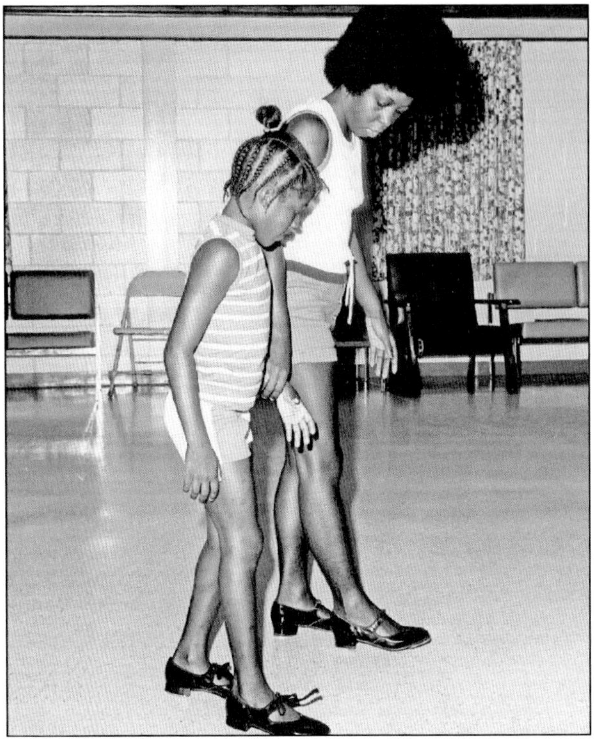

A young tap dance student is shown practicing at Rosewood Recreation Center. (Courtesy of AHC, PICA 24205.)

This old photograph highlights the bandstand at Rosewood Recreation Center. Well-known national African American entertainers performed on this stage at the close of World War II and through the 1950s. (Courtesy AHC, PICA 24212.)

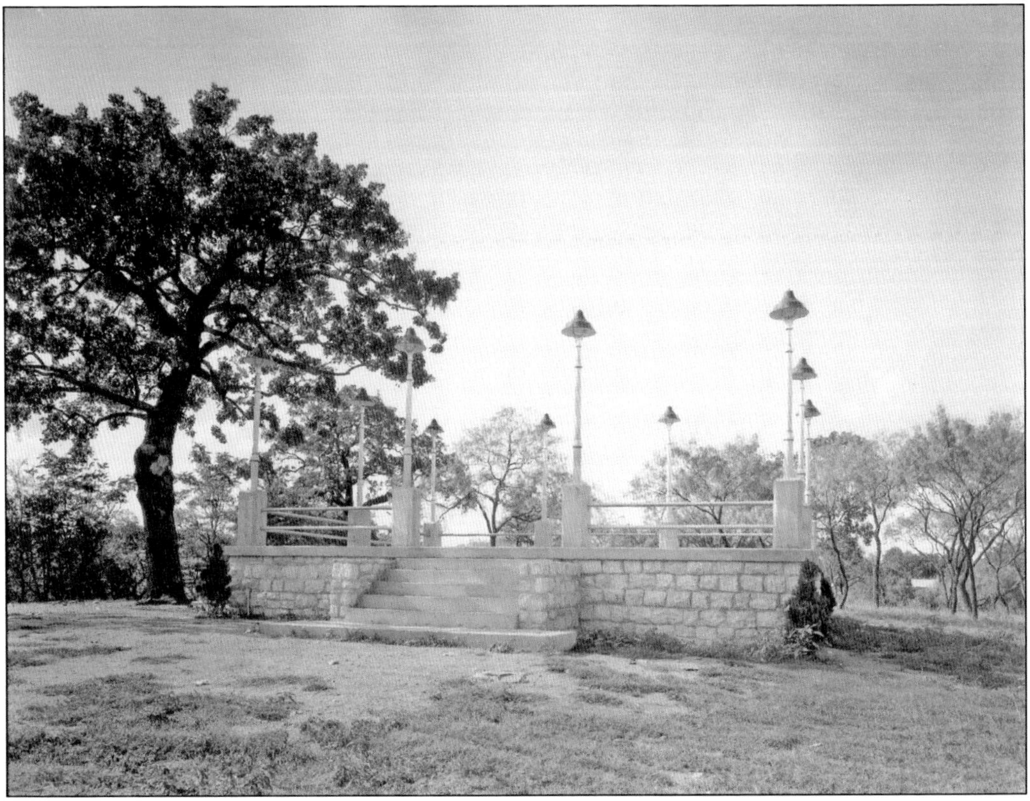

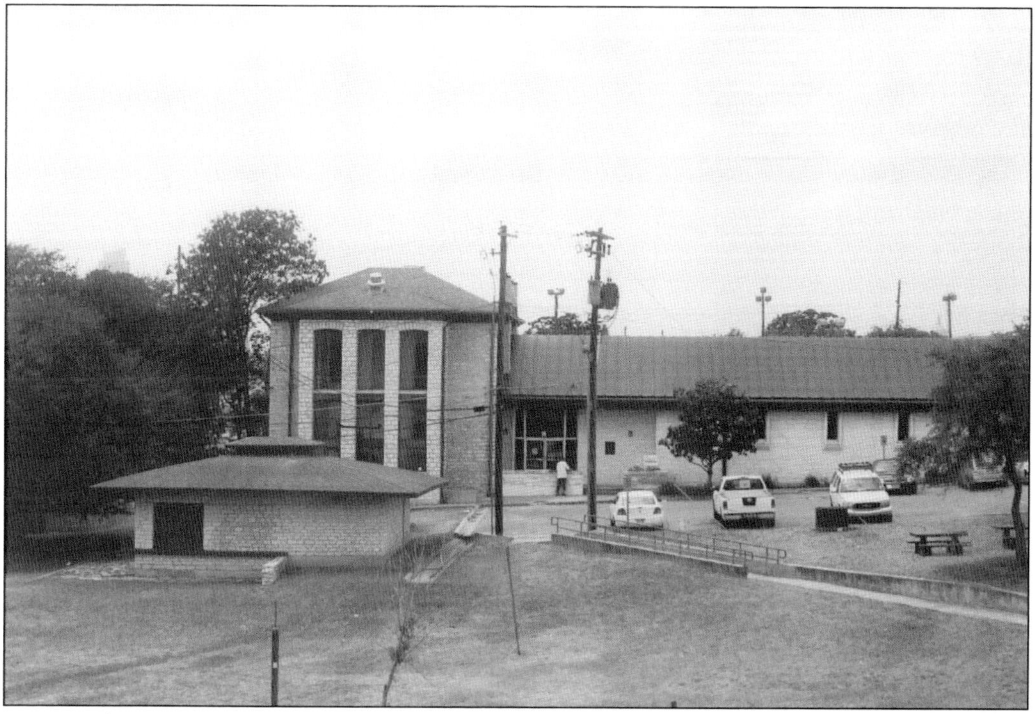

Rosewood Recreation Center is still a key institution in the community.

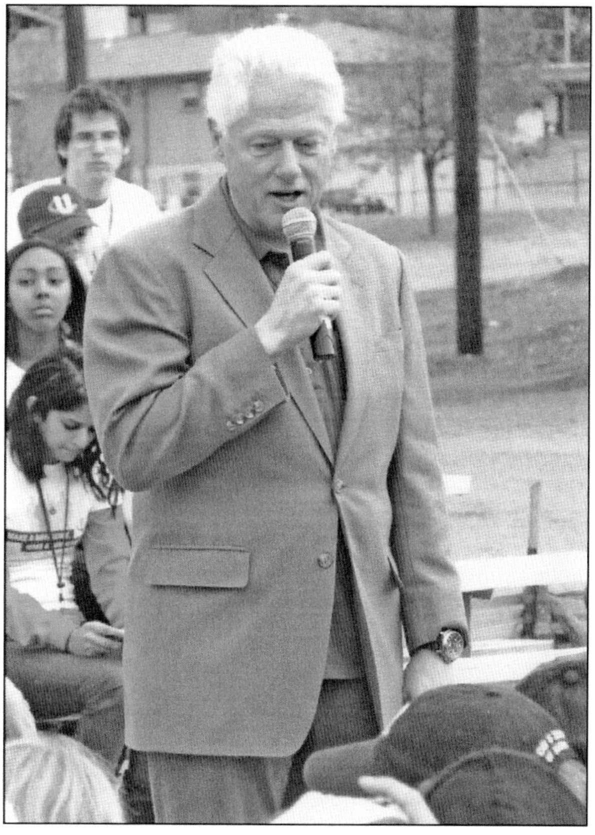

In 2009, the Clinton Global Initiative met at the Rosewood Recreation Center to organize a major University of Texas (UT) student project to help elderly, disabled, and poor Rosewood neighbors carry out a neighborhood-wide cleanup and improvement campaign. Pres. William Jefferson Clinton spoke to neighborhood residents and UT students at the center at the kickoff to the event, in which over 1,000 student volunteers participated.

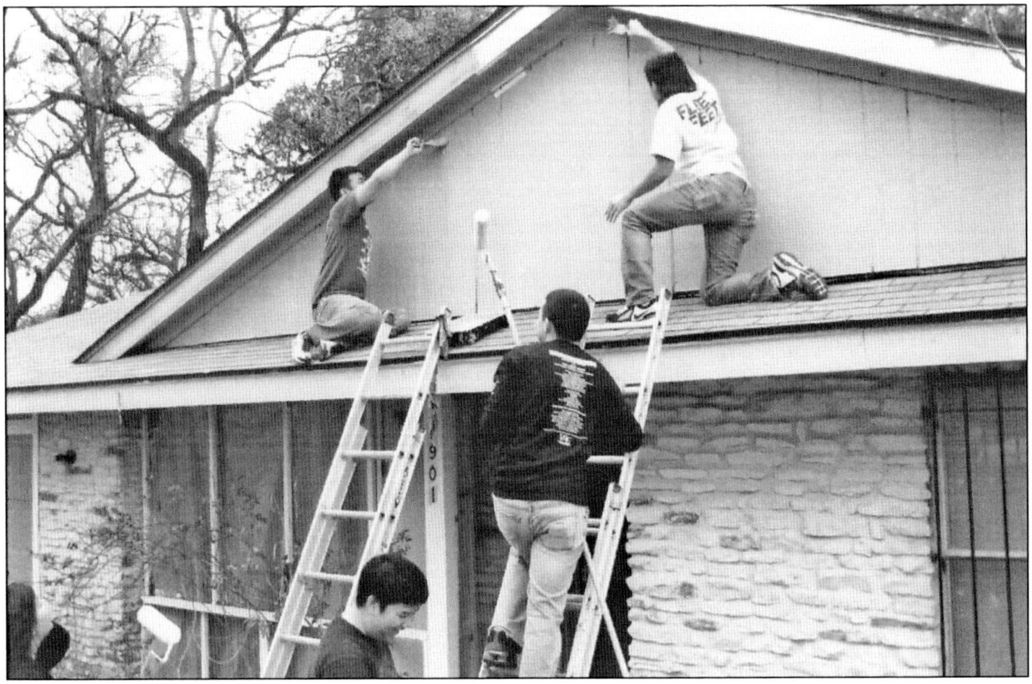

In the above photograph, student volunteers from the Clinton Global Initiative paint the exterior of Rosewood resident Tony Sanchez's home. Below, student volunteers who painted the exterior of Lee Thigpen's home pose for a group photograph.

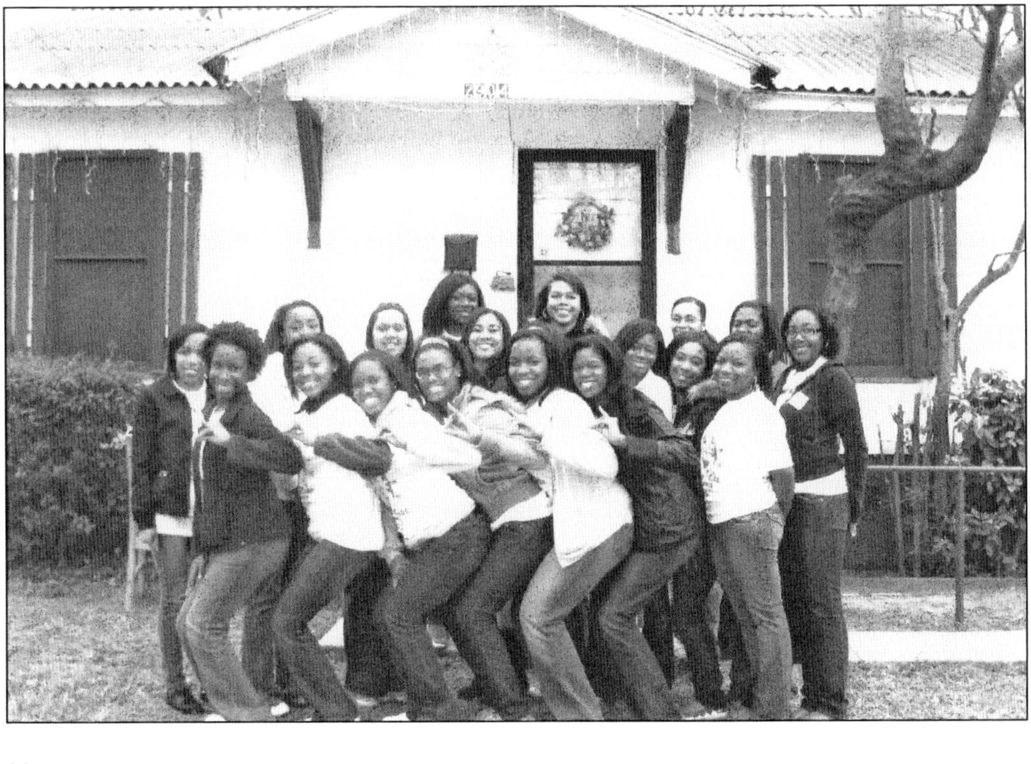

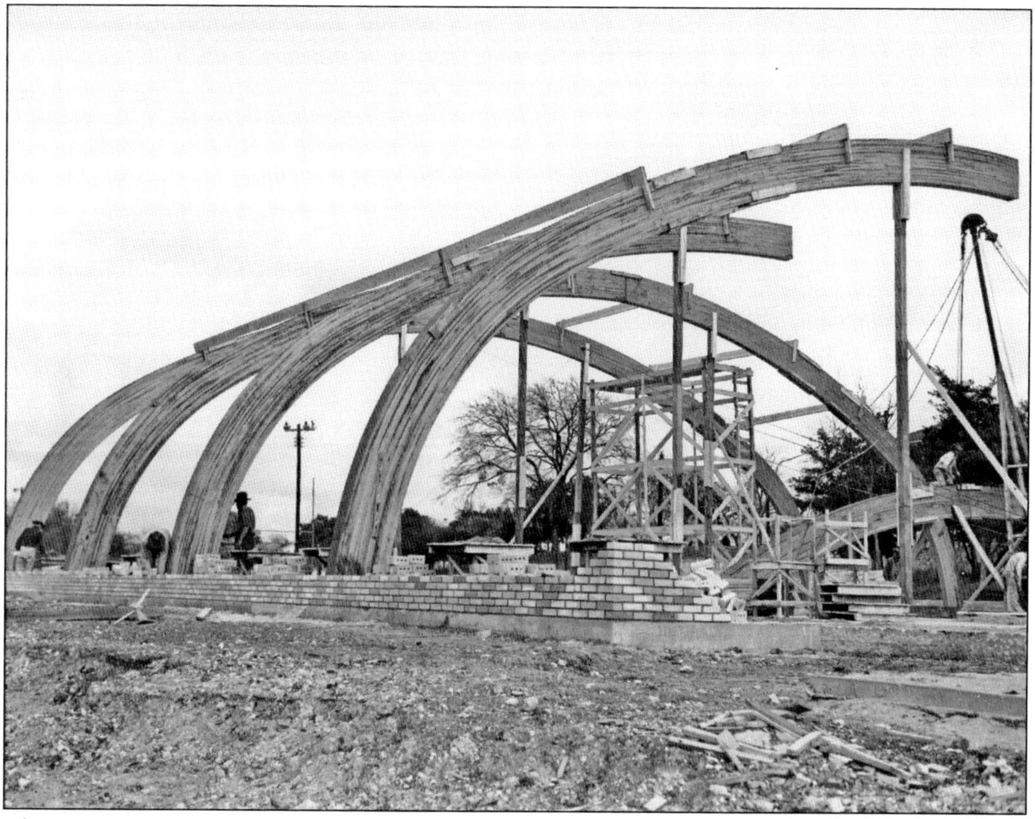

The Doris Miller Auditorium was dedicated to serving the recreational needs of local African American servicemen and their families during World War II. This photograph shows the building under construction. (Courtesy of AHC, PICA 24210.)

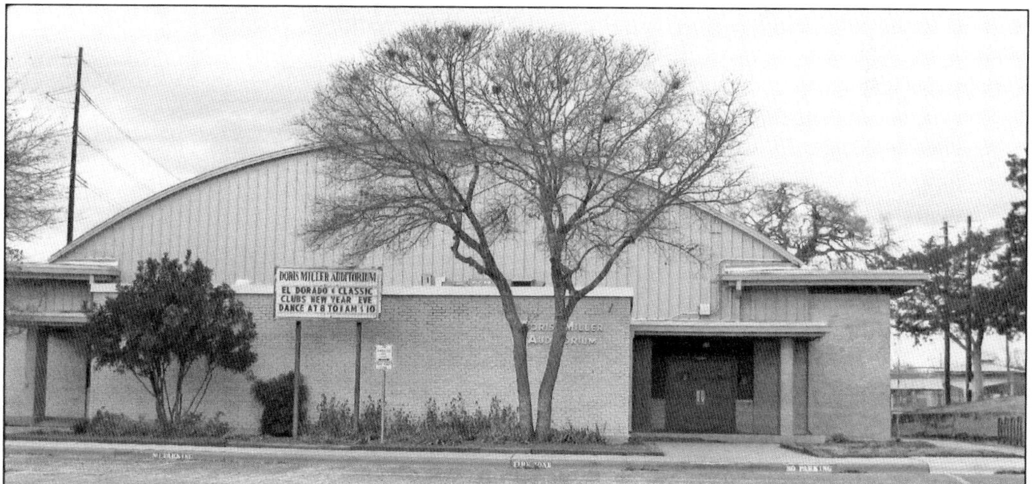

The Doris Miller Auditorium was named in honor of Doris "Dorie" Miller. Mr. Miller was born in Waco, Texas, and heroically lost his life serving in the US Navy during World War II. Mr. Miller was the first African American to be awarded the Navy Cross. He was played by actor Cuba Gooding Jr. in the 2001 movie *Pearl Harbor.*

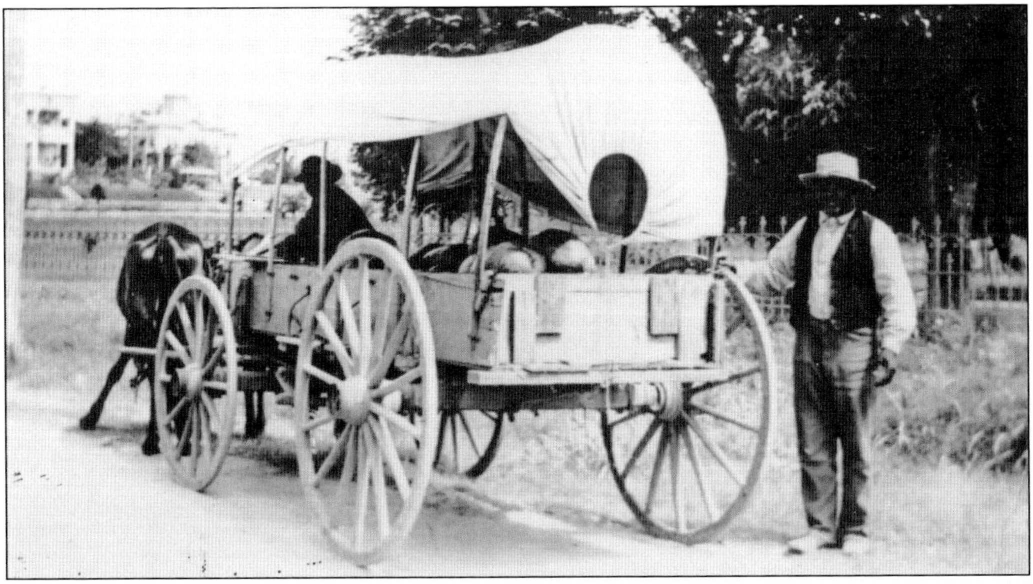

This photograph shows people on June 19, 1900, heading in their covered wagon to "East Woods" on East Twenty-fourth Street, where the official Emancipation Day celebration was to be held. June 19 was the day in 1865 when news of the Emancipation Proclamation reached Texas—two years after the fact. The exact location of the celebration has changed over the years, but whether it was Emancipation Park or Rosewood Park, Austin's major Emancipation Day, or Juneteenth, event has been in Rosewood for many years. (Courtesy of AHC, PICA 05483.)

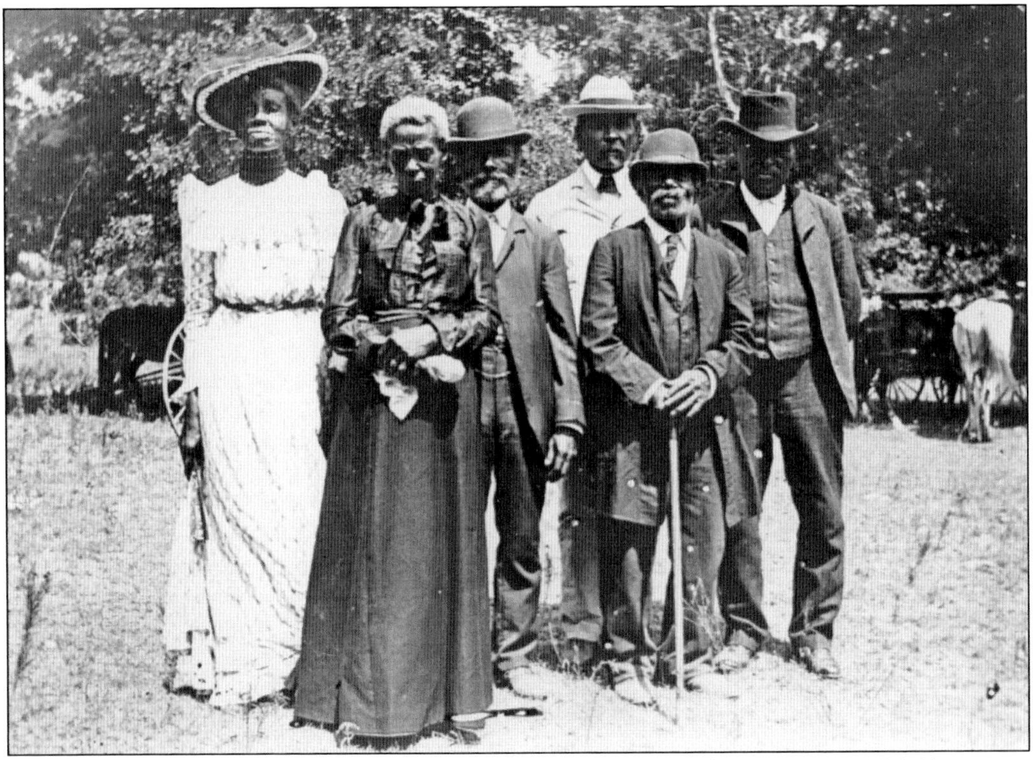

This image is from a Juneteenth celebration in 1900. (Courtesy of AHC, PICA 05476.)

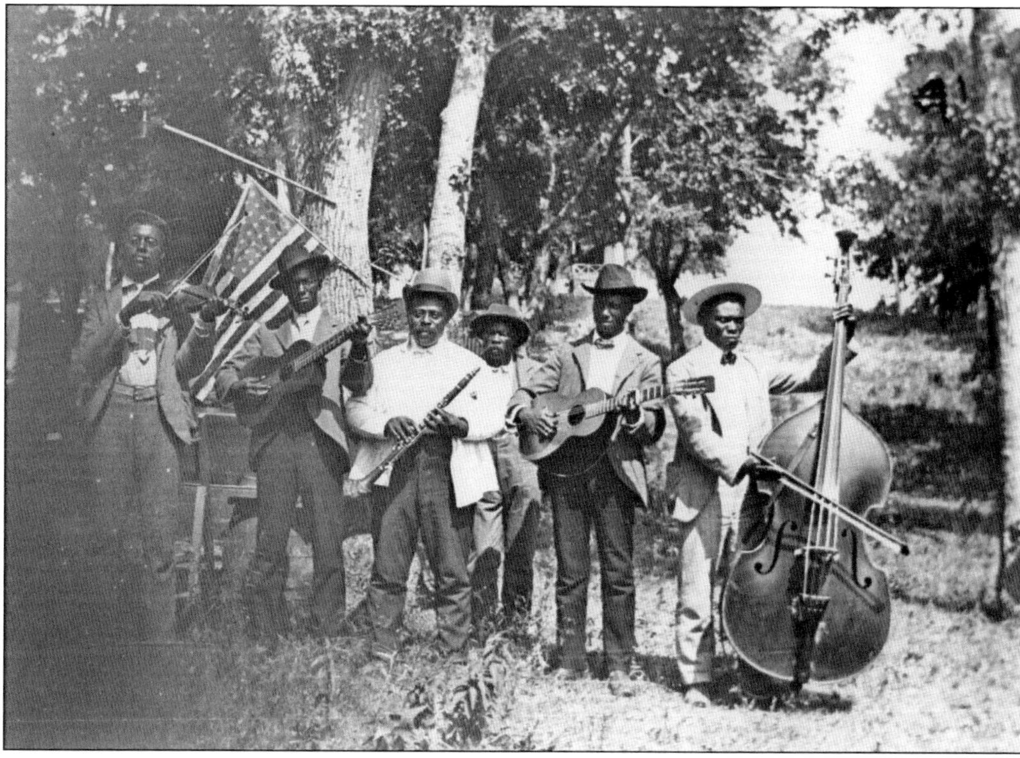

This band played at the 1900 Juneteenth celebration. (Courtesy of AHC, PICA 05481.)

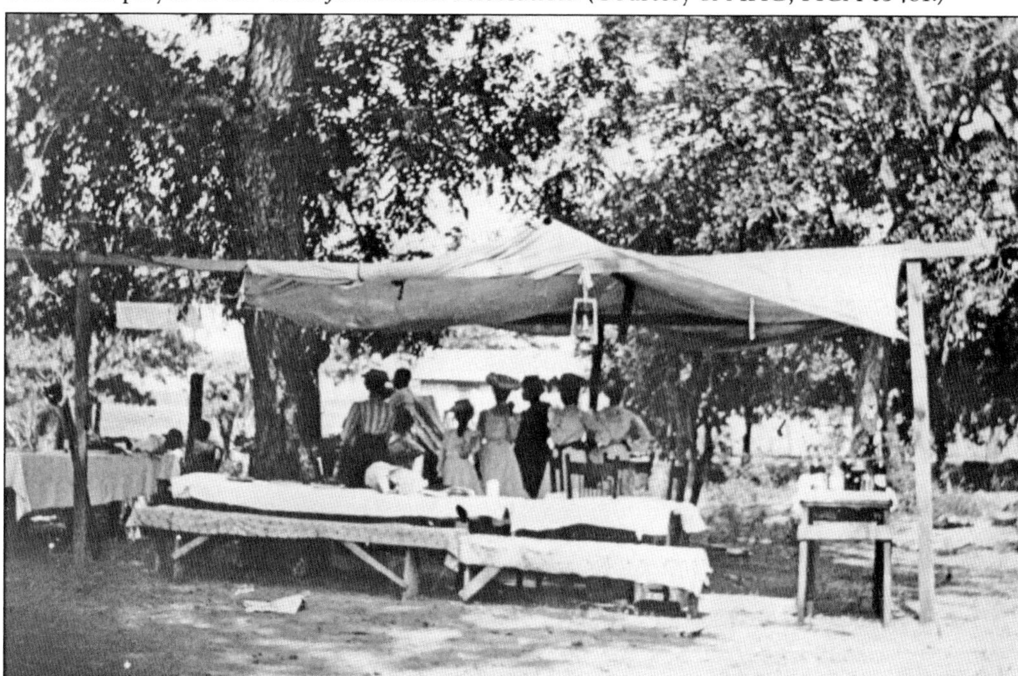

This picnic tent was set up by people celebrating Juneteenth in 1900. (Courtesy of AHC, PICA 05477.)

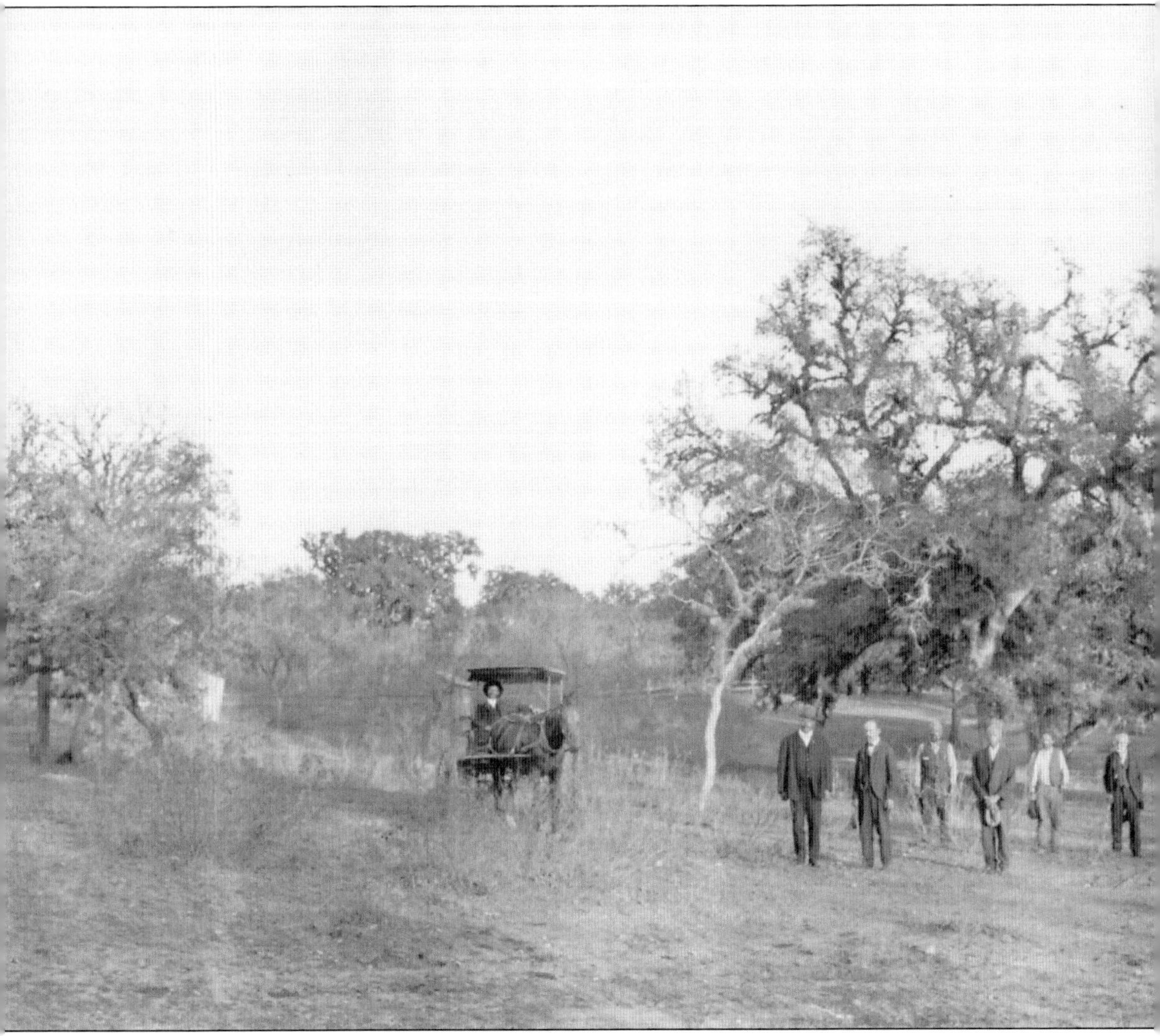

Frank Strain, his wife and five children lived in a house on New York Avenue in Foster Heights, Rosewood, in the late 1800s. Mr. Strain was the oldest son of Mahala Murchison, who has often been said to be the first African American resident of Austin. Recent research has found that there were, however, several hundred African Americans living in the Austin area in the mid-1800s,

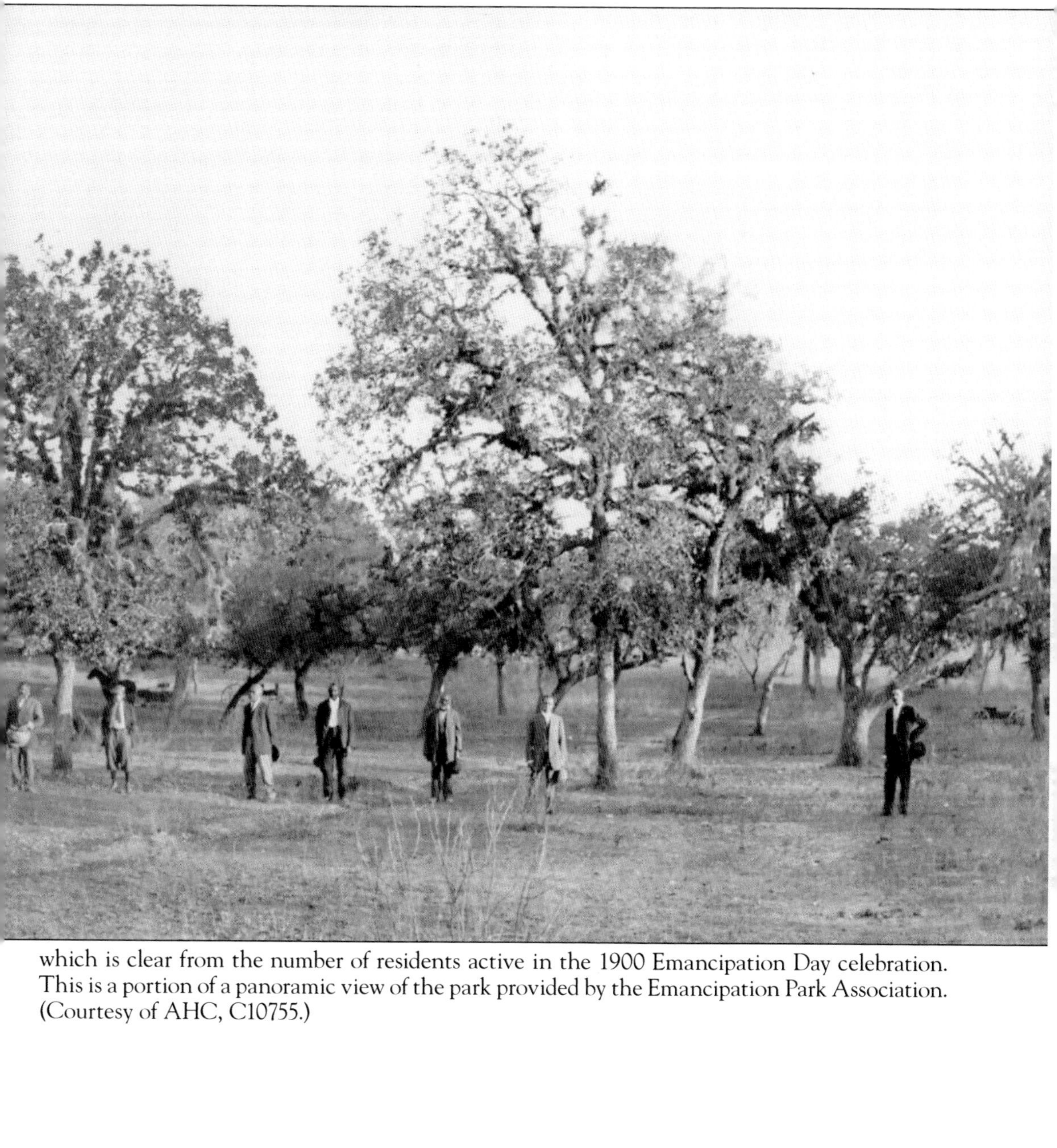

which is clear from the number of residents active in the 1900 Emancipation Day celebration. This is a portion of a panoramic view of the park provided by the Emancipation Park Association. (Courtesy of AHC, C10755.)

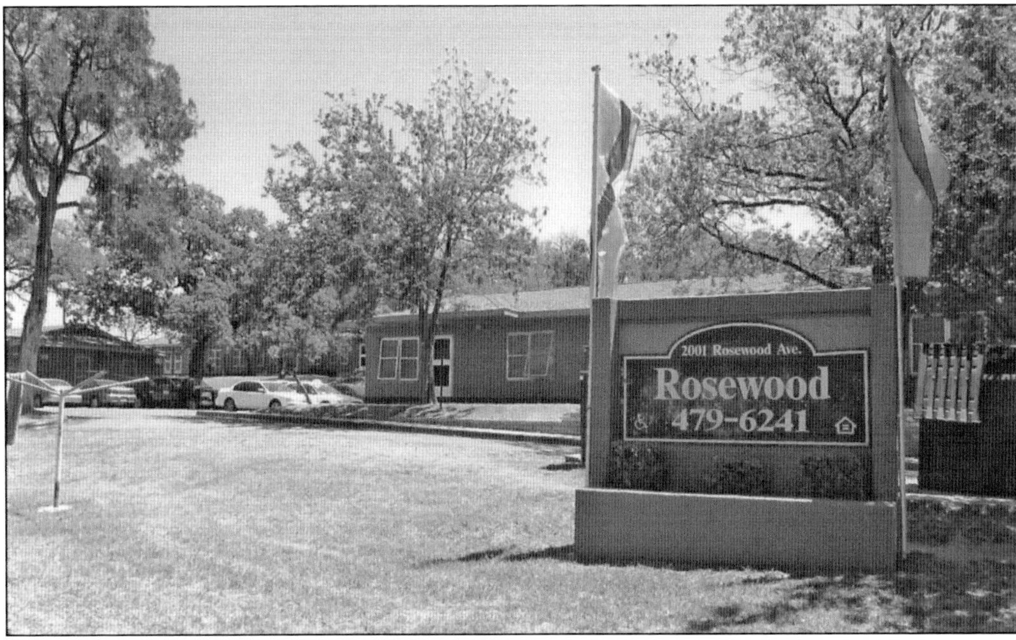

Some long-time Rosewood residents have different remembrances of the location of Emancipation Park. Some say it was located on what became the site of the Rosewood Project, the first housing by the City of Austin for low-income African Americans. Other Rosewood residents recall that Emancipation Park was located just east of present-day Downs Field on 12th Street. It is possible that the location actually changed over the years, since Rosewood Park itself has been the site of Juneteenth celebrations for several decades.

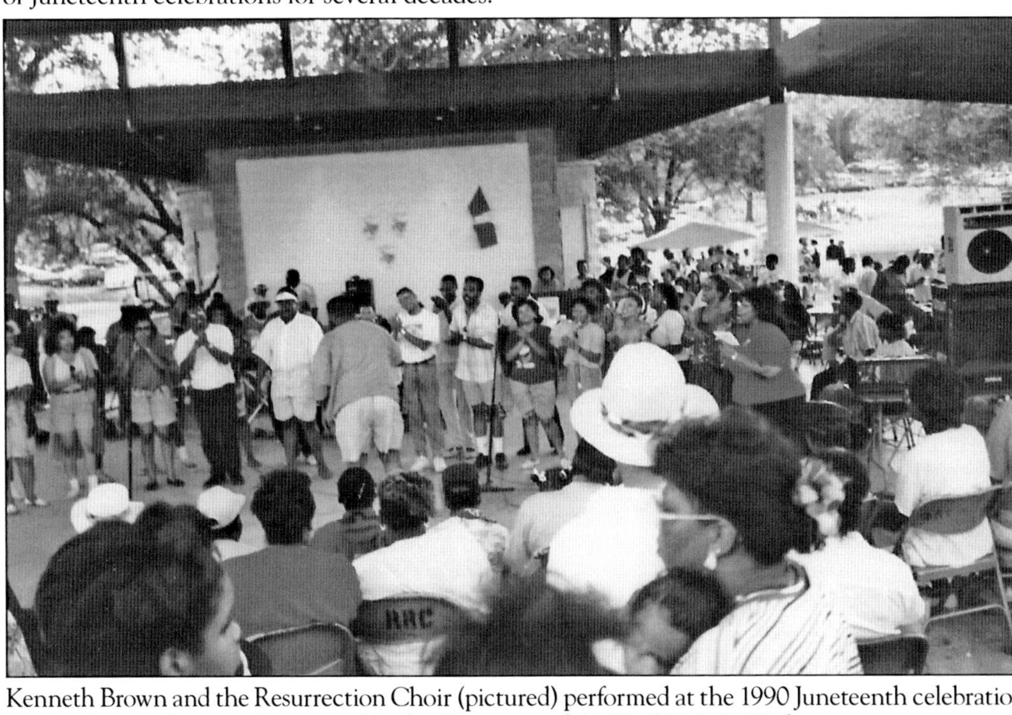

Kenneth Brown and the Resurrection Choir (pictured) performed at the 1990 Juneteenth celebration on the Gospel Stage in Rosewood Park. (Courtesy of AHC, PICA 28601.)

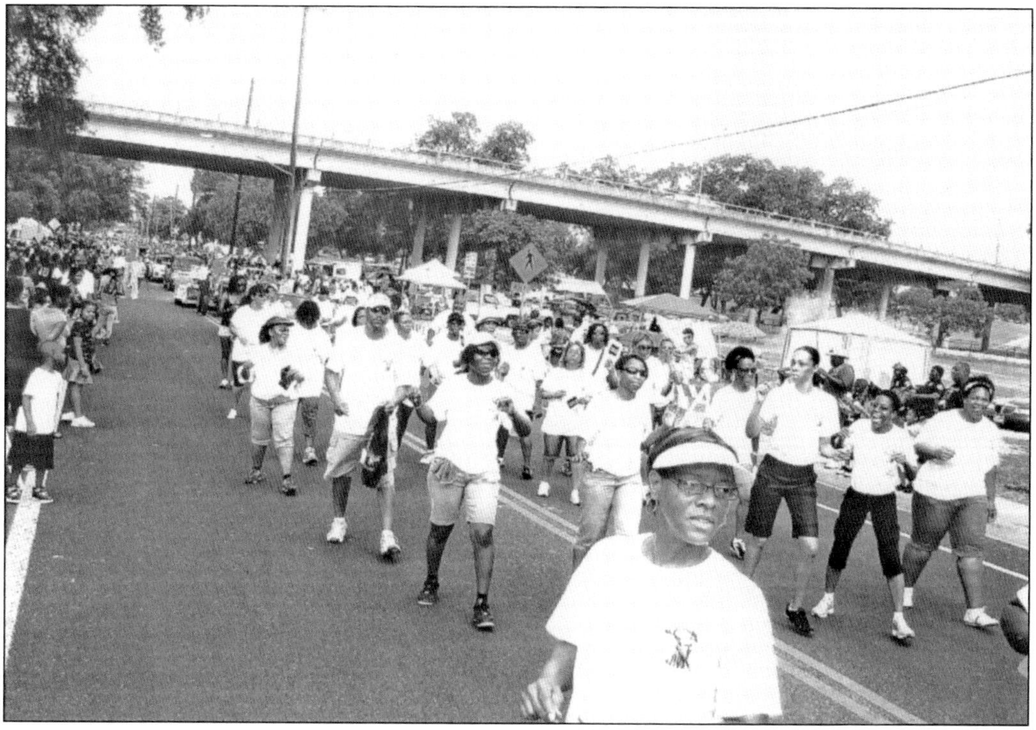

Participants in the Emancipation Day parade of 2010 prepare to enter Rosewood Park.

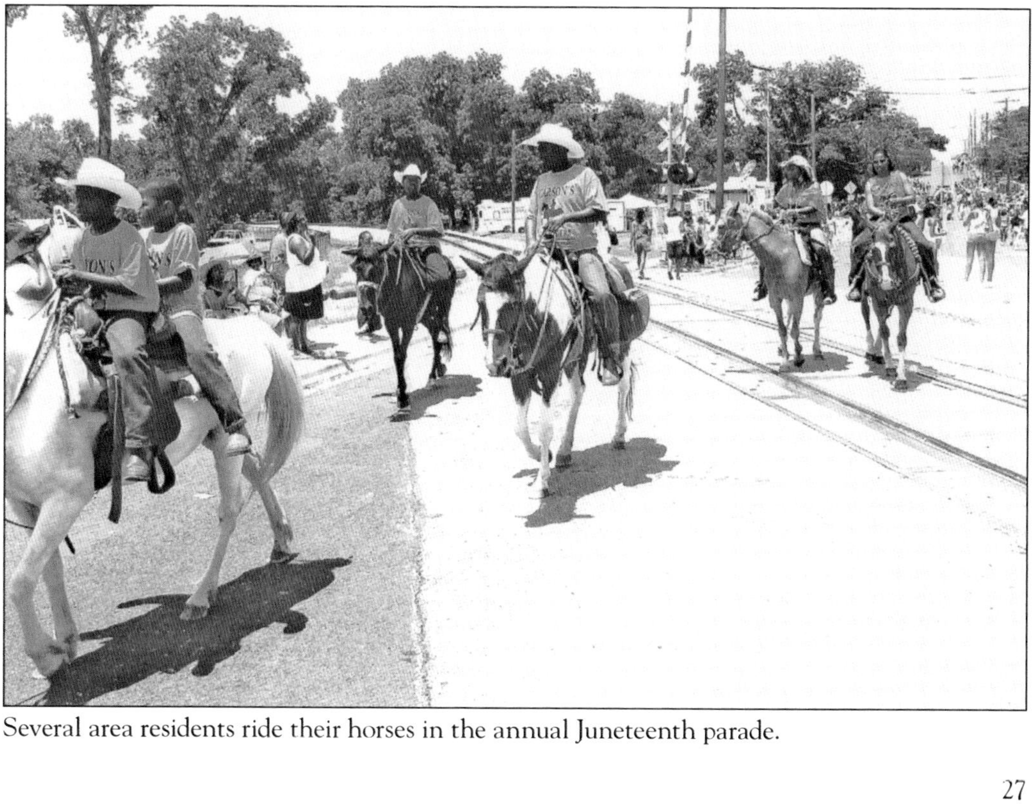

Several area residents ride their horses in the annual Juneteenth parade.

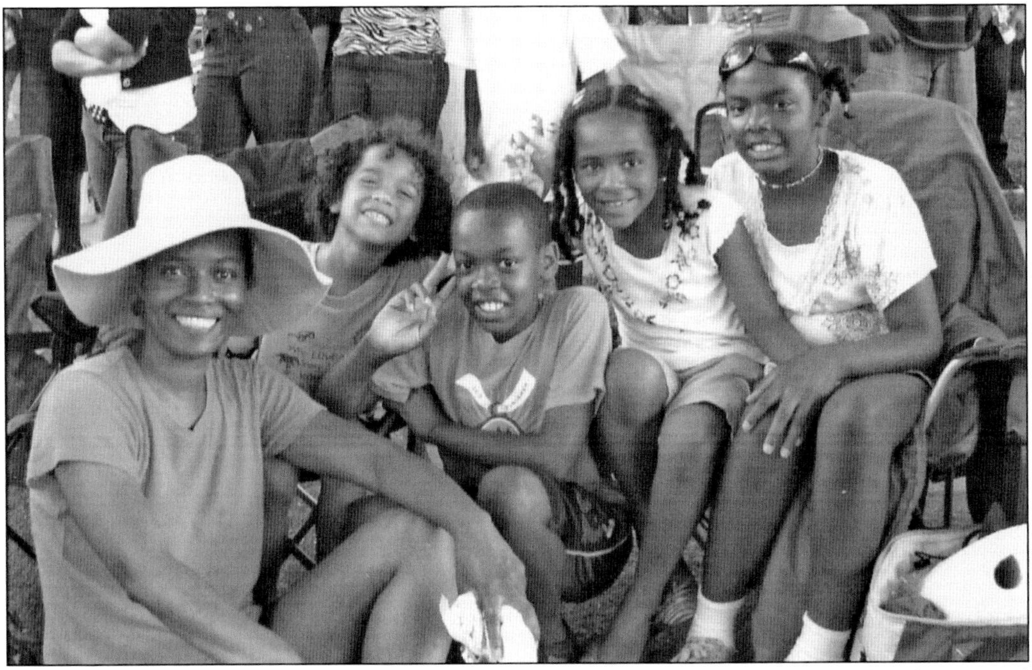

Denise Bunton and her family enjoy the 2010 Juneteenth celebration in Rosewood Park. Pictured here are, from left to right, Denise, Jordan, Aubrey, Alliyah, and Angel Bunton.

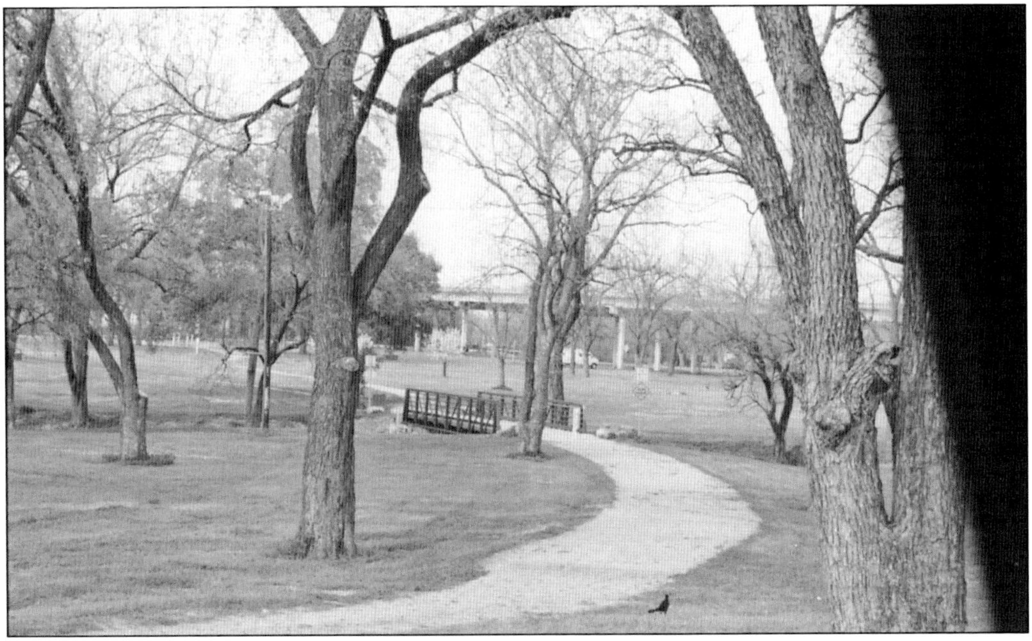

The city purchased the 17-acre Bertram-Huppertz farm sometime between 1875 and 1929. The parcel included what are now the Boggy Creek greenbelt and Rosewood Park. Lifelong resident Willie Simmons remembers raiding peach and plum trees along Nile Street and playing in Boggy Creek in his youth, when the area was still quite rural. The greenbelt remains a defining feature of Rosewood, paralleling Boggy Creek from northeast to southwest through the neighborhood. This is a portion of the trail in the greenbelt.

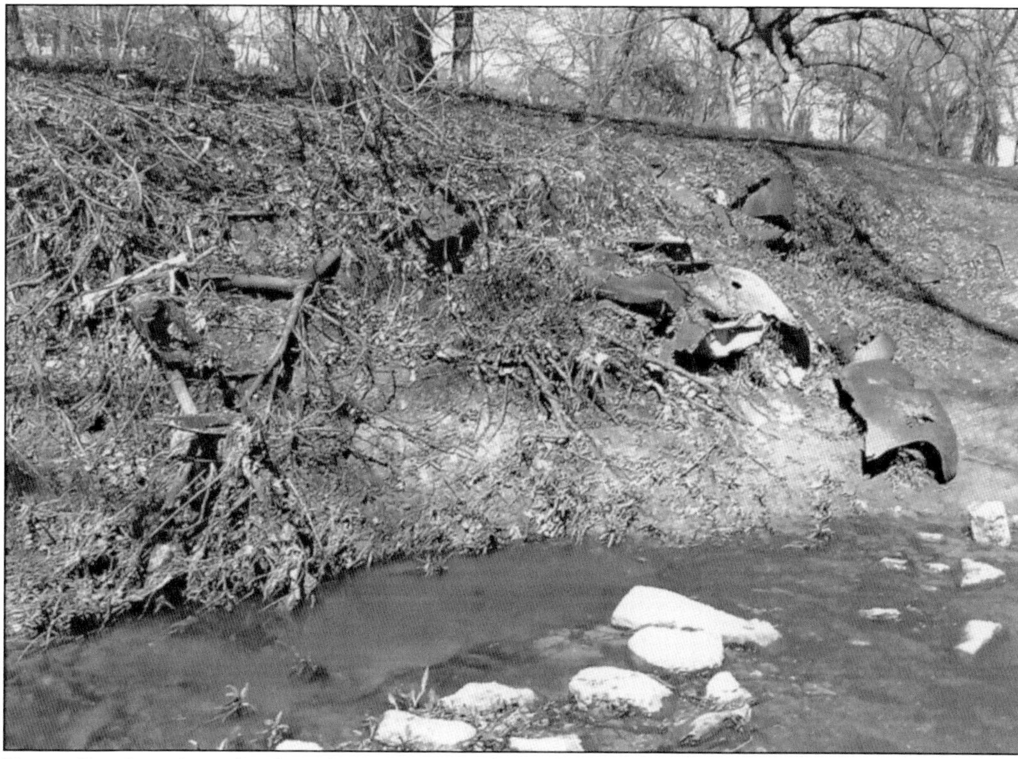

Boggy Creek and much of southern Rosewood was the site of the city dump during the early part of the 20th century. The dump was still being maintained when James Stewart of Nile Street was young. He remembered that he and his friends would pick out the metal and take it to metal scrappers. It was no longer used as a dump by the time the Hargrave Ranch was subdivided. Rusted car parts from the 1920s and 1930s can still be found in the bed of the creek.

Boggy Creek, like other creeks in Austin, was filled with sewage pipes for the city's sanitation system. The pipes were decommissioned several years ago, but will remain in place until the Austin Clean Water Project is completed around 2014.

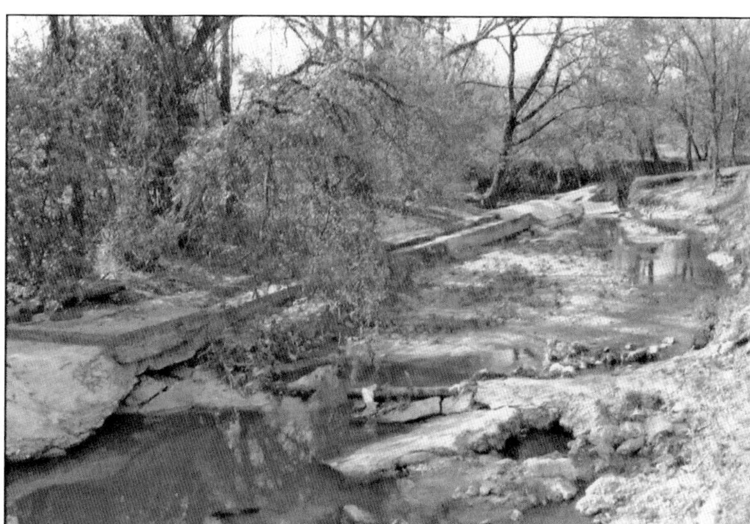

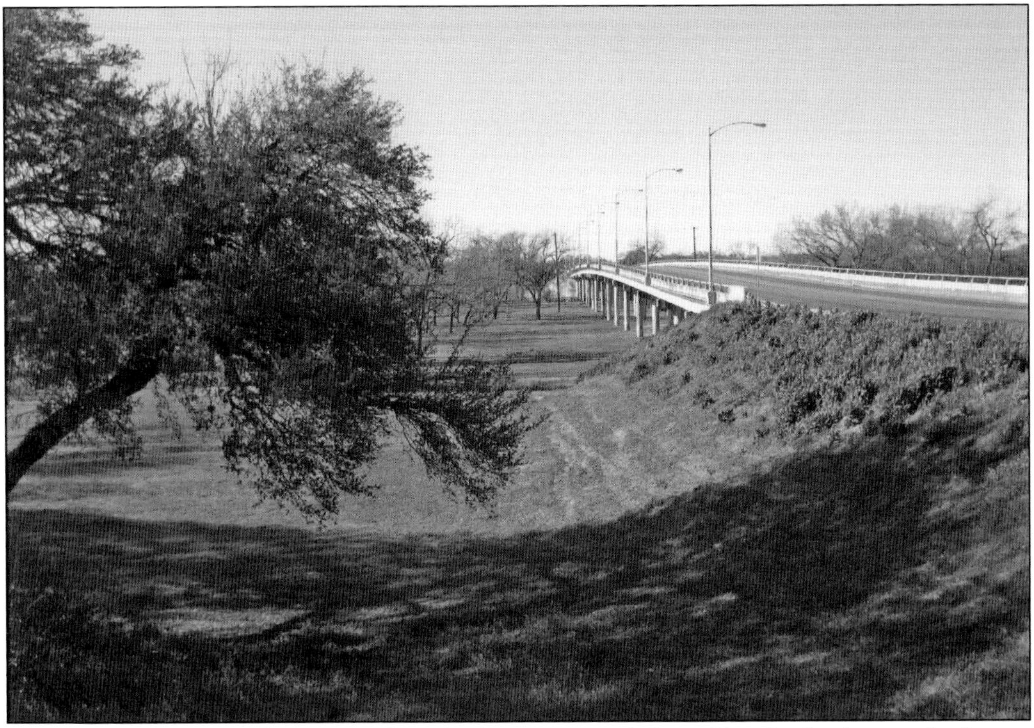

When the city began urban renewal in the late 1960s and the 1970s, this bridge was built over both Boggy Creek and Rosewood Avenue, effectively dividing the neighborhood and paving the way for major through traffic in the future.

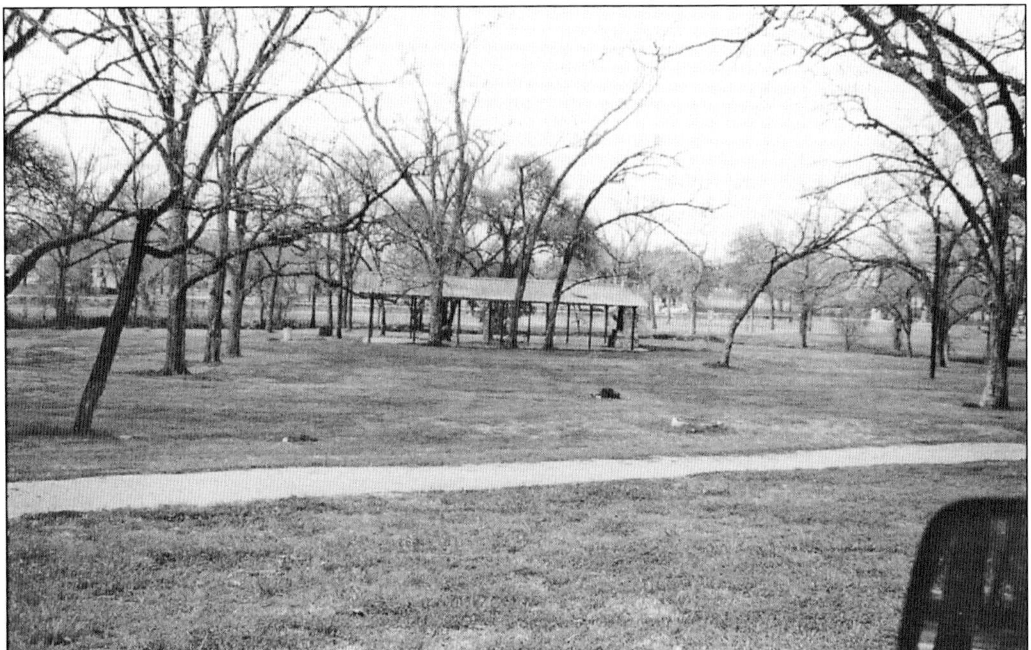

The city installed a covered picnic area in the greenbelt in the 1970s and added another one in 2008.

Michael Emery's family lived on Rosewood Avenue at the time of his birth. In those days, a good rainstorm would cause Boggy Creek to overflow its banks and create a lake where there had been a residential neighborhood. Mr. Emery and his wife, Beverly Johnson, live on Kuhlman Avenue today. Ms. Johnson works at the Alternative Learning Center, housed in the former Anderson High School. Mr. Emery works for KLRU-TV and keeps his television eye trained on African Americans in Austin with programs like *Juneteenth Jamboree*. (Photograph by Scott Newton, courtesy of Michael Emery.)

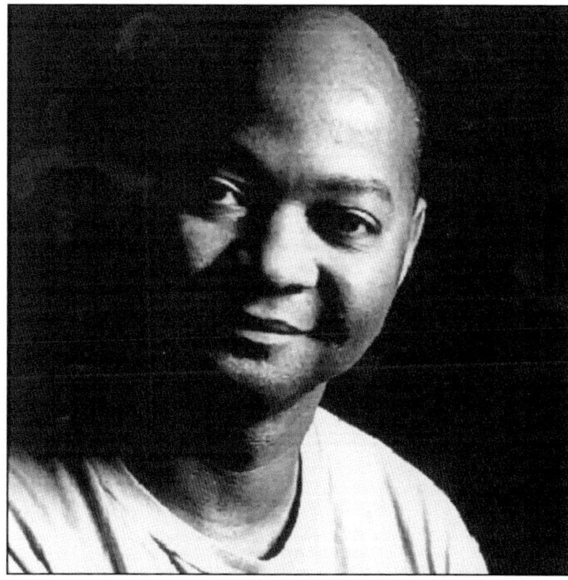

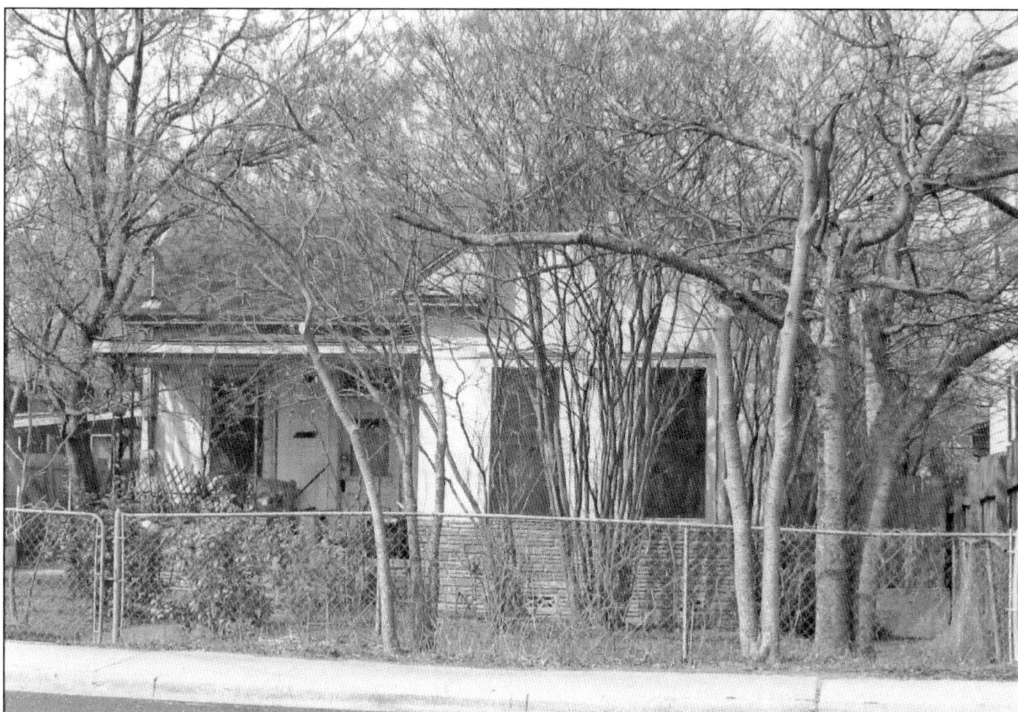

Clint Smith, a longtime Rosewood resident, grew up in this home on East Twelfth Street, built in the 1880s when the German settlers first came to Texas. Mr. Smith's family bought the house in the late 1930s, after another home that his father had built near the railroad tracks was condemned to make way for the city incinerator. When Mr. Smith was a young man, his mother, Willie Smith, started and managed a nursery in her home to enable young women with families to go to school. In the ensuing years, the former Smith-family home has housed the Sunshine Police Accountability Project, CopWatch, the Travis County Green Party, the Nader 2000 campaign, Clean Campaigns for Austin, the Instant Runoff Voting Coalition, and the National Organization for Women.

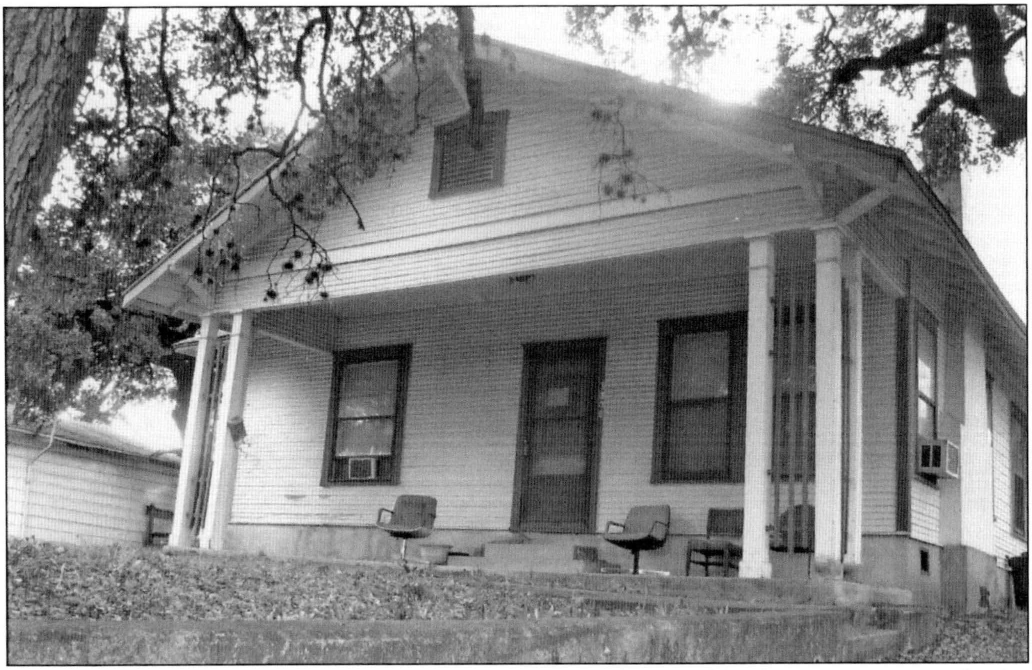

The eastern, larger portion of the Rosewood–Glen Oaks Neighborhood was originally the Hargrave Ranch. Hargrave and Kuhlman Streets first appeared in the Austin City Directory in 1935 but were listed as vacant. The first year that addresses were listed on Kuhlman was 1937. In 1939, Neal Street was listed in the Austin City Directory with one resident. This photograph shows the original Hargrave House.

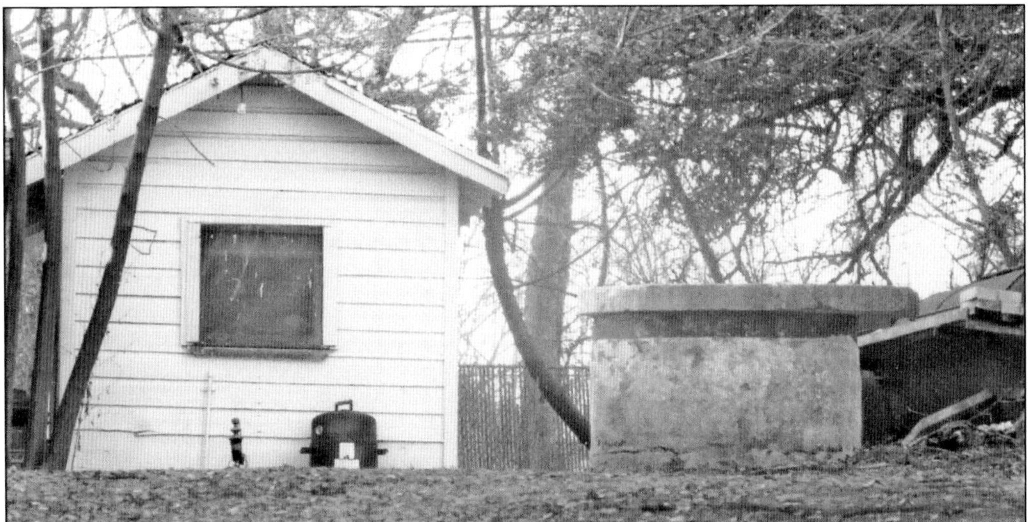

Ms. Hazel Nixon and her family moved into Kuhlman Avenue in the Rosewood–GlenOaks neighborhood in 1951 or 1952. At that time, Rosewood–Glen Oaks was like living out in the country. This shot is of the capped original Hargrave well. The older Hargrave parents, for whom Ms. Nixon's grandmother had worked, died in the 1940s and the children or grandchildren sold the property and subdivided the land. Glen Rae, Hargrave, Kuhlman, Neal, Nile, and Walter all appear with almost their current level of occupancy in the Austin City Directory for 1942.

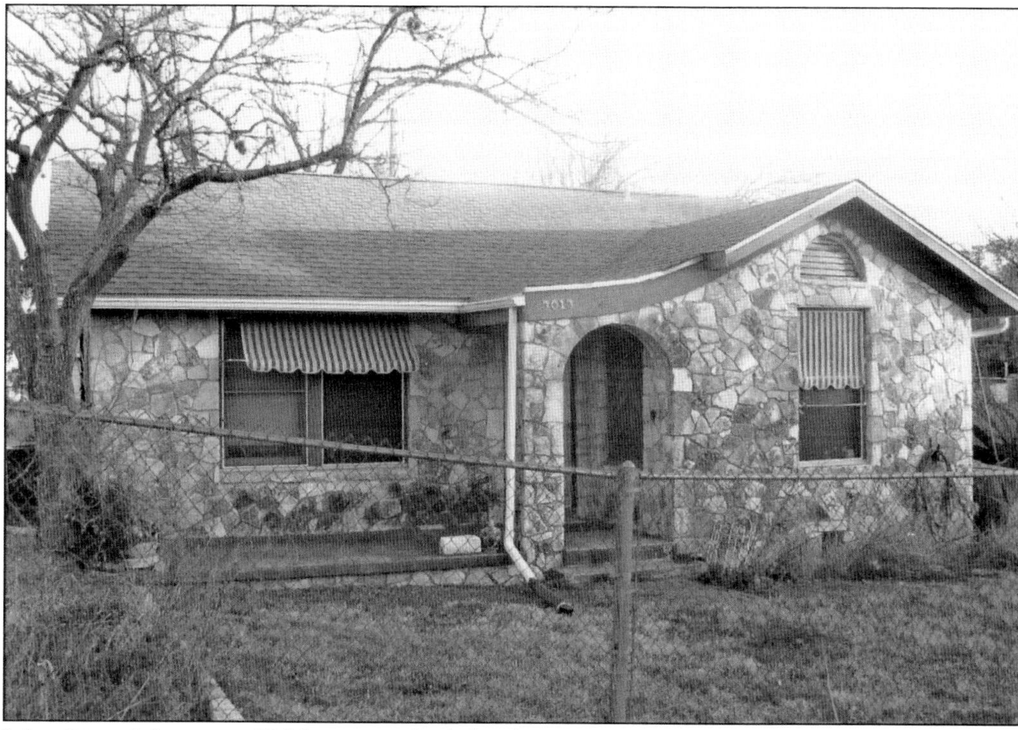

Jolyn Piercy's home on Kuhlman was built by the Hargraves for their adult children before the land was subdivided. For years, Ms. Piercy found handmade square nails, handmade barbwire, and other old artifacts in her yard whenever she dug. There was no city water in the area until the late 1960s. Ms. Piercy has been an active Rosewood–Glen Oaks Neighborhood Association member since its inception.

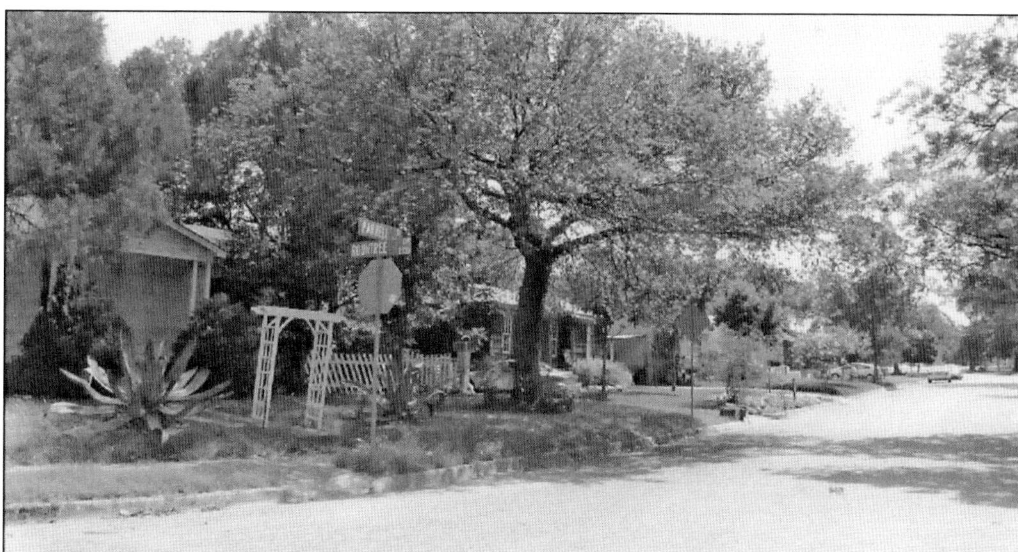

Three neighborhoods in the northern part of the Rosewood Neighborhood Planning Area were built in the 1950s. Streets in the Austin Heights neighborhood—including Rountree, Rannell, Eckert, and Higgins—first appear in the city directory in 1952.

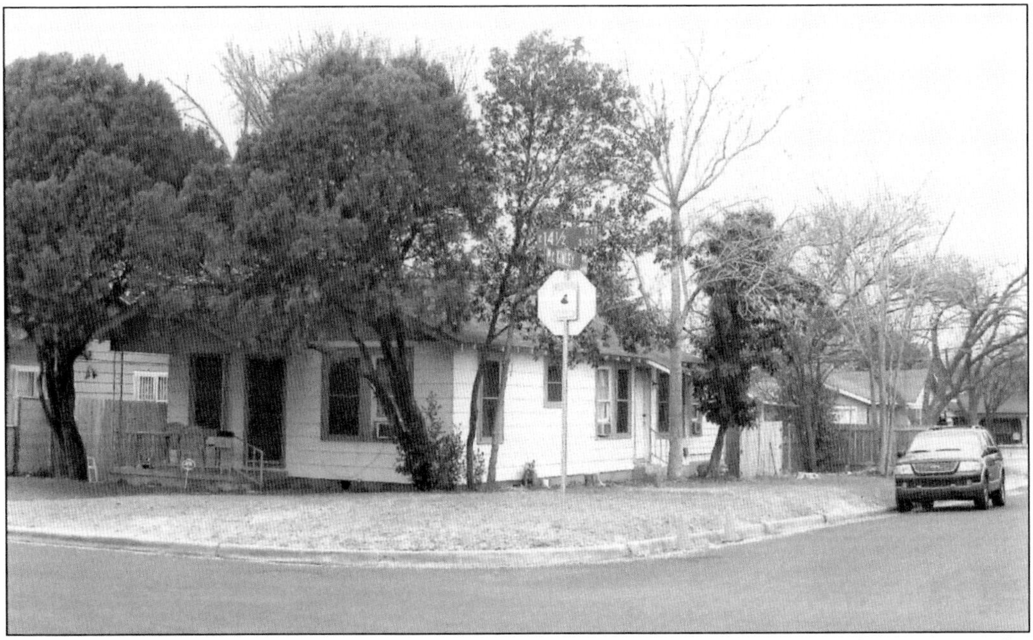

Streets in the McKinley Heights neighborhood also first appear in 1952, as do streets in the Clifford-Sanchez neighborhood. Oak Springs Drive does not appear until 1953. In his memoirs, Volma Overton noted: "[McKinley Heights] was one of the best neighborhoods for Blacks who were financially able to purchase and maintain upscale homes to live." At the same time, however, most of Rosewood and Salina were unpaved and full of "shotgun houses" in poorly maintained condition.

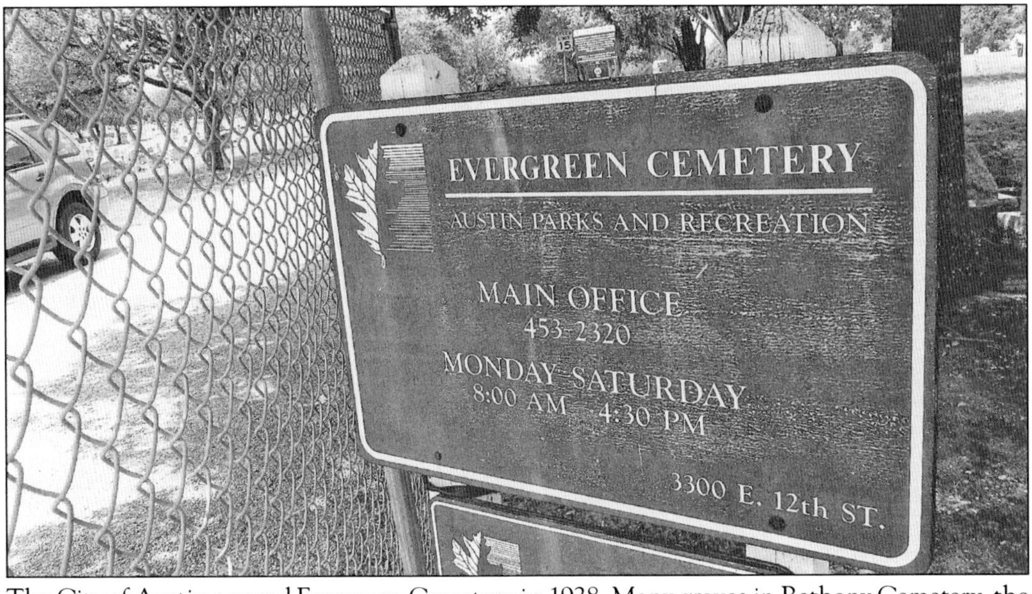

The City of Austin opened Evergreen Cemetery in 1928. Many graves in Bethany Cemetery, the original East Austin African American cemetery, were exhumed and the remains transferred to nearby Evergreen. Willie Wells, featured in chapter four, was originally interred at Evergreen, and later moved to the Texas State Cemetery. Recent Rosewood residents who have passed away were also interred in Evergreen.

Two

EDUCATION

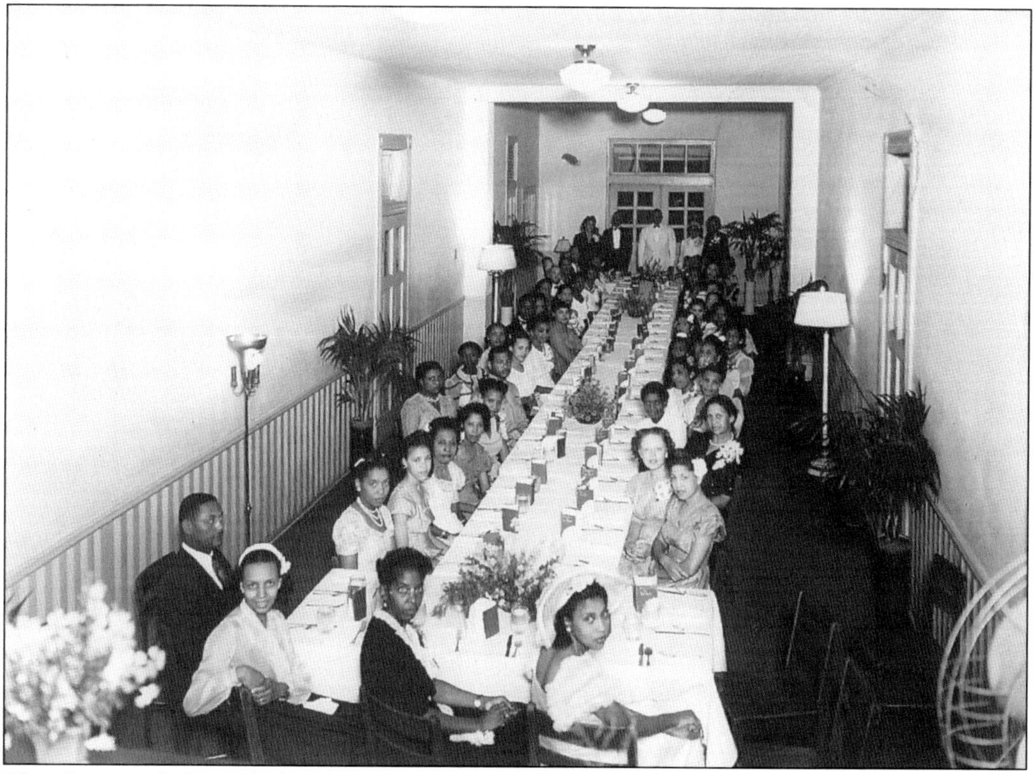

This photograph shows the bittersweet closing ceremony for the Blackshear and Rosewood Elementary Schools. Prior to *Brown v. Board of Education of Topeka* in 1954, which declared state laws that established separate public schools for black and white students unconstitutional, African American students in Austin attended segregated schools including Blackshear Elementary and Rosewood Elementary. (Courtesy of the George Washington Carver Museum and Cultural Center.)

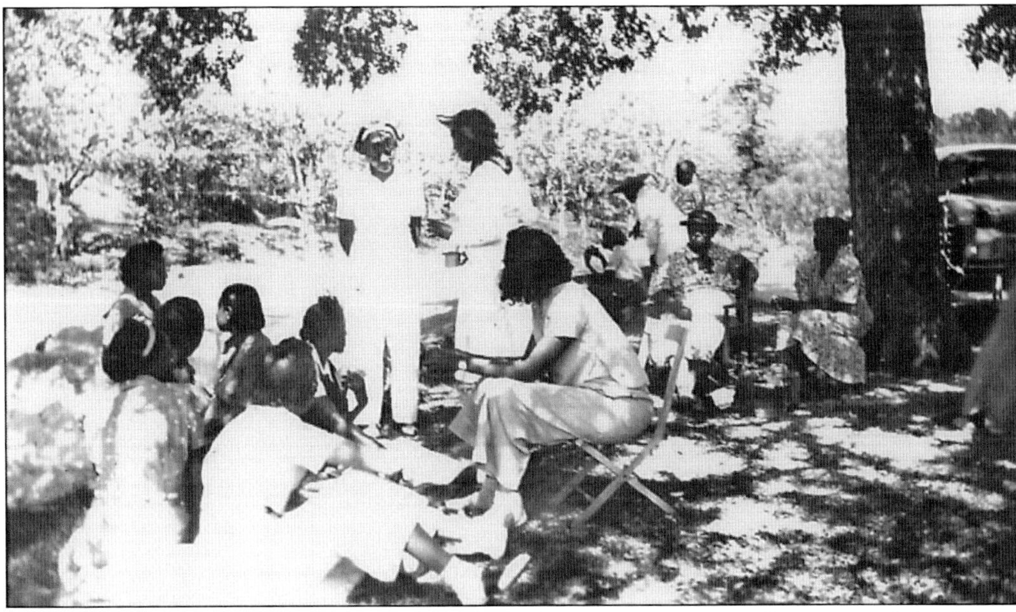

In this photograph, Rosewood students and teachers enjoy a picnic. (Courtesy of the George Washington Carver Museum and Cultural Center.)

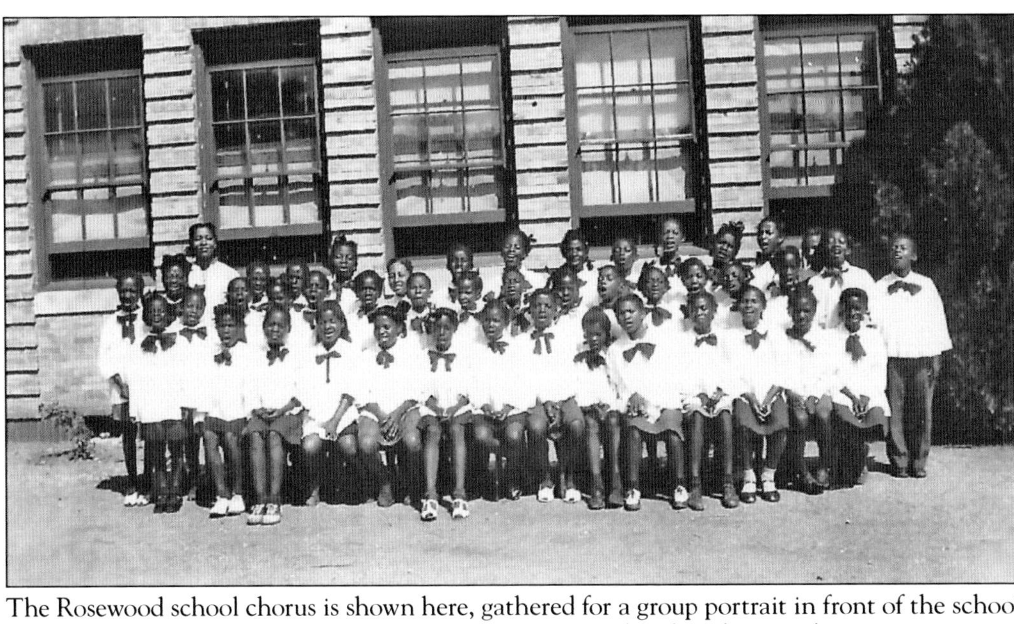

The Rosewood school chorus is shown here, gathered for a group portrait in front of the school. (Courtesy of the George Washington Carver Museum and Cultural Center.)

This is a closeup of some of the members of the Rosewood school chorus. (Courtesy of the George Washington Carver Museum and Cultural Center.)

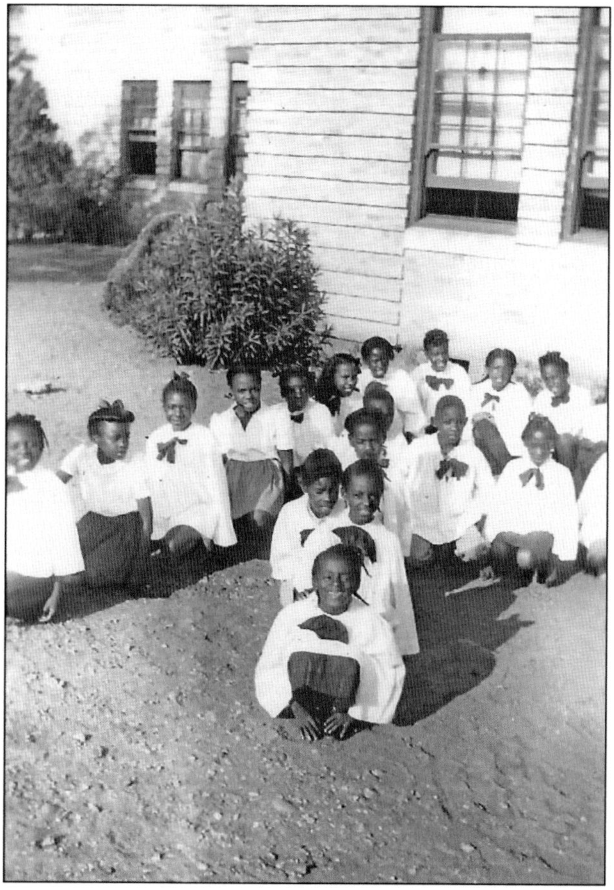

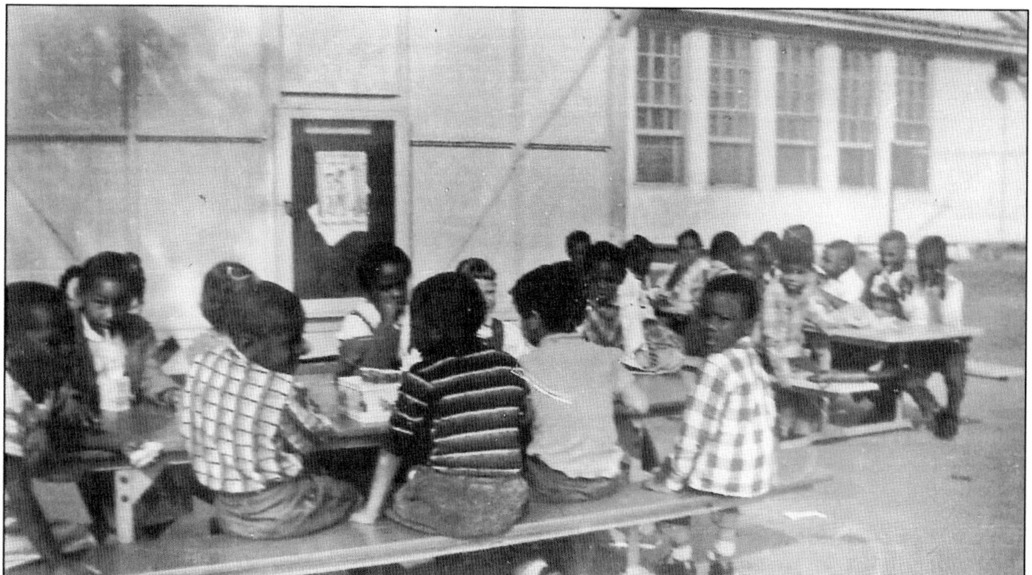

This photograph of lunchtime at Rosewood Elementary School shows several students enjoying the break. (Courtesy of the George Washington Carver Museum and Cultural Center.)

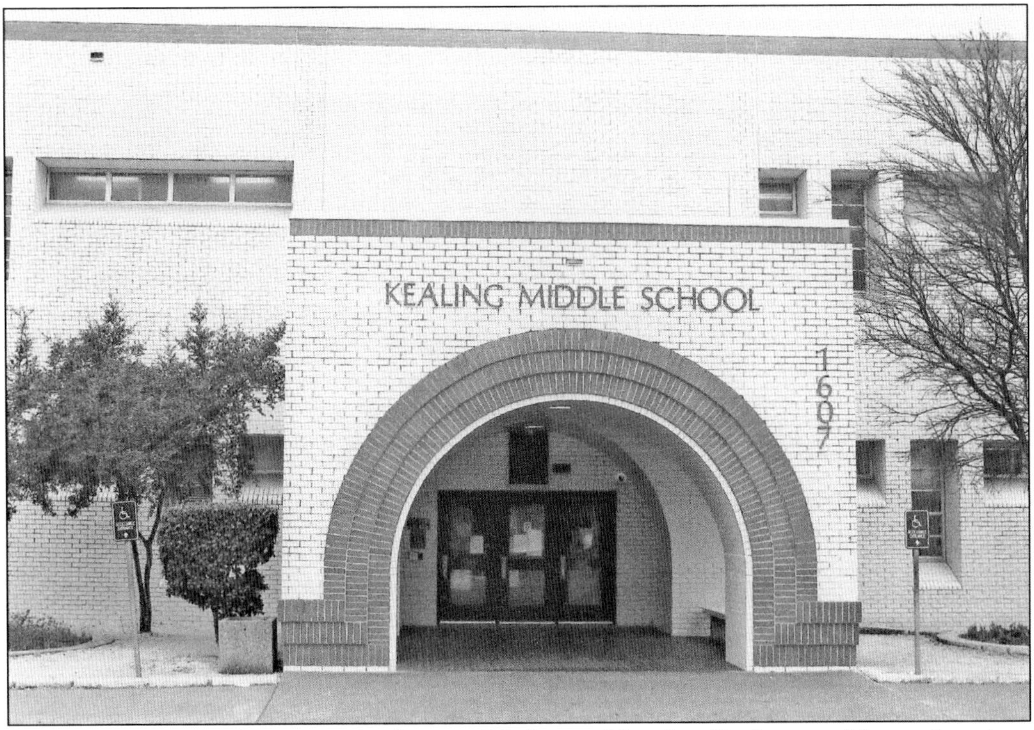

Kealing Middle School was named in honor of Hightower Theodore Kealing, an African American educator and author who lived in Austin in the 19th century. The institution opened in 1930 as the first junior high school for African American students. The first principal, Prof. I.Q. Hurdle (seen in the photograph of the Anderson High School classroom on page 43), held that position until 1939. The second principal, Prof. T.C. Calhoun, held the position until 1971, when Kealing was closed along with all other exclusively African American Austin schools. In 1986, the school building was reopened as a junior high school for neighborhood youth and for students in the new math and science magnet program. The magnet program was expanded to include liberal arts in the 1990s. In 2004, a sixth-grade program was added to the curriculum.

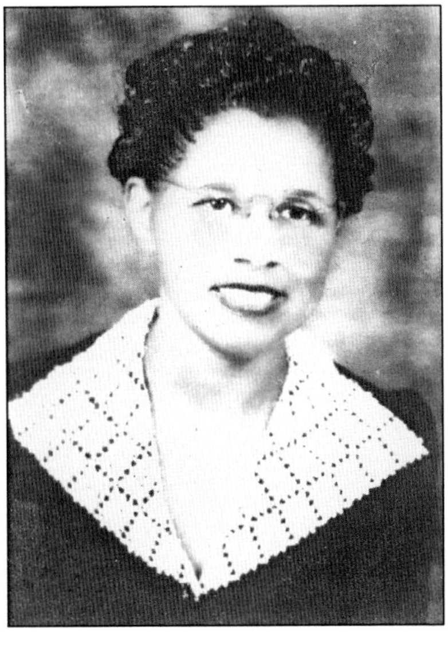

Onie B. Conley, an Austin native, graduated from Samuel Huston College and received her master's degree from Columbia University. She taught physical education, and later science, at Kealing Middle School, where she began teaching at age 19. Ms. Conley taught at Kealing for 43 years. (Courtesy of Conley-Guerrero Senior Activity Center.)

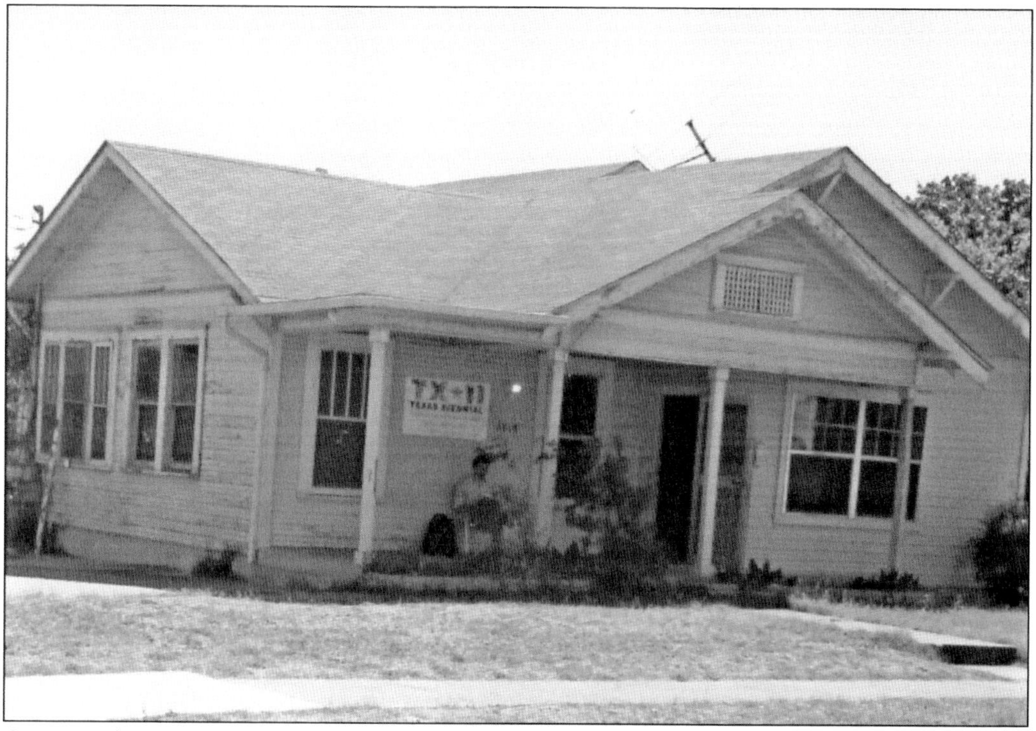

Onie Conley's longtime home was at 1314 Rosewood Avenue. Since her passing, the house has hosted various social service providers.

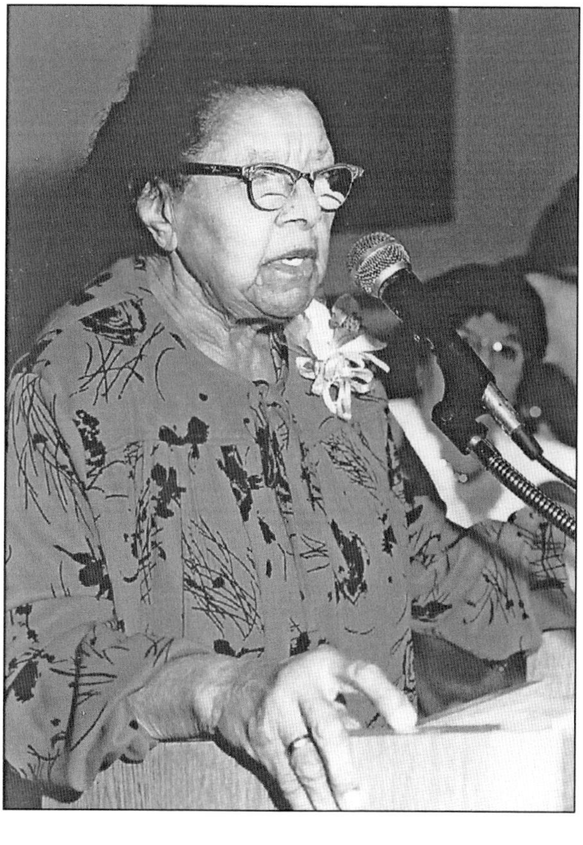

The Heart's Ease Circle of King's Daughters was organized in 1894 to care for the aged. At first, the organization rented a house on East Tenth Street but later purchased its own space. By the 1940s, the group had grown to more than 40 members serving 16 residents, and the space was made available to other nonprofit organizations for a number of years. By the 1970s, only two King's Daughters worked to provide financial assistance: Betty G. Poole and Onie B. Conley (pictured at right). Ms. Conley arranged to donate the property to the Conley-Guerrero Senior Center Guild, which in turn sold the property in 1995 to fund activities at the center. (Courtesy of Conley-Guerrero Senior Activity Center.)

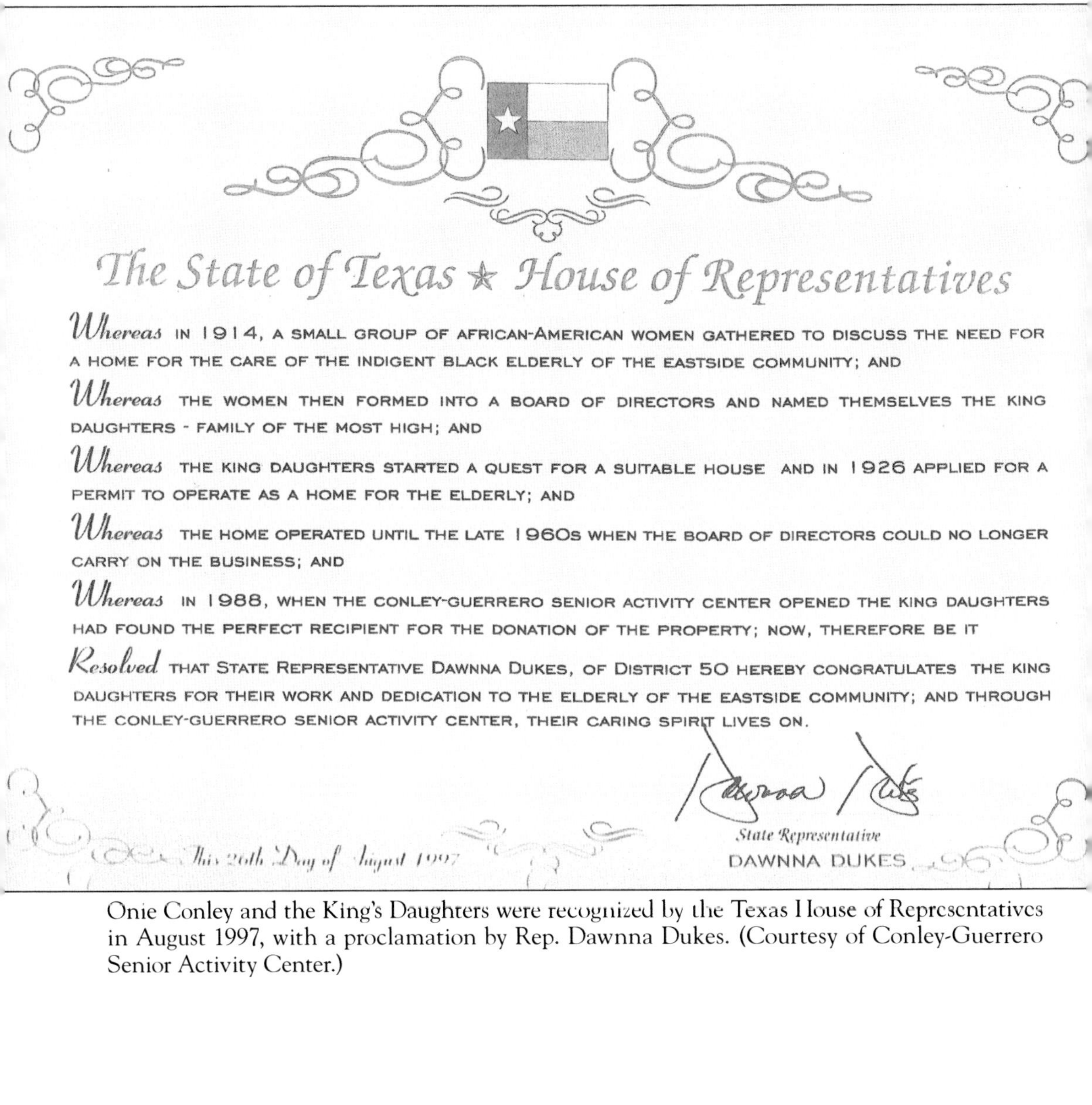

The State of Texas ★ House of Representatives

Whereas IN 1914, A SMALL GROUP OF AFRICAN-AMERICAN WOMEN GATHERED TO DISCUSS THE NEED FOR A HOME FOR THE CARE OF THE INDIGENT BLACK ELDERLY OF THE EASTSIDE COMMUNITY; AND

Whereas THE WOMEN THEN FORMED INTO A BOARD OF DIRECTORS AND NAMED THEMSELVES THE KING DAUGHTERS - FAMILY OF THE MOST HIGH; AND

Whereas THE KING DAUGHTERS STARTED A QUEST FOR A SUITABLE HOUSE AND IN 1926 APPLIED FOR A PERMIT TO OPERATE AS A HOME FOR THE ELDERLY; AND

Whereas THE HOME OPERATED UNTIL THE LATE 1960S WHEN THE BOARD OF DIRECTORS COULD NO LONGER CARRY ON THE BUSINESS; AND

Whereas IN 1988, WHEN THE CONLEY-GUERRERO SENIOR ACTIVITY CENTER OPENED THE KING DAUGHTERS HAD FOUND THE PERFECT RECIPIENT FOR THE DONATION OF THE PROPERTY; NOW, THEREFORE BE IT

Resolved THAT STATE REPRESENTATIVE DAWNNA DUKES, OF DISTRICT 50 HEREBY CONGRATULATES THE KING DAUGHTERS FOR THEIR WORK AND DEDICATION TO THE ELDERLY OF THE EASTSIDE COMMUNITY; AND THROUGH THE CONLEY-GUERRERO SENIOR ACTIVITY CENTER, THEIR CARING SPIRIT LIVES ON.

This 26th Day of August 1997

State Representative
DAWNNA DUKES

Onie Conley and the King's Daughters were recognized by the Texas House of Representatives in August 1997, with a proclamation by Rep. Dawnna Dukes. (Courtesy of Conley-Guerrero Senior Activity Center.)

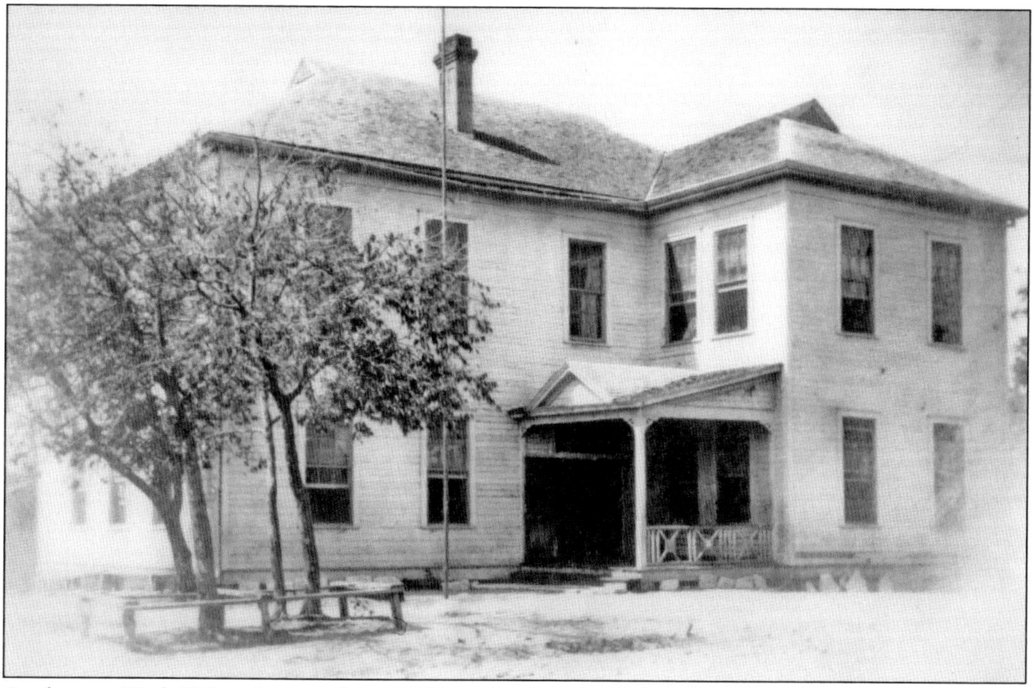

Anderson High School opened in 1907 as the Austin Colored High School. This two-story, framed building was located at the northwest corner of Olive and Curve Streets. Anderson was moved several times before it was finally closed. Regardless of location, this high school educated generations of Rosewood residents and served as a center of community life for East Austin's African Americans. (Courtesy of AHC, PICA 20860.)

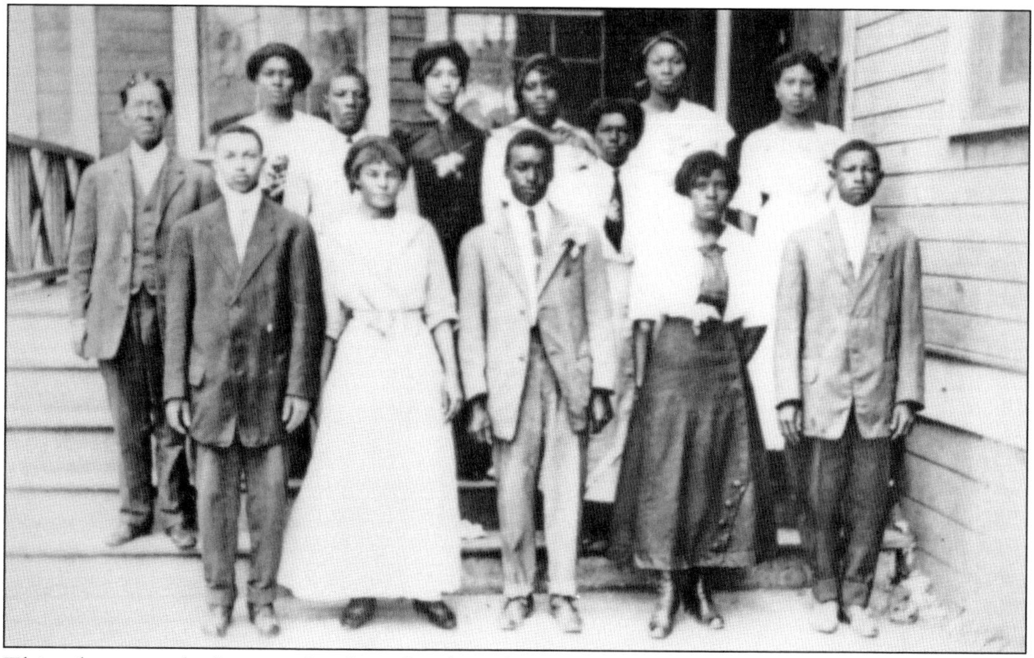

This photograph depicts the first faculty of Anderson High School. (Courtesy of AHC, PICA 20861.)

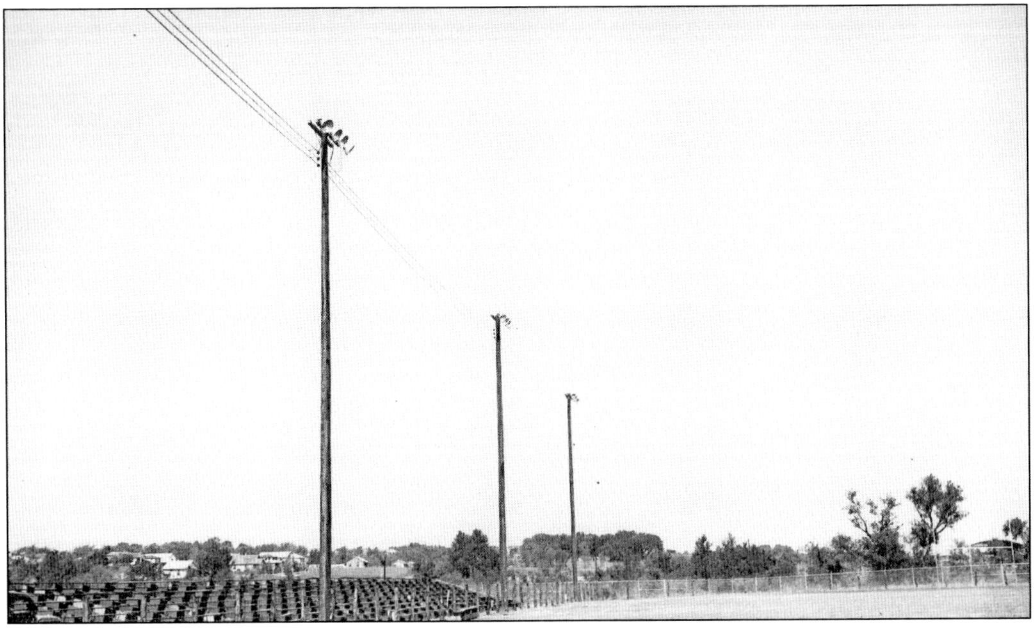

Anderson High School's Yellow Jacket Field got electric lights, which allowed for Friday night football games, which was the highlight of the community. The stadium was filled to capacity for the games. Track was also important, and the high school had a big and well-supported marching band that performed at all events. (Courtesy of AHC, PICA 20629.)

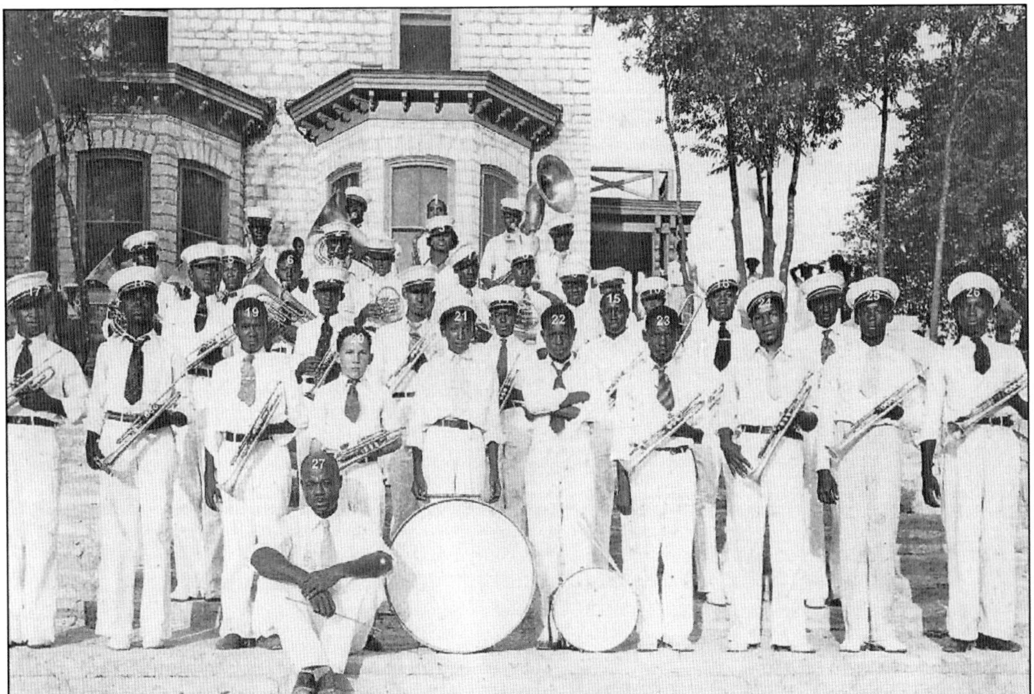

This photograph shows the first Anderson High School Yellow Jacket Band. Charter members included Hermie Edwards, Raymond Edmonson, Ullysis Fowler, and Roy Patterson. Band director Prof. B.L. Joyce is seated in front (No. 27). (Courtesy of Michael Emery.)

George Ellis Emery was in the Anderson High School Band. He is No. 16 in the previous photograph. In the early 1950s, Mr. Emery designed the family's new house on Kuhlman Avenue in Glen Oaks Addition, just south of the "new" L.C. Anderson High School, where he taught school. Their closest neighbor, the late Hazel Nixon, was the first African American to reside in the new Glen Oaks subdivision. She had worked for the family that previously owned the land. In the 1960s, Mr. Emery's wife purchased a condemned house in the Clarksville area, which was a former freedom town in West Central Austin, and moved it into the backyard of her double-sized lot. (Courtesy of Michael Emery.)

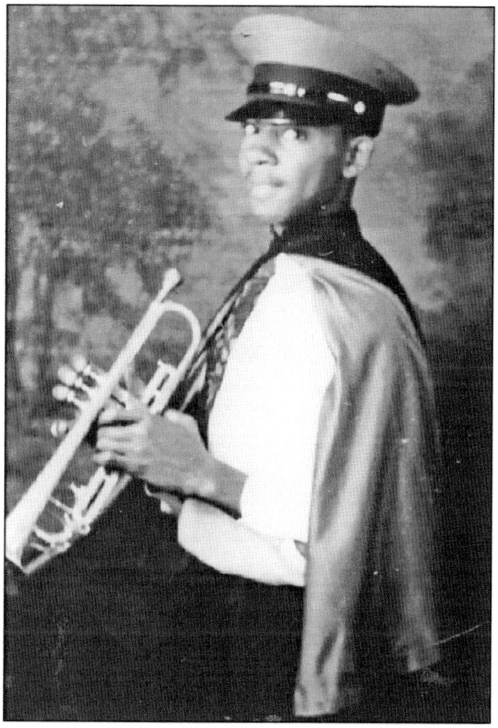

A classroom in Anderson High School shows Prof. I.Q. Hurdle standing in the back at the right. (Courtesy of AHC, CO2689.)

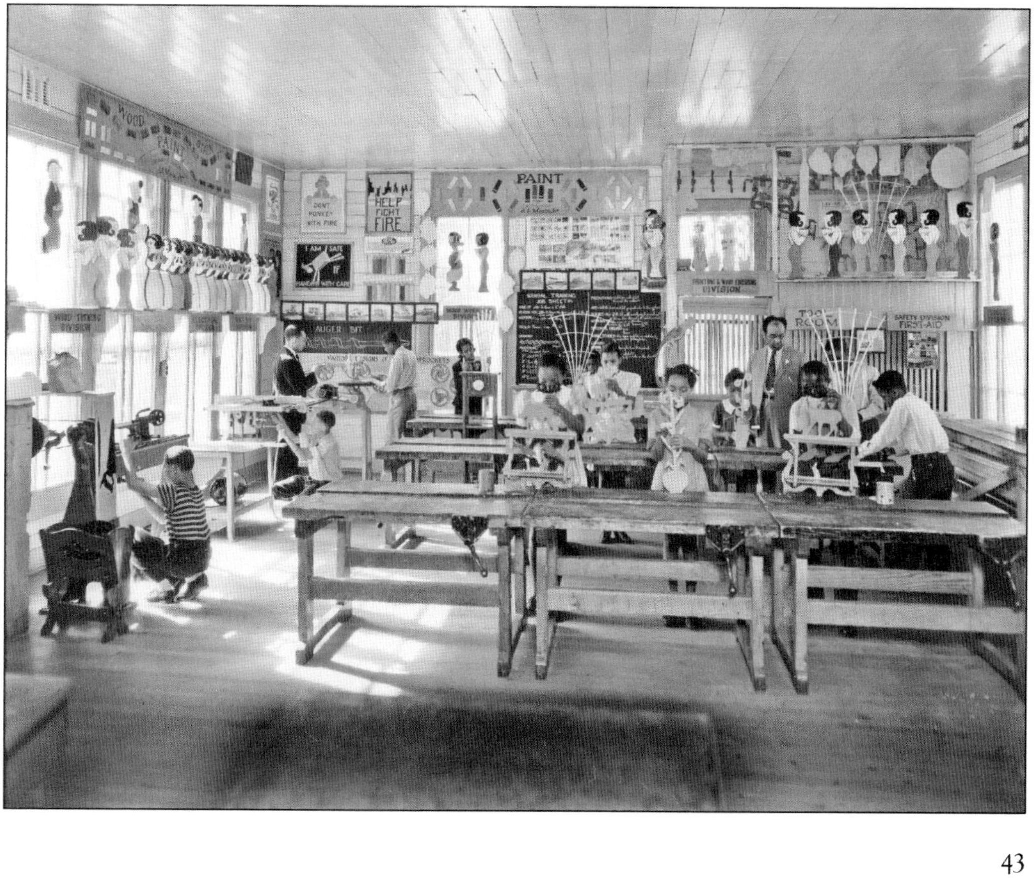

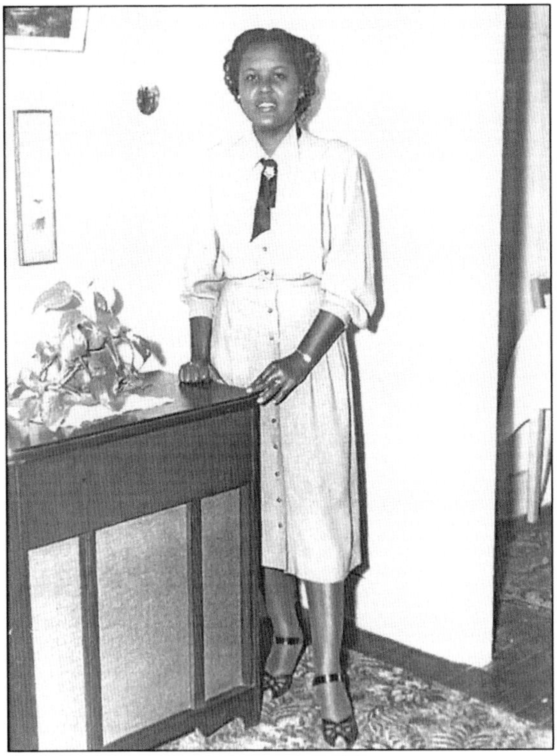

Viola Wilson is seen here in her younger years, when she lived in Rosewood. She was a member of the 1939 graduating class of the old Anderson High School, located just west of present-day Rosewood. After she married John Bell Wilson, they bought a home on Glen Rae Street, then part of Lorraine Heights. Ms. Wilson recalls attending Juneteenth celebrations at the original Emancipation Park, which was closed when the Austin Housing Authority built today's Rosewood Project on the site. (Courtesy of Viola Wilson.)

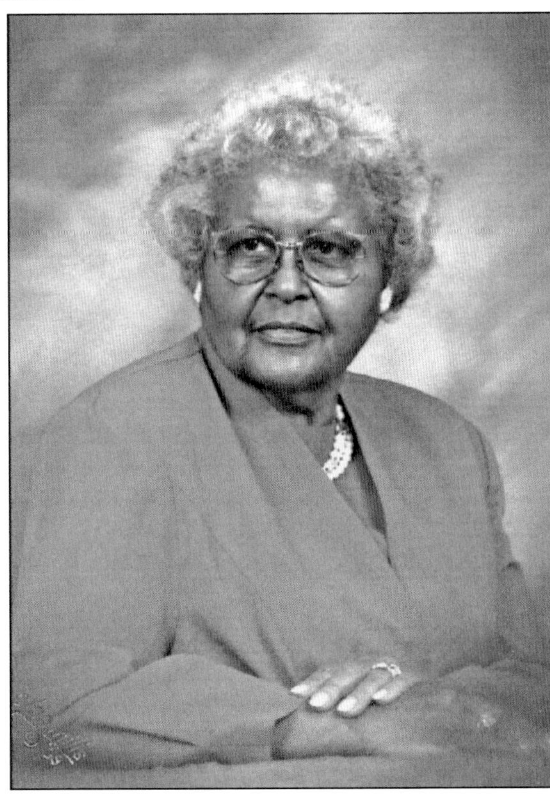

Ms. Wilson today lives with her daughter but retains a keen interest in Rosewood, where her son and grandson still live. (Courtesy of Viola Wilson.)

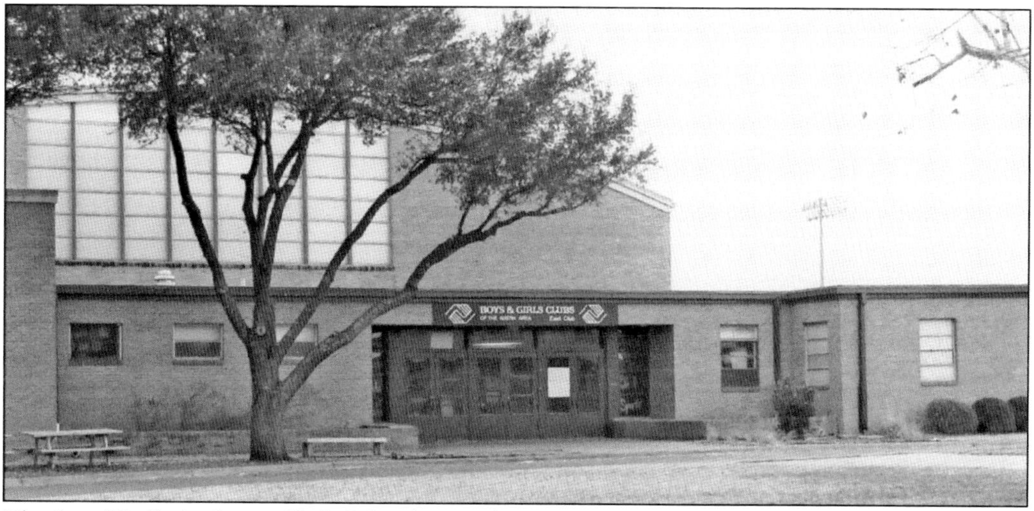

The "new" L.C. Anderson High School opened at 2601 Thompson Street in 1953. The school was named for L.C. Anderson, born in 1853 to slave parents, who served as second principal of Prairie View College for 34 years. The school included 25 classrooms, a lunchroom, laboratories, an auditorium, two gymnasiums, and administrative offices. Following the desegregation of Austin public schools in 1971, the students were bused to campuses all over the city. The facility was a campus for Austin Community College for a number of years and currently houses a Boys and Girls Club, a special Austin Independent School District program, and the newly revitalized Yellow Jacket Field.

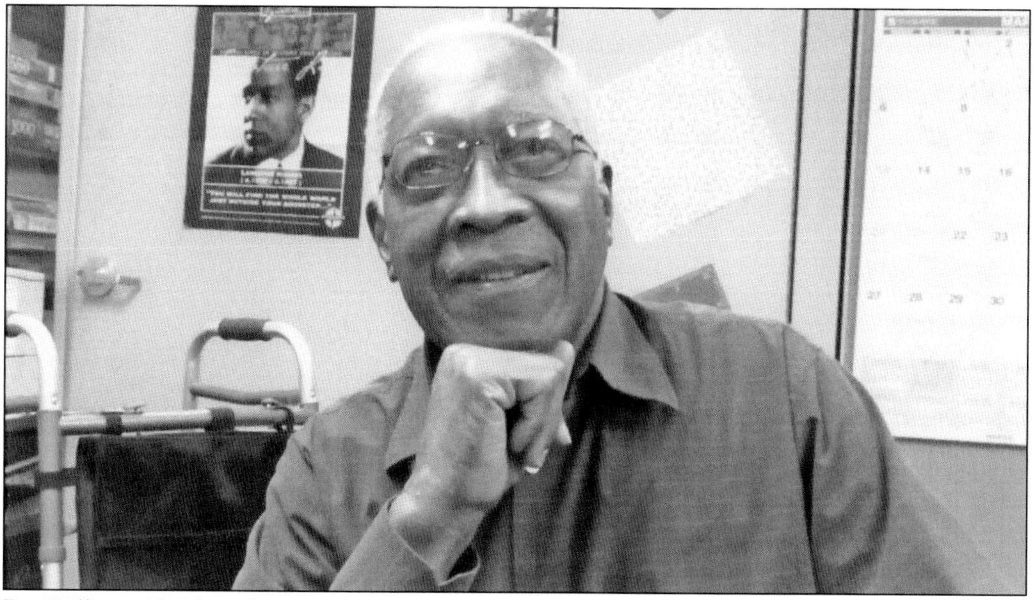

Dr. William Charles Akins's roots are in the Rosewood Neighborhood. He attended Blackshear Elementary, Kealing Junior High, and the old Anderson High School. He also graduated from Huston-Tillotson College and attended Prairie View A&M. He was a child of the Depression and an only child. His father was a tenant farmer during the days of segregation. Dr. Akins's family lived on Washington Avenue where it intersected with Rosewood Avenue and Chestnut Street, when Chestnut Street was mostly rural. He recalls walking to most places most of the time, but sometimes they would walk to the "end" of the streetcar line at Twelfth and Chicon Streets to catch a ride to town. Dr. Akins notes, "I was blessed to become a teacher."

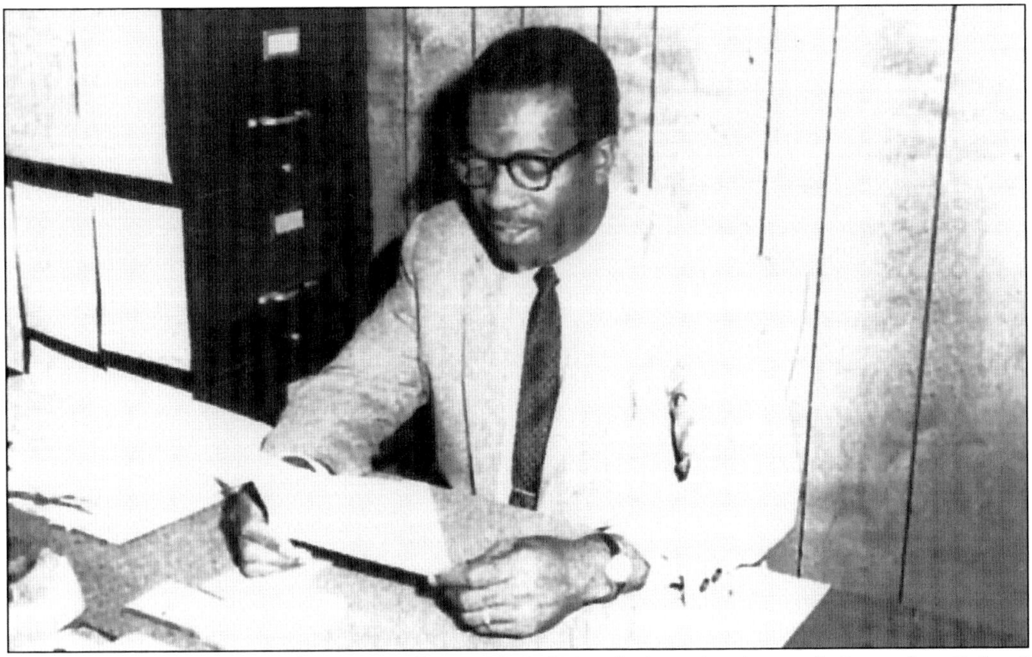

In 1964, Dr. Akins was teaching at Anderson High School when the Austin Independent School District (AISD) made its first attempt to integrate faculty. When he was transferred to Johnston High School, a new mixed school, he was the AISD's only African American teacher at any high school other than Anderson. At the same time, Bertha Means was moved from Anderson to Allen Junior High. (Courtesy of Mr. Willie Simmons, photograph by the Yellow Jacket.)

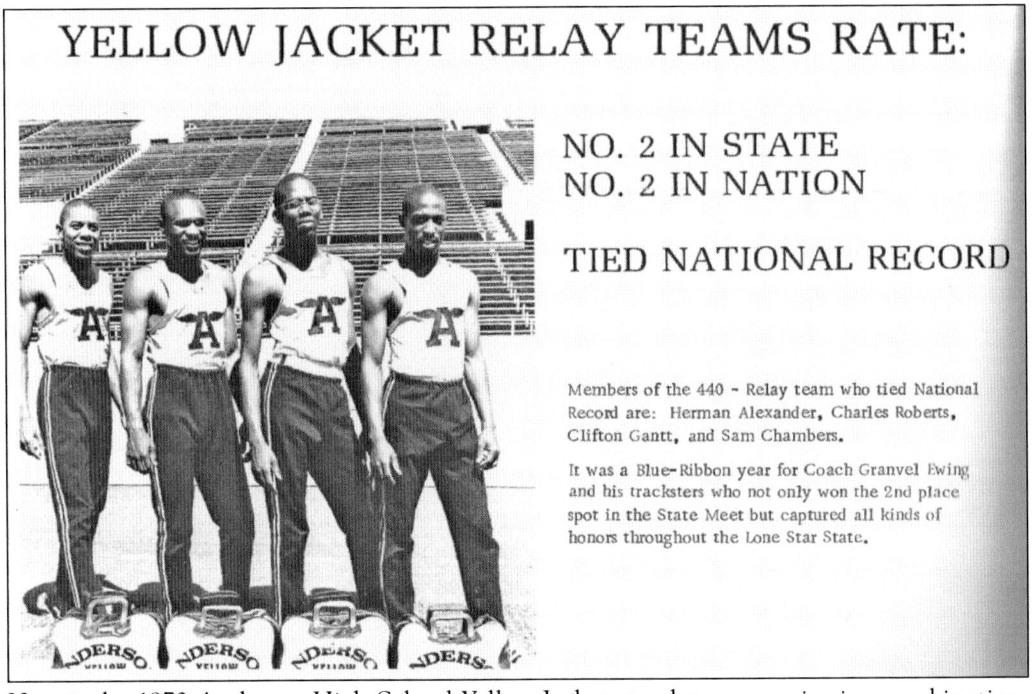

YELLOW JACKET RELAY TEAMS RATE:

NO. 2 IN STATE
NO. 2 IN NATION

TIED NATIONAL RECORD

Members of the 440 - Relay team who tied National Record are: Herman Alexander, Charles Roberts, Clifton Gantt, and Sam Chambers.

It was a Blue-Ribbon year for Coach Granvel Ewing and his tracksters who not only won the 2nd place spot in the State Meet but captured all kinds of honors throughout the Lone Star State.

Here is the 1970 Anderson High School Yellow Jackets track team, a winning combination. (Courtesy of Willie Simmons, photograph by the Yellow Jacket.)

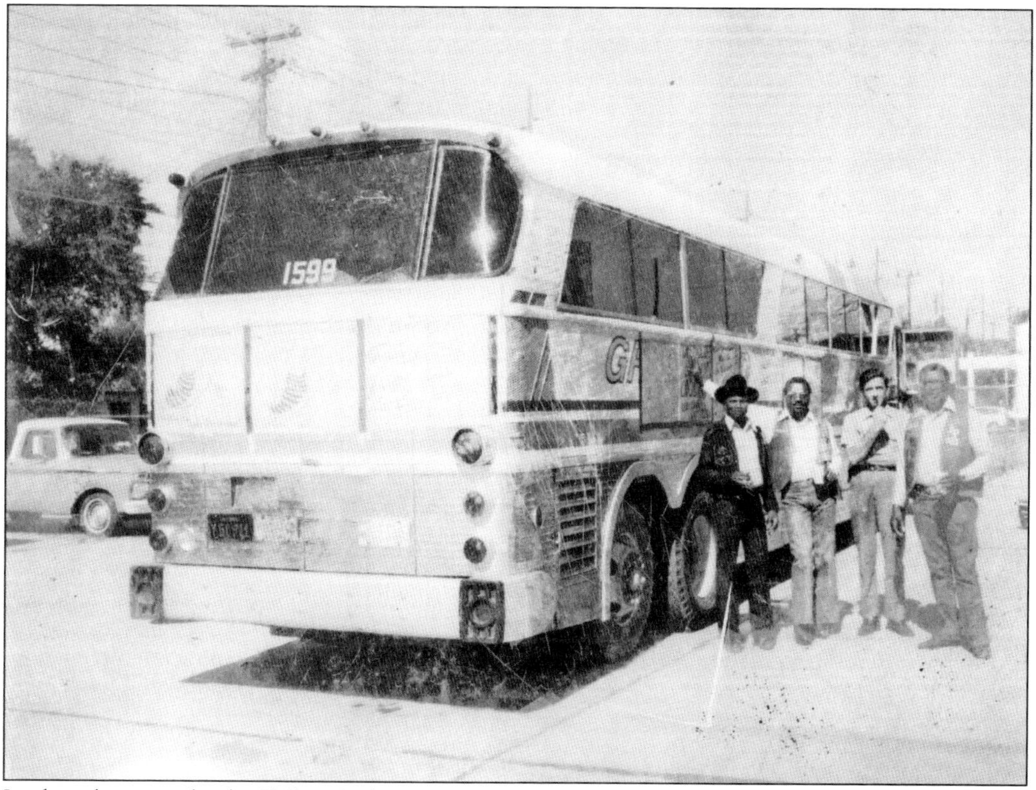

In this photograph, the Yellow Jacket Citizen Band Club boards a bus to attend an away game. (Courtesy of AHC, AR.2001.002[Y-2].)

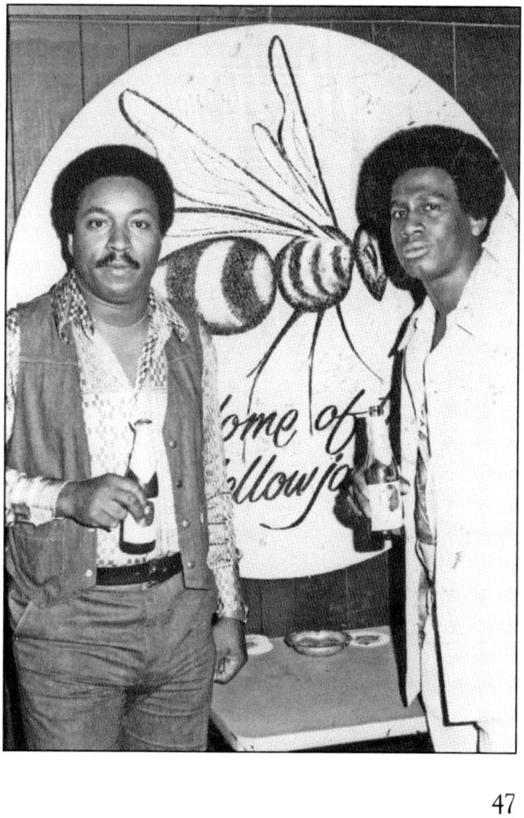

Coach Alvin Moore (left) of the Huston-Tillotson University baseball team is attending a Yellow Jacket event with another fan. Coach Moore still coaches the team, which plays on Downs Field on East Twelfth Street in Rosewood. (Courtesy of AHC, AR.2001.002.)

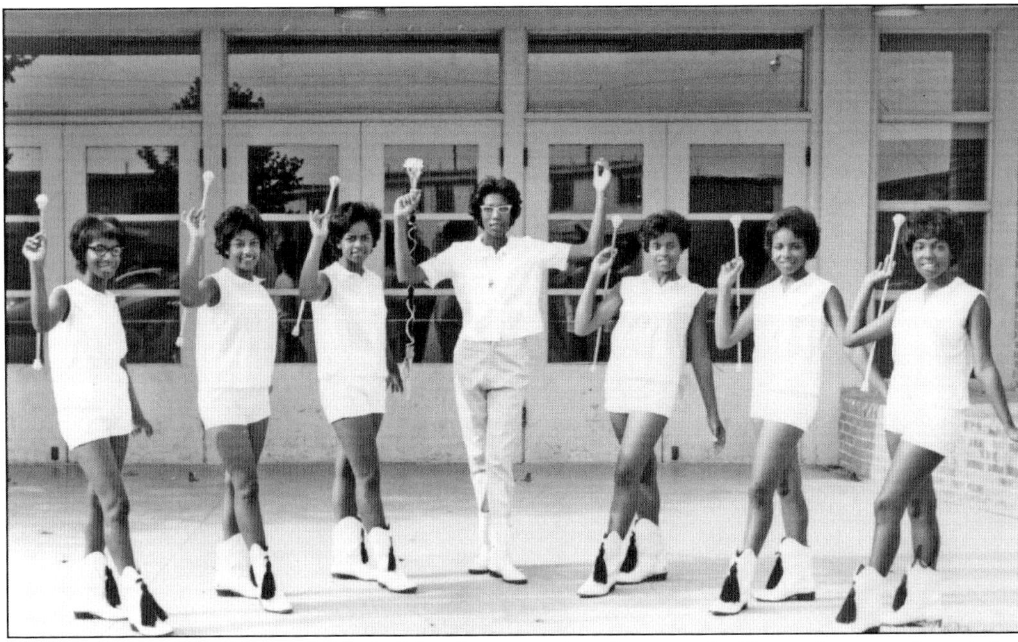

Drum majorettes for Anderson High School pose in this photograph. Shown here are, from left to right, Joan Arnold, Nancy Houston, Addie Powell, Nelda (Wells) Spears (current Travis County tax assessor–collector), Brenda Pleasant, Gloria Arnold, and Brenda Douglas. Anderson High School graduates include many current and recent Austin government officials. In late July 2011, Ms. Spears announced her retirement as tax assessor–collector. (Courtesy of AHC, PICA 29927.)

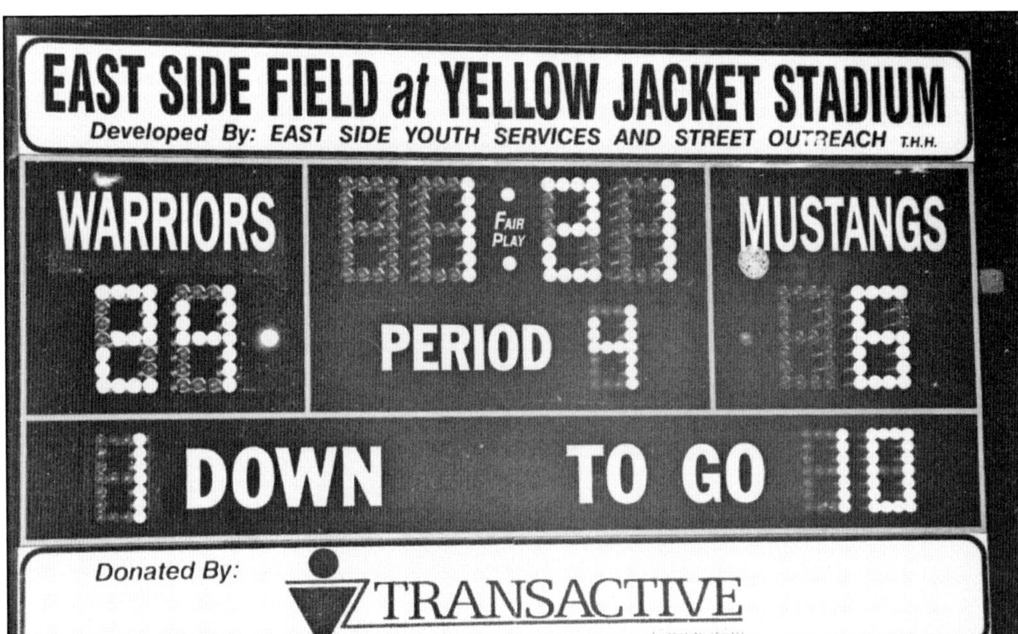

Fans anxiously watched the Yellow Jacket Stadium scoreboard during games. (Courtesy of AHC, P8620.)

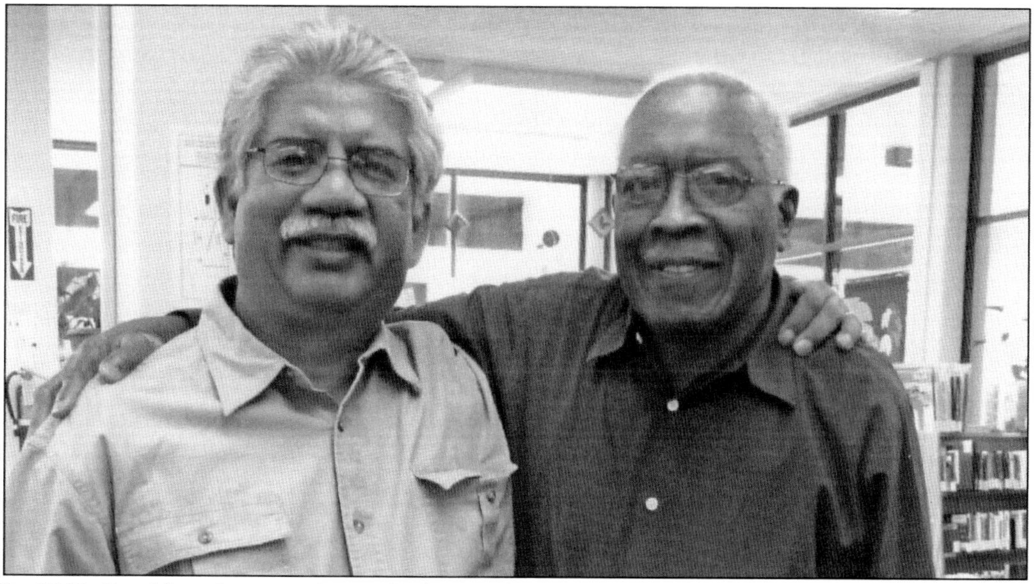

In 1968, Dr. Akins became dean of Johnston but returned to Anderson the following year as assistant principal. Author Gilberto Rivera (left) was one of Dr. Akins's (right) social studies students at Johnston. In 1973, after Anderson High was closed in Rosewood, a new school named Anderson High was opened in Northwest Austin. IBM had just moved to Austin, and several high-level African American IBM officials, such as future city council member Berl Handcox, had children at the new Anderson. The surrounding area was a very conservative, upper-middle-class community, but eventually tensions between African American and white students leveled off. Dr. Akins remained principal there for 10 years. Huston-Tillotson granted him an honorary doctorate in 1982 as an alumnus and pioneer in integration in the Austin area.

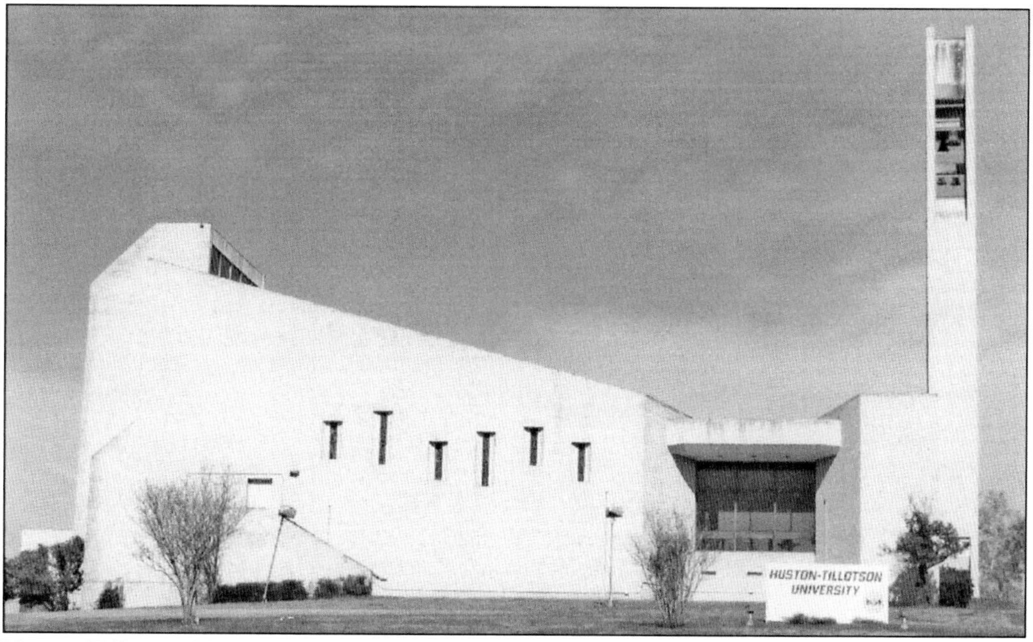

Huston-Tillotson University, located just west of the Rosewood neighborhood, was formed from the merger of Samuel Huston College and Tillotson College in 1952.

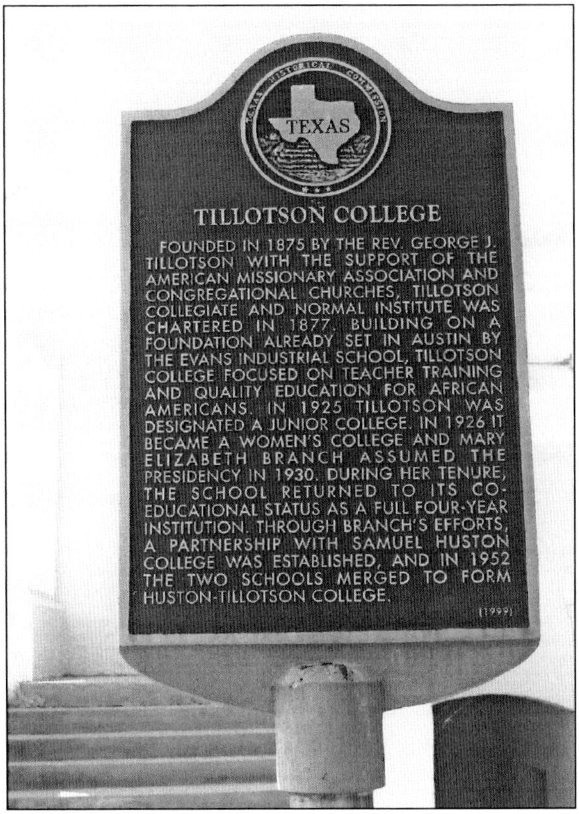

Founded in 1875 by the Reverend George J. Tillotson with the support of the American Missionary Association and the Congregational churches (now United Church of Christ), Tillotson Collegiate and Normal Institute was chartered in 1877. Building on a foundation already set in Austin by the Evans Industrial School, Tillotson College focused on teacher training and quality education for African Americans. Allen Hall was its first building. (Courtesy of Huston-Tillotson University.)

Evans Industrial Hall, which currently houses the education program, still sits on what was Austin's second-highest hill and the highest point of the present Huston-Tillotson campus. In 1925, Tillotson was designated a junior college, and in 1926, it became a women's college. Mary Elizabeth Branch assumed the presidency in 1930. (Courtesy of Huston-Tillotson University.)

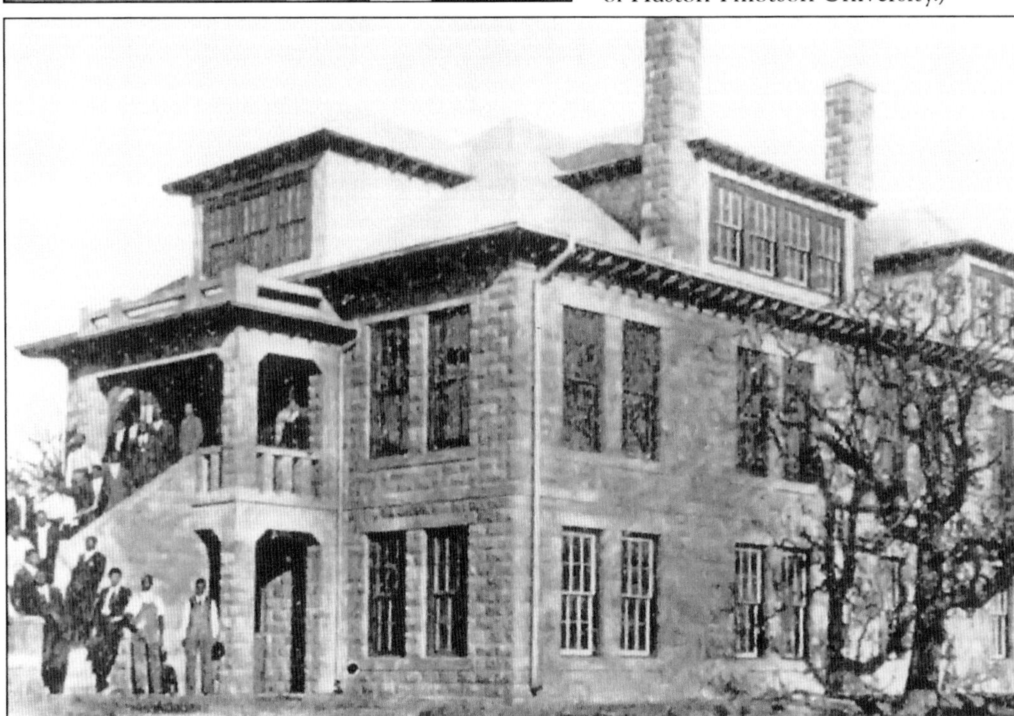

Samuel Huston College traces its history to 1876, when the Reverend George W. Richardson founded a college in Dallas for the education of African American youth. St. Paul's Methodist Episcopal Church was leased for the private school, named Andrews Normal School. The school moved to Austin in 1878 and held classes in what is now Wesley United Methodist Church. The construction of Interstate 35 through the Samuel Huston campus facilitated a merger in 1952 that formed Huston-Tillotson College, now known as Huston-Tillotson University. The campus is the site of many arts and cultural events, including the annual celebration of Dr. Martin Luther King Jr. Day. (Courtesy of Huston-Tillotson University.)

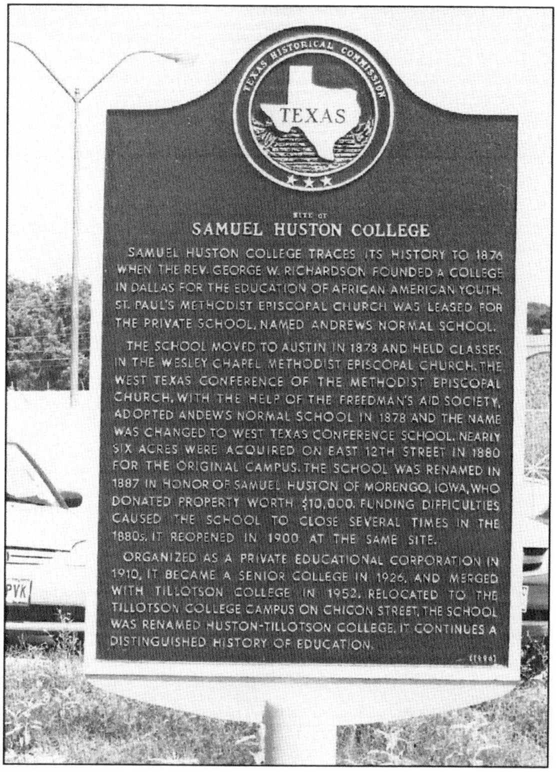

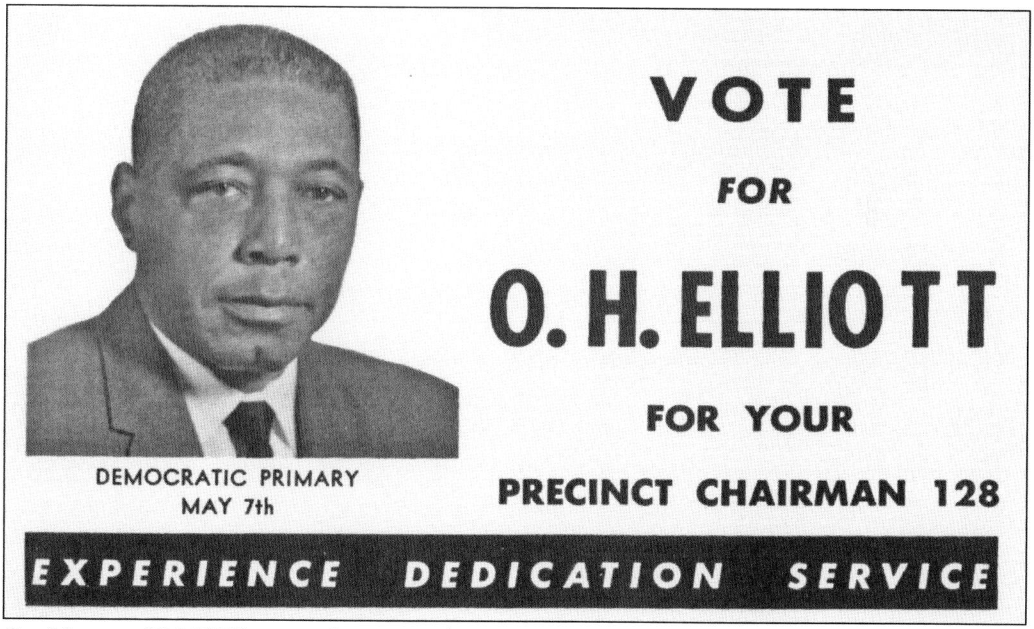

Ora Herman "O.H." Elliott was born in Arkansas and graduated from the University of Kansas. He served as business manager and instructor at Samuel Huston College, then as business manager at Clark College in Atlanta, Georgia, and returned to Austin when Samuel Huston College became Huston-Tillotson College. He and his family lived in the Chestnut Neighborhood, just northwest of Rosewood. (Courtesy of AHC, AR 2007.017[1-27-Front].)

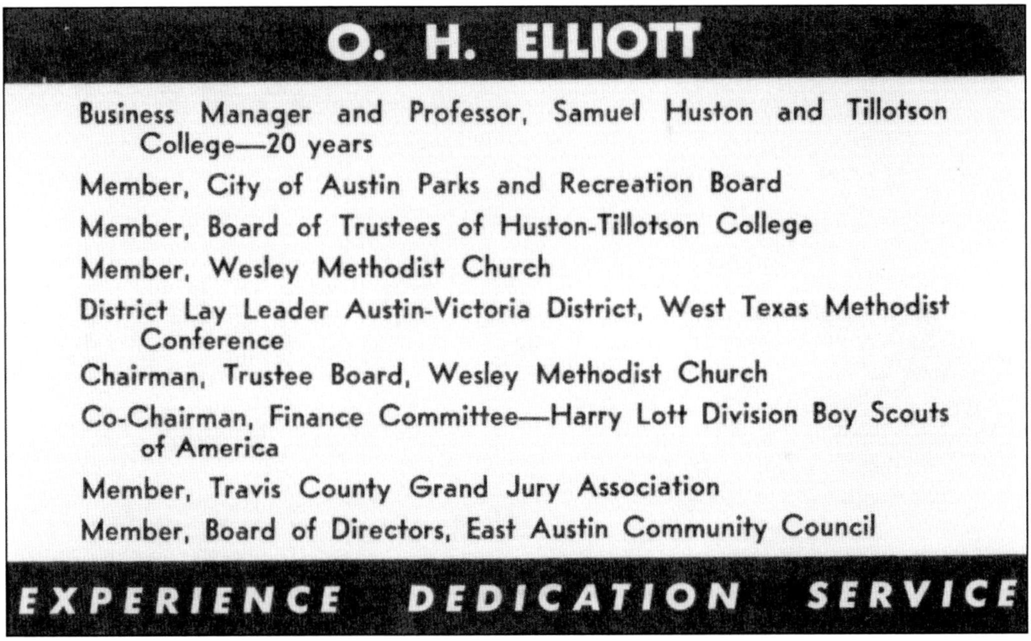
O. H. ELLIOTT

Business Manager and Professor, Samuel Huston and Tillotson College—20 years

Member, City of Austin Parks and Recreation Board

Member, Board of Trustees of Huston-Tillotson College

Member, Wesley Methodist Church

District Lay Leader Austin-Victoria District, West Texas Methodist Conference

Chairman, Trustee Board, Wesley Methodist Church

Co-Chairman, Finance Committee—Harry Lott Division Boy Scouts of America

Member, Travis County Grand Jury Association

Member, Board of Directors, East Austin Community Council

EXPERIENCE DEDICATION SERVICE

Mr. Elliott was active in the Travis County Democratic Party, served as a member of the City of Austin Parks and Recreation Board, chairman of the Harry Lot Division of the Boy Scouts of America, grand secretary of the Most Worshipful St. Joseph Grand Lodge, and chairman of the Trustee Board of the Wesley United Methodist Church. He was also a founding member of the Capital City Lions Club and the *Capital City Argus*, an African American newspaper. This photograph shows a card from Elliott's campaign for chair of local precinct 128. (Courtesy of AHC, AR 2007.017[1-27-Back].)

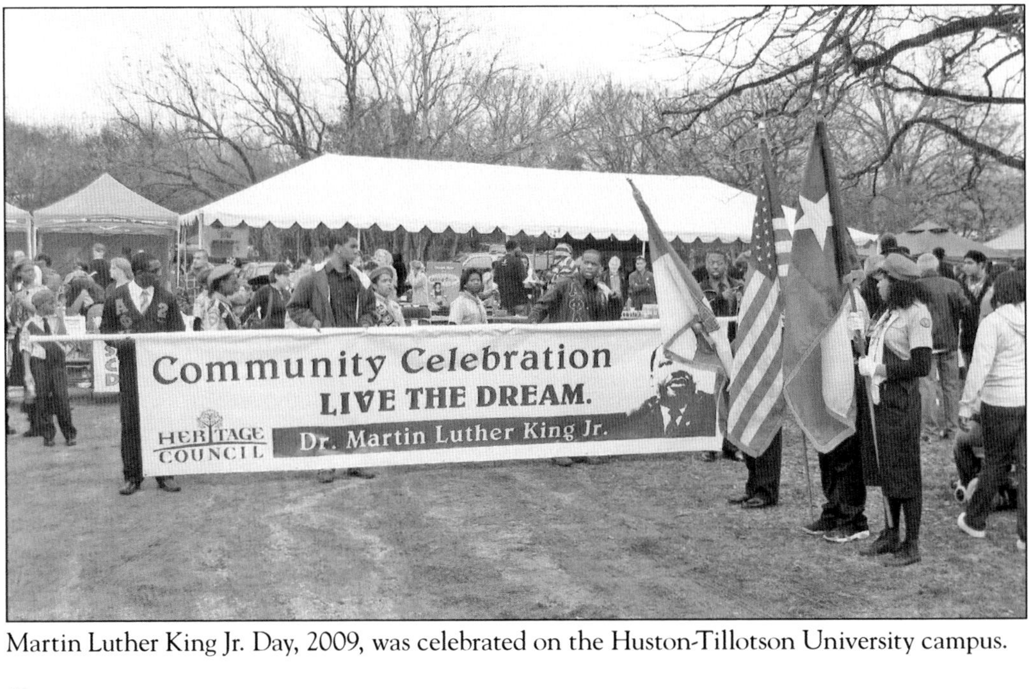

Martin Luther King Jr. Day, 2009, was celebrated on the Huston-Tillotson University campus.

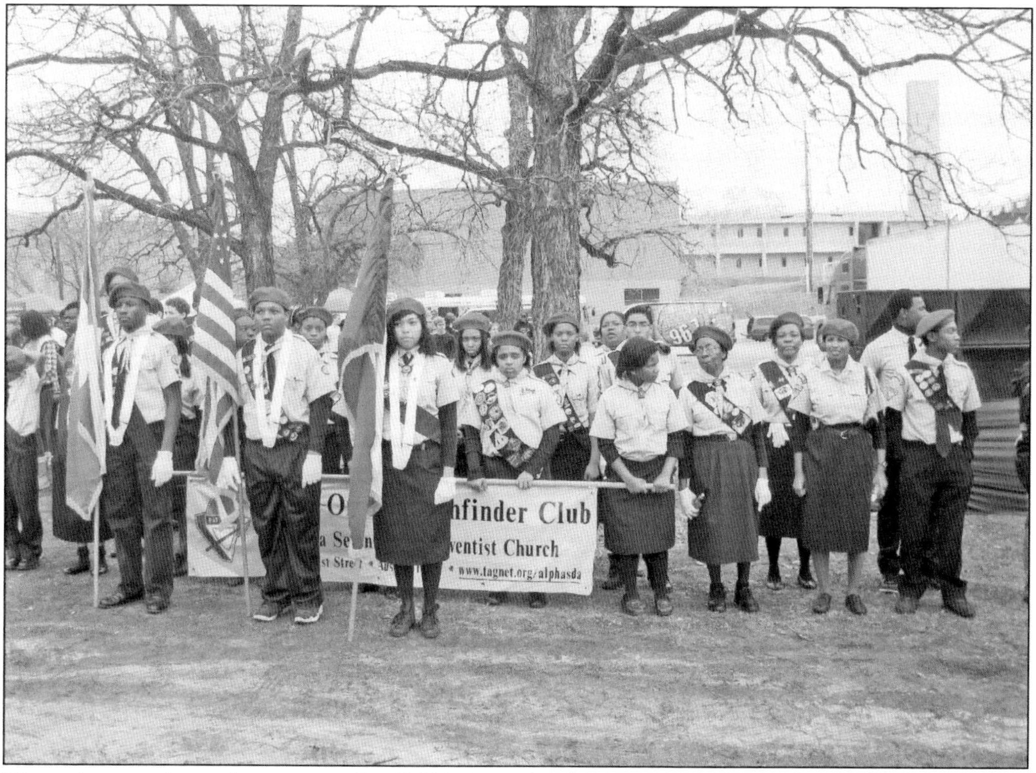

The color guard stands at rest at the 2009 Martin Luther King Jr. Day event at Huston-Tillotson.

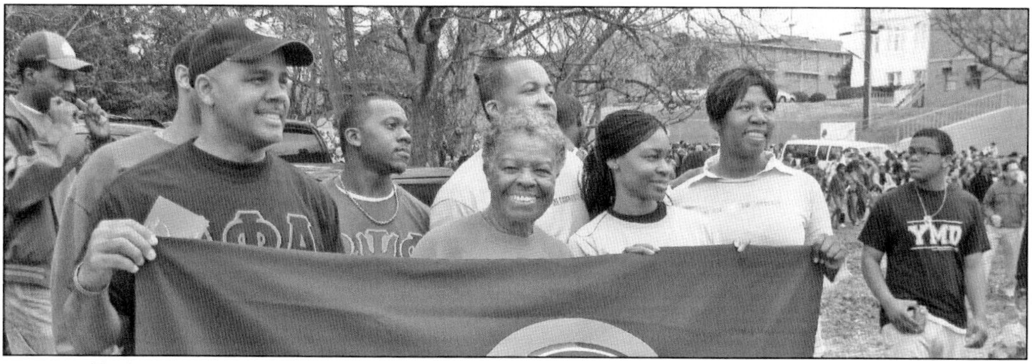

Rep. Wilhelmina Ruth Delco (center, behind the flag) attended the Martin Luther King Jr. Day celebration. Representative Delco, born in Chicago, was educated there and at Fisk University in Nashville. When she and her husband relocated to Austin, she became an active participant and then leader in the Parent Teacher Association in her children's school. Representative Delco was the first African American elected to the AISD Board of Trustees in 1968. After a successful term on the school board, she ran a successful campaign for the Texas House of Representatives. She served in the Texas State Legislature for 20 years.

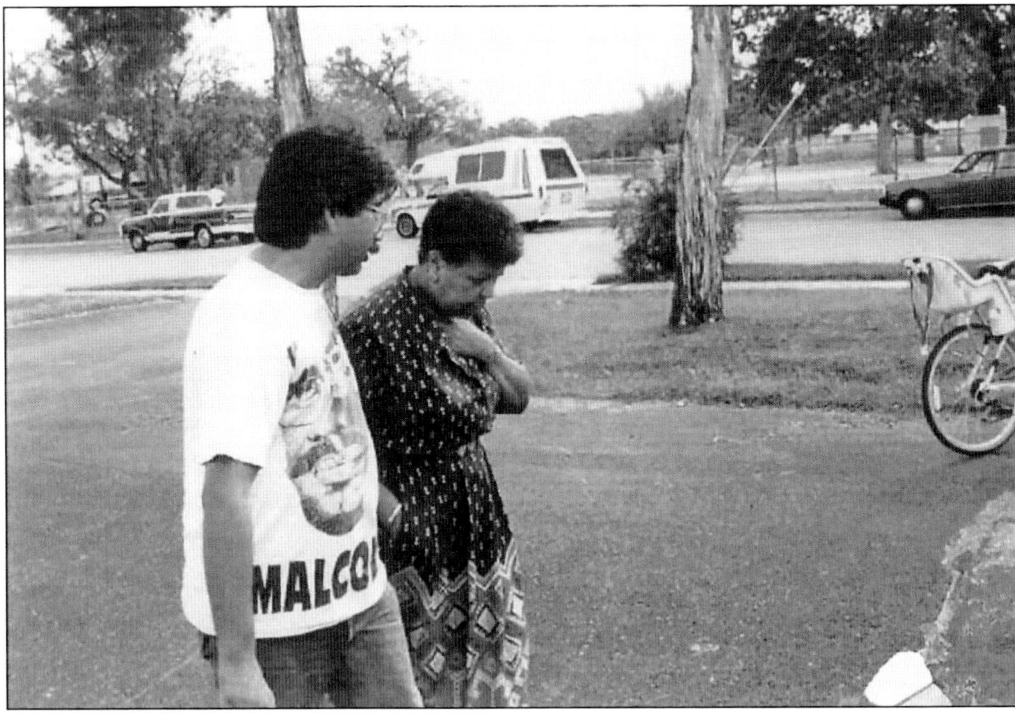

Author Gilberto Rivera is pictured with Representative Delco in the 1980s during a Rosewood neighborhood cleanup. (Courtesy of Tony Hall.)

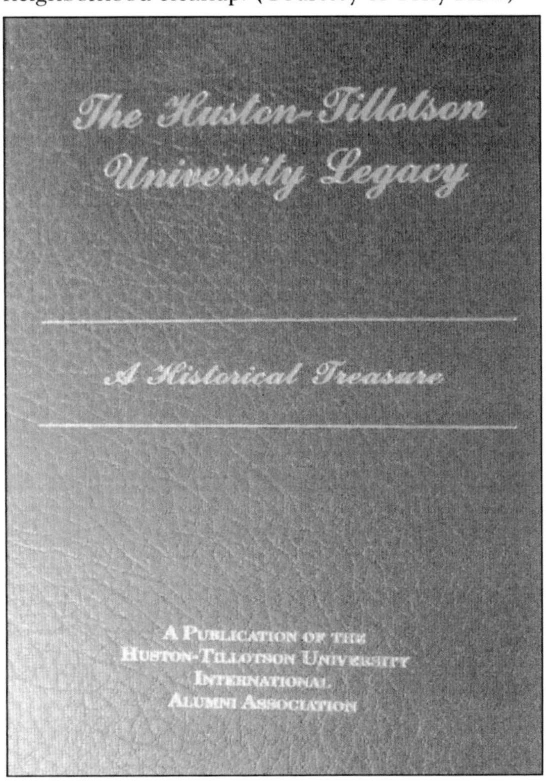

Dr. Wilhelmina E. Perry and August N. Swain researched and wrote *The Huston-Tillotson University Legacy: A Historical Treasure*. Dr. Perry is the daughter of Dr. William H. Jones, president of Tillotson College from 1944 to 1952. This book celebrates the unique history and contribution of the university to the city of Austin, the African American community of Austin, and the neighborhoods surrounding the university. The first page notes, "The original schools appeared in the 1870s . . . each represented Reconstruction Era efforts to further higher education opportunities for emancipated slaves and their children . . . The school has now revised itself to serve the interests of education in a desegregated, pluralistic society." This important volume celebrates the many alumni of Huston-Tillotson, including education administrator Dr. William Charles Akins, civil rights leader Volma Overton, and city council member Dr. Charles E. Urdy.

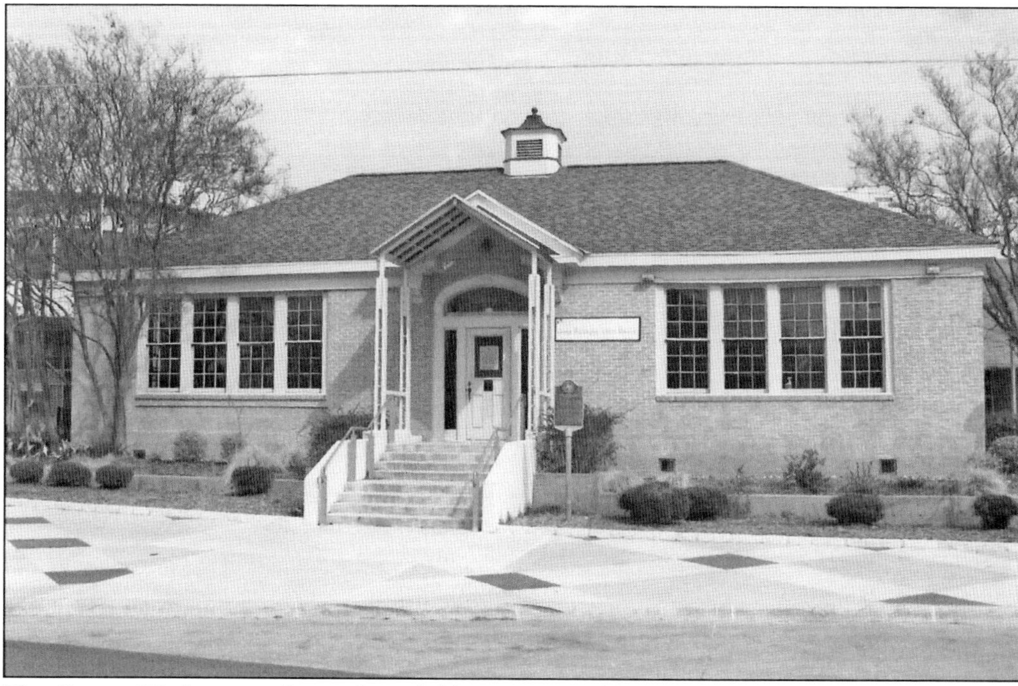

The George Washington Carver branch library was established in 1933 at 1165 Angelina Street, when the city built a new central library and moved the 1,800-square-foot original central library building to Rosewood to serve African American citizens. In 1979, the original Carver branch library was converted to the Carver Museum.

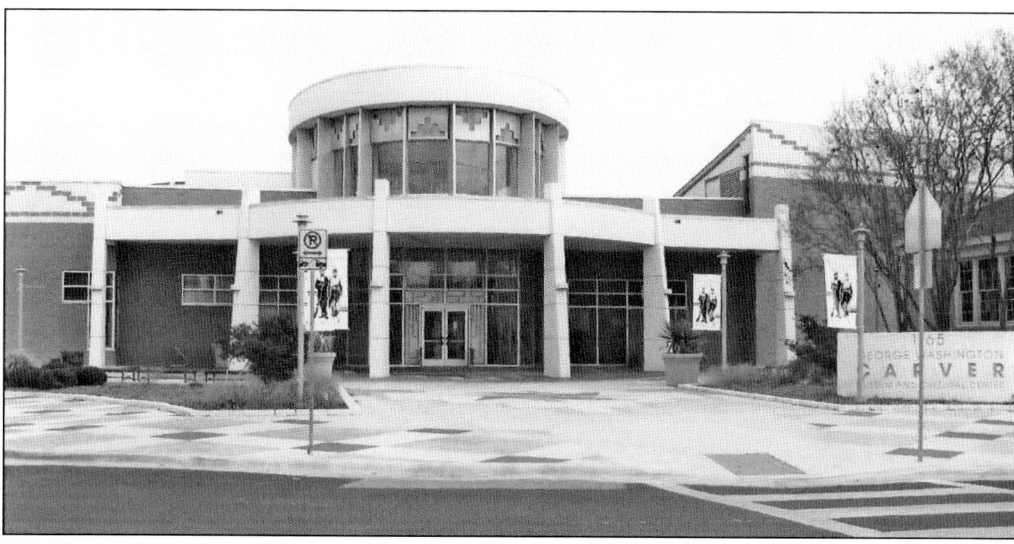

The George Washington Carver Museum, Library and Cultural Center Complex is located on Angelina Street just west of Rosewood, where the original branch library was located in 1933. The old branch library became the museum when, in 1979, the city built a new 10,000-square-foot library facility to better serve the community. Then, in 2004, the library was upgraded with expanded space for public-use computers, meeting rooms, and a youth area. In addition, a new 30,755-square-foot cultural center, complete with various meeting rooms, a stage, and teaching space was built in conjunction with the expansion of the library.

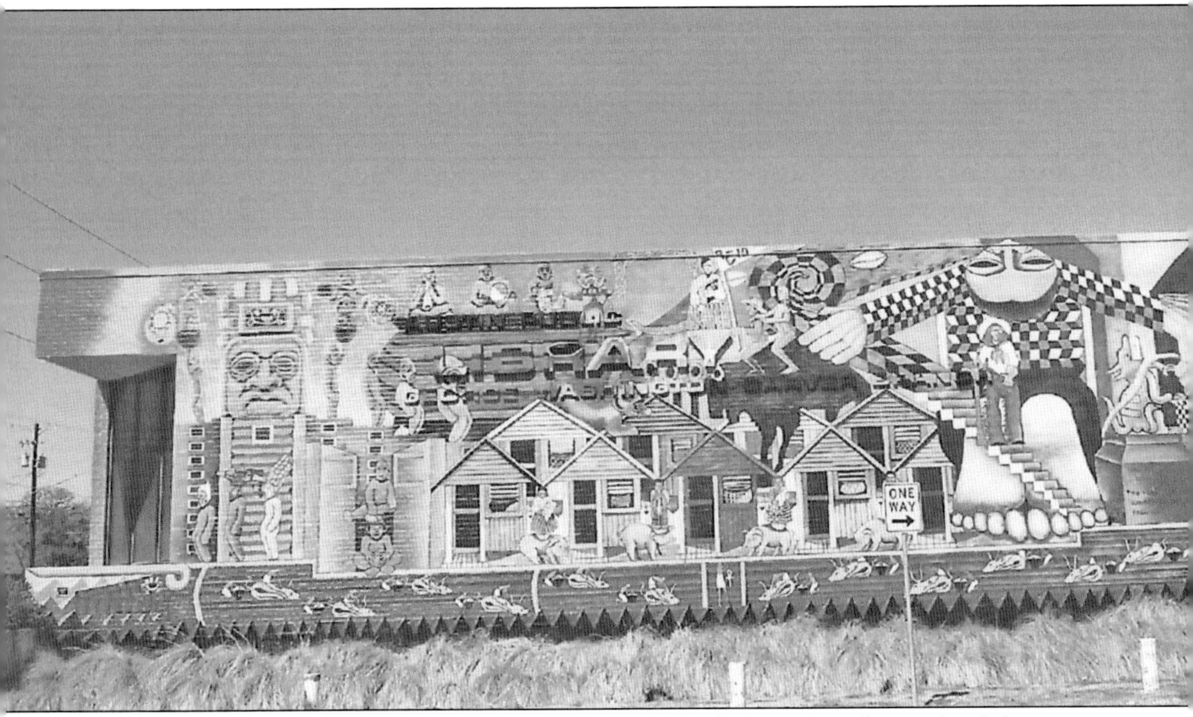

The Sesquicentennial Mural, "The Middle Passage"—dedicated to those who did not survive the Middle Passage as slaves on the transatlantic ships—was created by artist John Fisher in 1986 on the southern wall of the George Washington Carver Library. Mr. Fisher fully restored the mural in 1999.

Three

Business

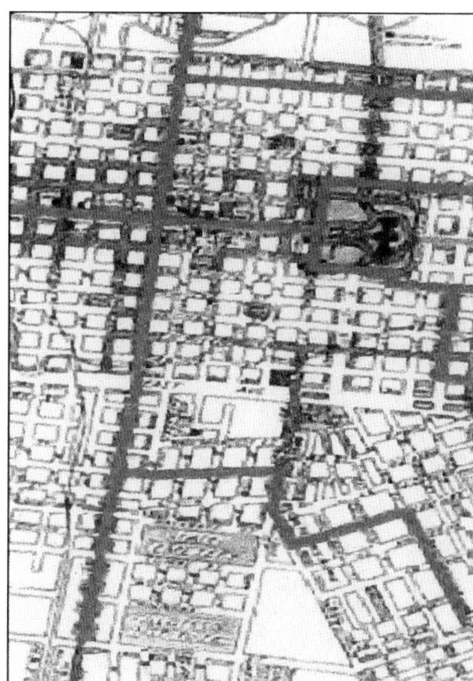

According to an *Austin Statesman* account on March 23, 1955, the Republic of Texas laid out Austin in 1839 with Congress Avenue as the main street. In 1871, the City of Austin introduced its first urban rail line in the form of trolley cars that served downtown and major north-south and east-west arterials. Clint Smith, a former Rosewood resident, recalls that, growing up in the late 1930s, Twelfth and Chicon Streets were the end of the streetcar line. (Courtesy of the Texas General Land Office.)

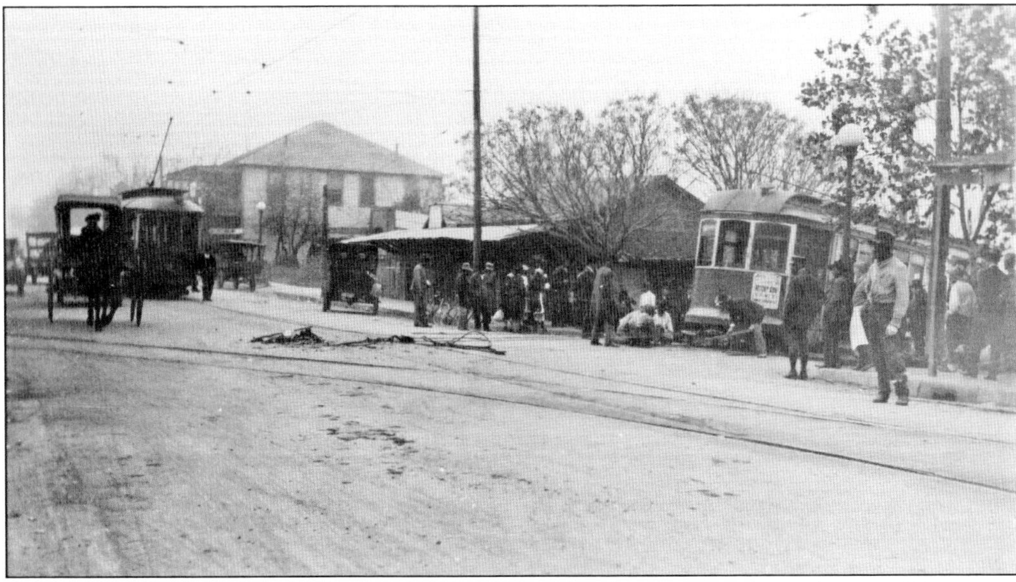

Here is a streetcar at the corner of Waller and East Sixth Streets, just southwest of Rosewood. (Courtesy of AHC, PICA 18803.)

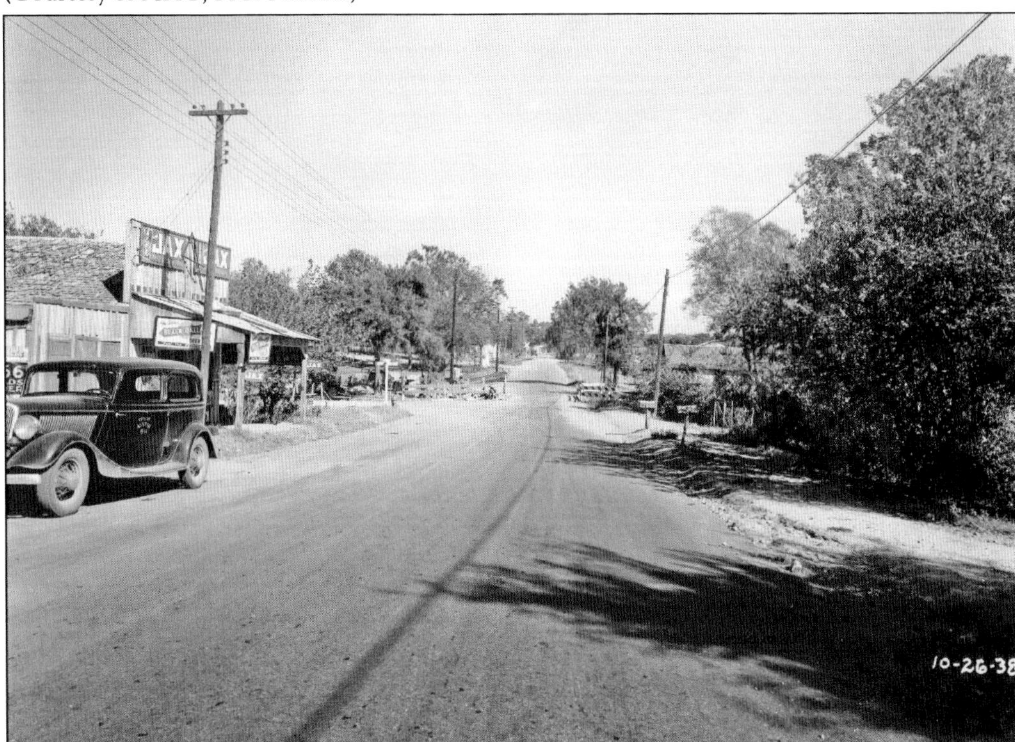

This is a view of Rosewood Avenue at Chestnut Street on October 26, 1938. The construction in progress was to widen the bridge over Boggy Creek. By the 1940s, the Rosewood business community included Fats Walker Tailor Shop, the Deluxe Ice House, the Deluxe Cab Company, the Rocco Service Station, Marshall Barber Shop, Dr. Washington's office, Jolly's Grocery Store, McClain's Grocery Store, Smith's Plumbing, and B&L Heating and Air. (Courtesy of AHC, PICA 02354.)

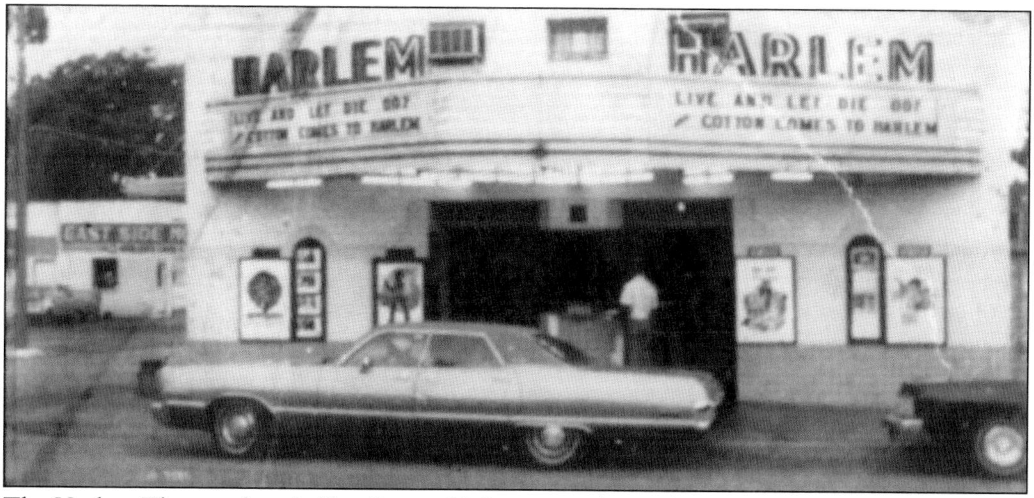

The Harlem Theater, founded by George H. Jones, was located in the business corridor and was filled with neighborhood residents for every show. From the 1930s through the 1950s, Rosewood residents can recall African Americans going to the movies comfortably at the Harlem Theater, but if they wanted to attend a movie at the Ritz on East Sixth Street downtown, they had to sit in the balcony, segregated from white moviegoers. (Courtesy of AHC, AR.2001.002[H-2].)

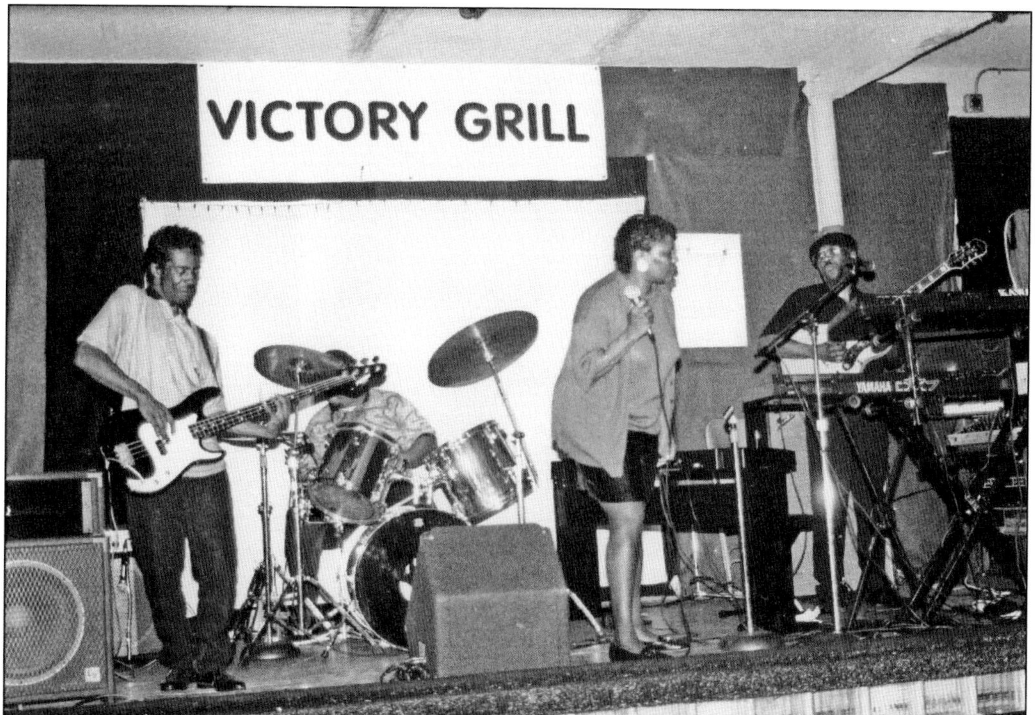

During the late 1940s and 1950s, music lovers went to the east side of town to hear live bands at clubs on "the cuts" (East Eleventh) and at "the end" (East Twelfth). During this time, the area became an entertainment center for African Americans. Here, Sugar Williams and A Touch of Class perform at the Victory Grill several decades later. (Courtesy of AHC, AR.2001.002[V-1].)

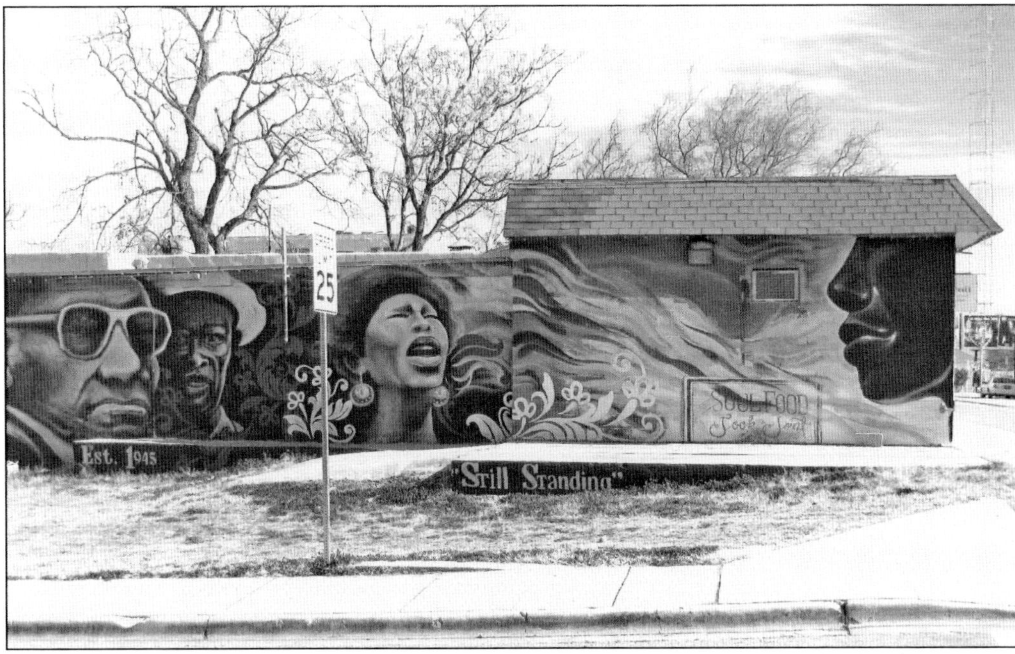

This mural is on the north wall of the Victory Grill, just west of Rosewood. This business is a restaurant and bar with an indoor venue for live music, which supports Austin's ability to remain the "live music capital of the world."

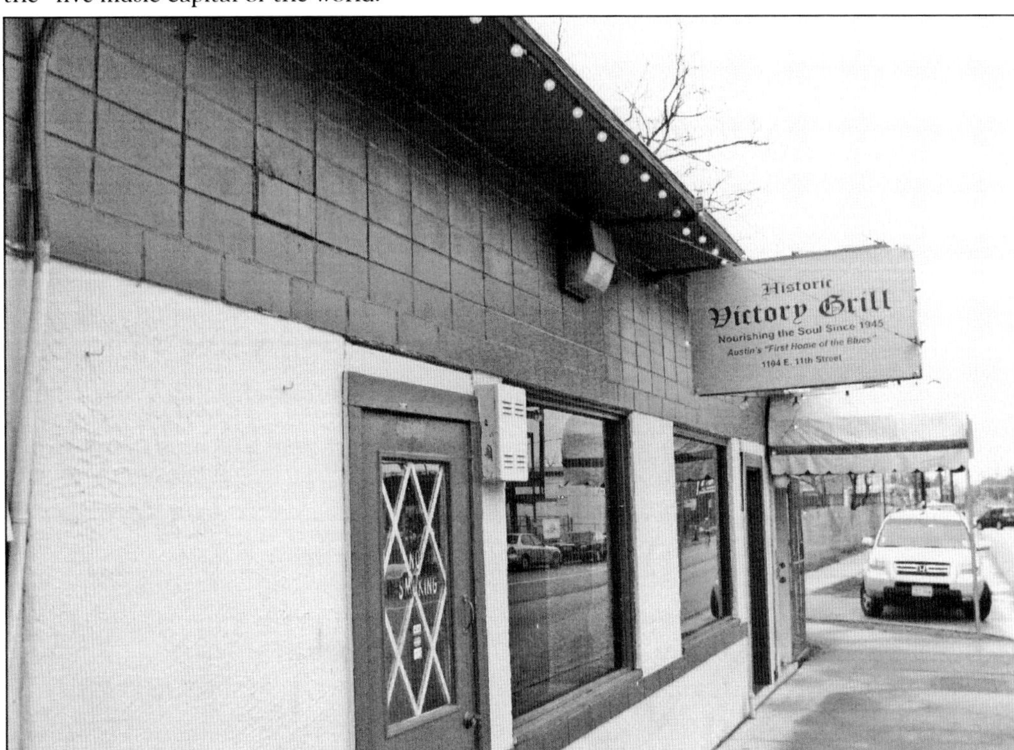

Shown here is the front of the Victory Grill, on East Eleventh Street.

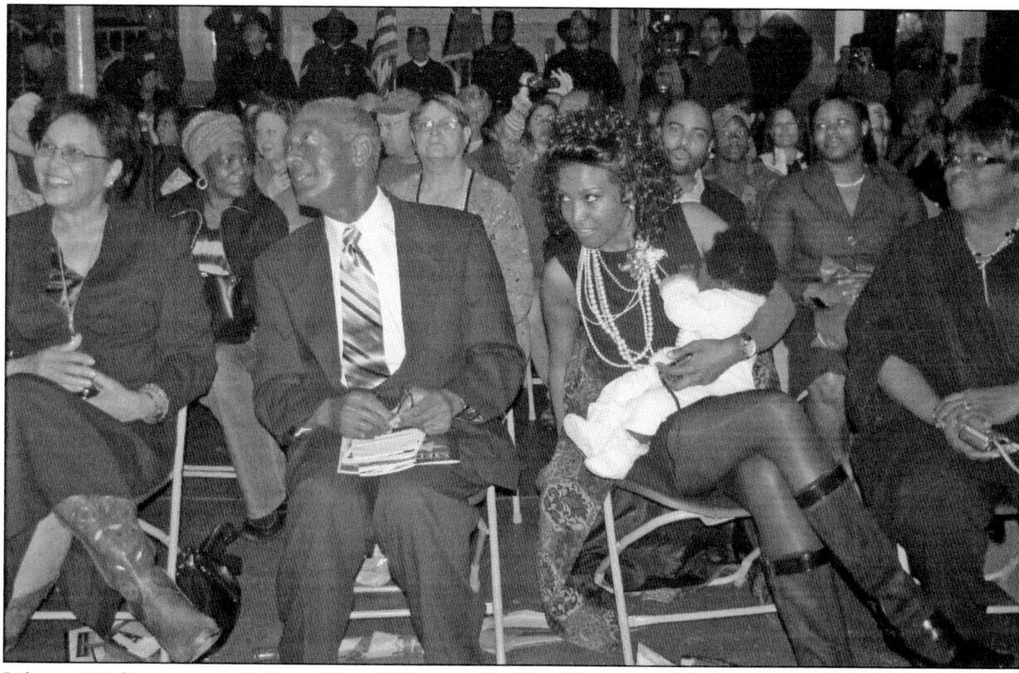

Johnny Holmes opened the original Victory Grill on Rosewood Avenue on VJ Day (Victory over Japan Day, August 16, 1945). Holmes's children, Johnny Holmes Jr. (not pictured), Raymond L. Holmes (second from left), and Myrtle Lafaye Holmes (far right), were present for the dedication on February 9, 2010, of an official Texas Historical Marker for the venue. The Texas Historical Commission recognized the historic Victory Grill with the marker, which commemorates the significance of the establishment during and after World War II.

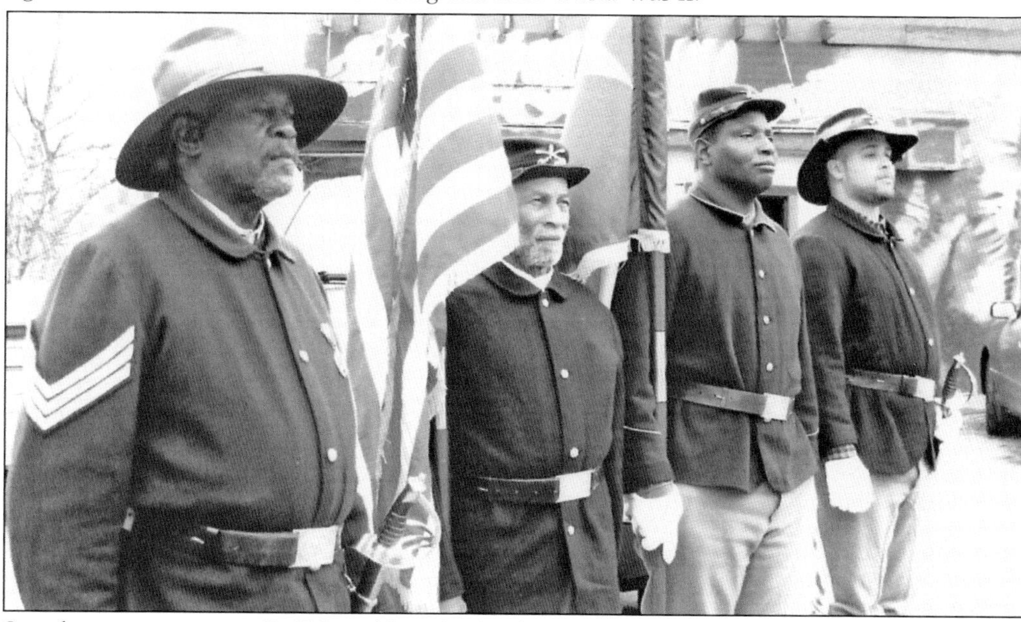

Standing at attention as Buffalo Soldiers for the dedication of the historical marker at the Victory Grill are, from left to right, Luis Padilla, Selton Williams, Nathaniel Booker, Horace P. Williams, and David Boevers (not pictured).

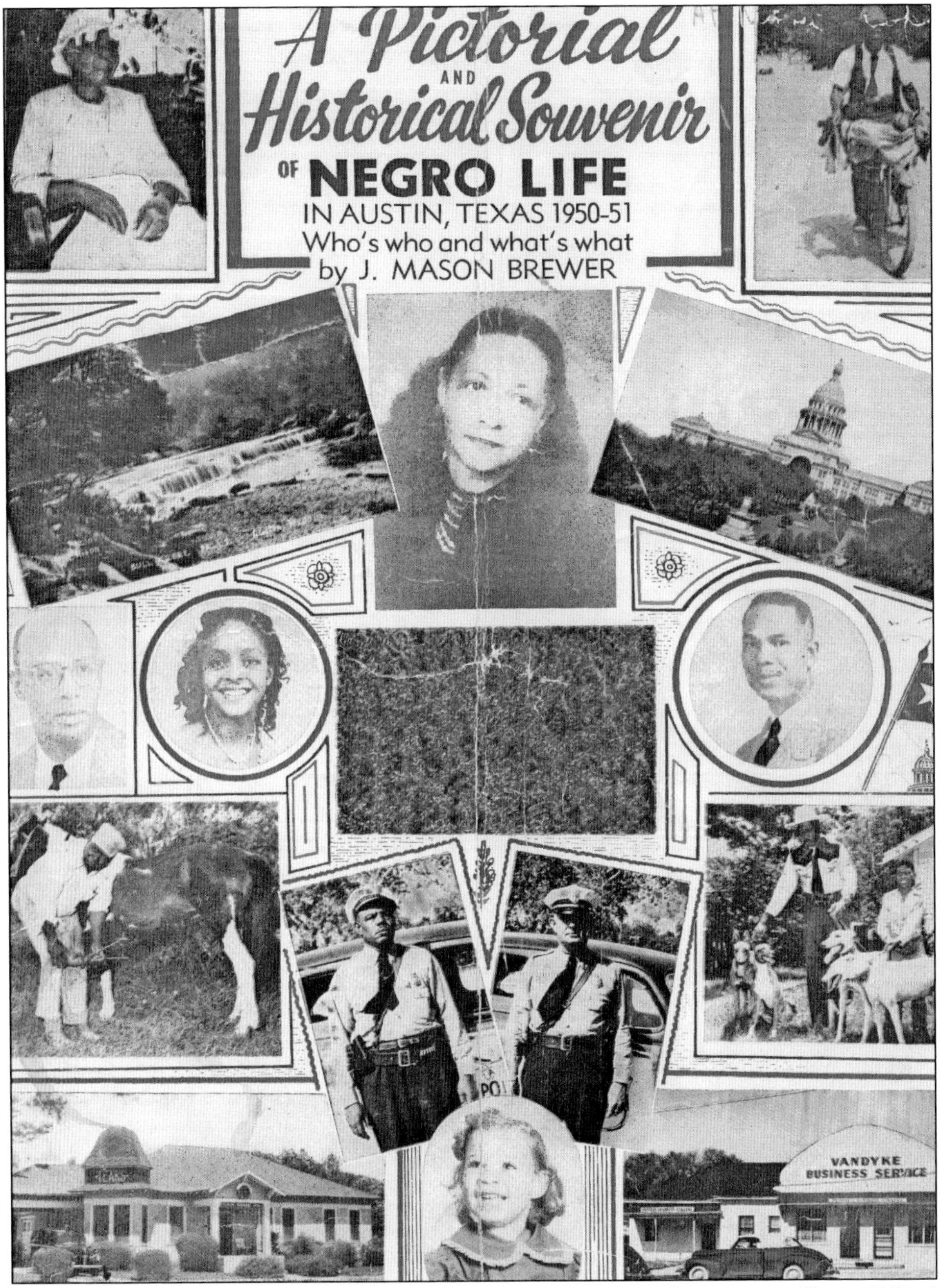

In 1951, J. Mason Brewer compiled *A Pictorial Souvenir of Negro Life in Austin, Texas 1950–1951.* Numerous businesses advertised in the document, including: Talley's News Nook and Lee's Shoe Repair at 1087 East Twelfth Street , Franklin's Barber Shop at 1014B East Eleventh, Caldwell's Barber Shop at 1208A East Twelfth, Chew-Chat Inn at 3001 East Twelfth, Hillside Drug Store at 1209 East Eleventh, E.L. Anderson Service Station at 1328 East Twelfth, Harlem Cab Co. at 1129 1/2 East Twelfth, Jasper's Real Estate and Lumber Company at 3003 East Twelfth, Jewell's Parisienne Beauty Shoppe at 1014 East Twelfth, Southern Dinnett at 1010 East Eleventh, Bell Tailors at 1197 Chicon, and Marvel Cleaners at 1710 East Eleventh. (Courtesy of AHC, 325.26Br-Pictorial.)

William M. Tears Sr., at the time the first African American on the Austin police force, serving from 1895 to 1901, became the first African American undertaker in the city. He left the police force to found Tears Mortuary in 1901. At the time, it was located at 514 East Sixth Street in what is now downtown Austin.

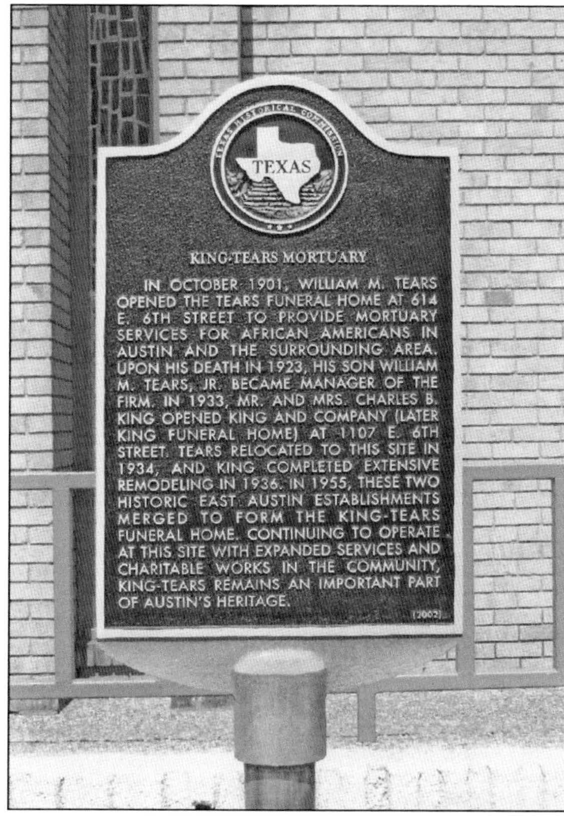

In 1955, the Tears Funeral Home merged with the King Funeral Home to become King-Tears Mortuary, located at 1300 East Twelfth Street. The funeral home, featured in Mr. Brewer's 1951 souvenir, was then operated by Milton C. Tears, the second son of the founder. King Tears Mortuary is still in business today. Dr. John Q. Taylor King Sr., Huston-Tillotson University's longest-serving president, served as president of King Tears after his retirement from Huston-Tillotson.

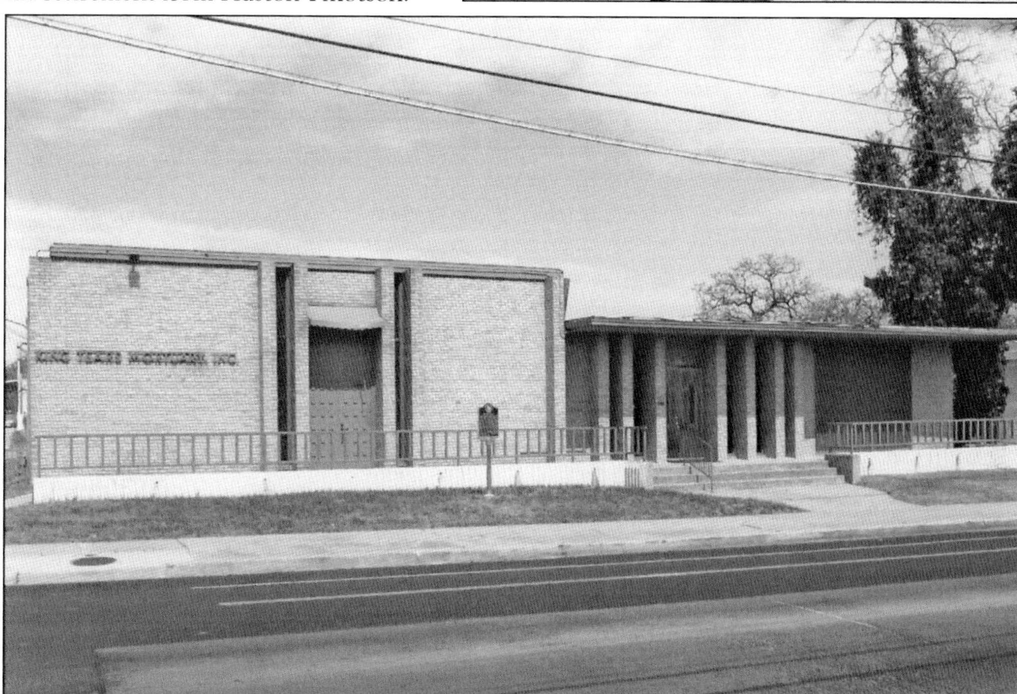

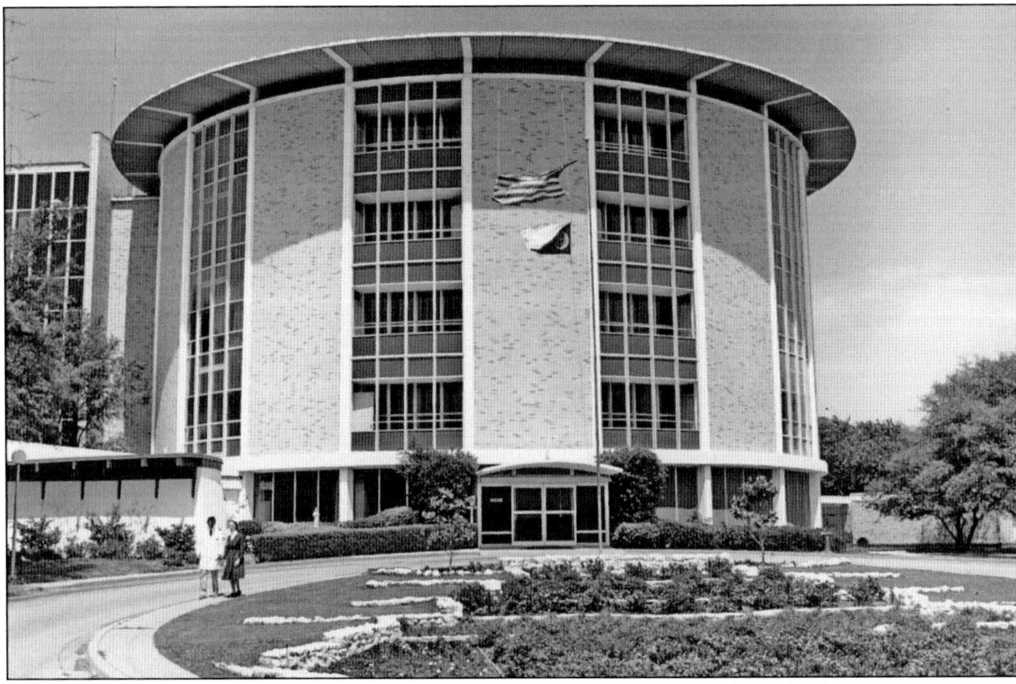

Holy Cross Hospital was built on the grounds of Holy Cross Catholic Church in 1940. It was the only local hospital where African American physicians were permitted to practice medicine. According to the web page on Holy Cross Catholic Church maintained by the Catholic Diocese of Austin, the Franciscan Missionary Sisters of the Immaculate Conception, the first religious women to practice medicine in the United States, staffed Holy Cross. The hospital moved from the church grounds to this larger facility on Martin Luther King Jr. Boulevard in 1951. When Holy Cross Hospital closed in 1989, there was no longer a hospital anywhere in Rosewood or in all of East Austin. (Courtesy of AHC, PICA 28987.)

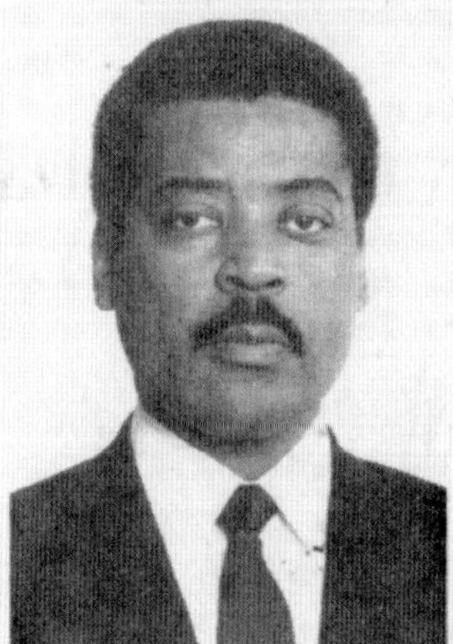

Pharmacist **O.C. Houston** is well know for his pharmaceutical services and for his kindness and concern for others. The owner of Hospital Pharmacy is active in the NAACP, and several other organizations.

O.C. Houston has been the owner and head pharmacist of Hospital Pharmacy, 2115 East Martin Luther King Jr. Boulevard in Rosewood, for more than 30 years. The caption with this photograph from the *Villager* notes that he was well known not only for his pharmaceutical services but also for his concern for others, as demonstrated by his participation in the NAACP and other service-minded organizations. (Courtesy of AHC, AR.2001.002[H-4].)

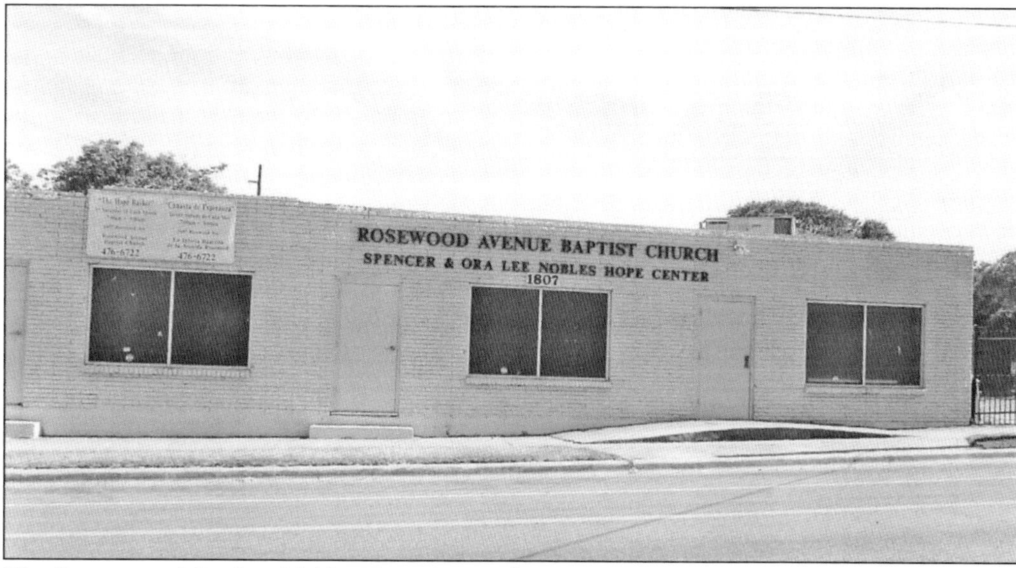

The Spencer and Ora Lee Nobles Hope Center, located on Rosewood, was the site of the Spencer and Ora Lee Nobles Barbecue restaurant. Ora Lee Nobles was born at home, on East Ninth Street, assisted by a midwife. Nobles noted, in an interview in *Historic Resources Survey of East Austin, Texas* in 2000, that the neighborhood was always integrated with African Americans, Mexican Americans, and whites. The streets in the area were not paved, and Ms. Nobles's mother fought to get city sewers, paved streets, and gas service in the 1940s. Ms. Nobles's parents were working people, but her father was one of the few people in the neighborhood to own a car and a garage, so he gave rides on his way to work to neighbors who worked downtown.

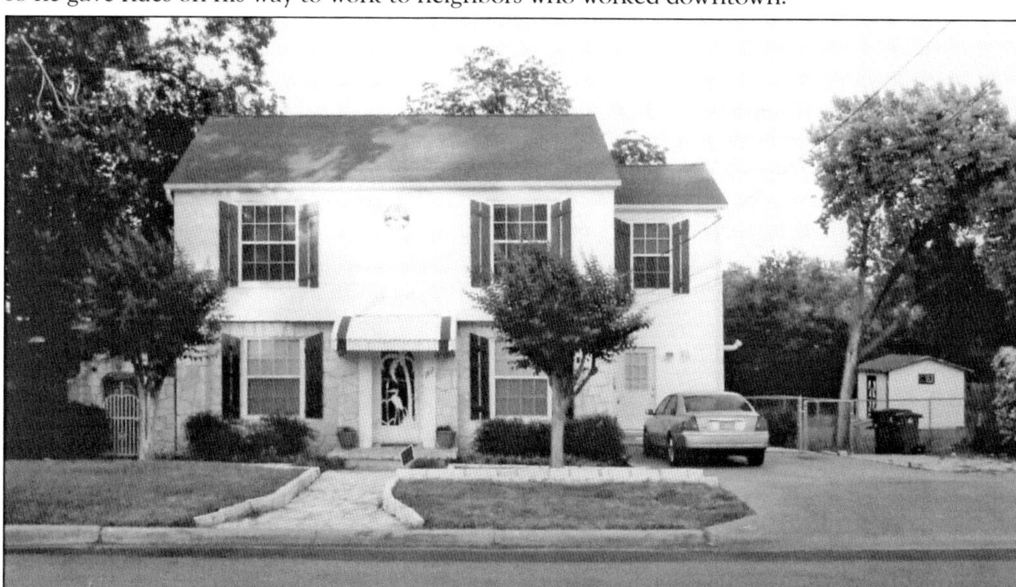

Dr. Everett H. Givens was one of the first African American dentists in Austin, living just northwest of Rosewood in this house, built in 1938, when he had his practice. Dr. Givens was also a civic leader. Dr. and Ms. Givens had a pool in the backyard with a pool house, and they were well known for their hospitality and generosity. Pres. Lyndon B. Johnson was among Dr. Givens's personal friends.

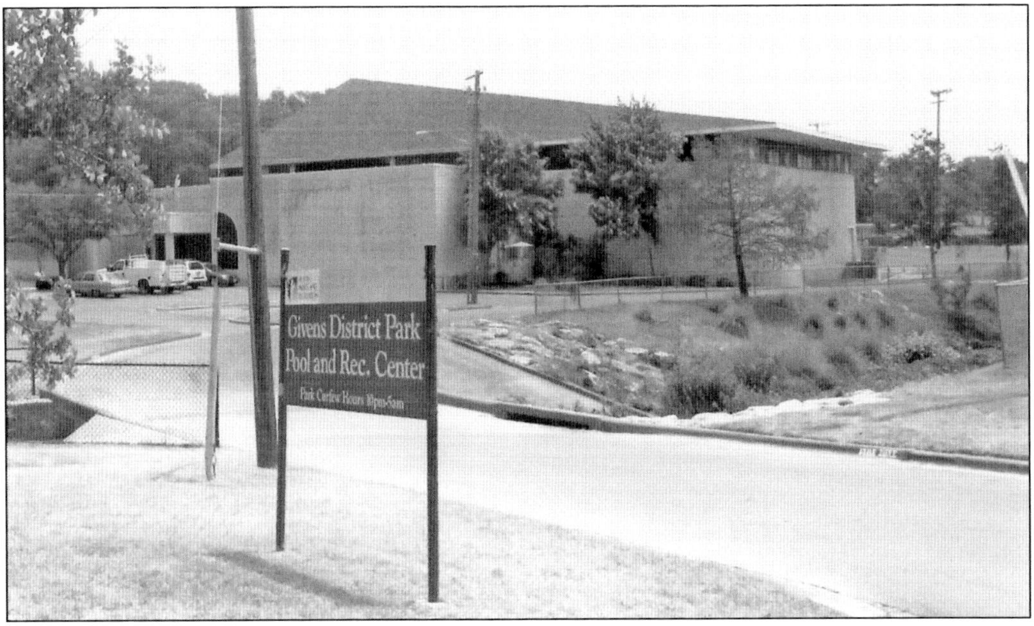

In 1974, the Austin City Council adopted the City Parks and Recreation Advisory Board recommendation to rename Oak Springs Park as Dr. Everett H. Givens Park, in honor of Dr. Givens. Givens Park includes a recreation center, swimming pool, pavilion, two lighted tennis courts, playscape, picnic area, and two softball fields.

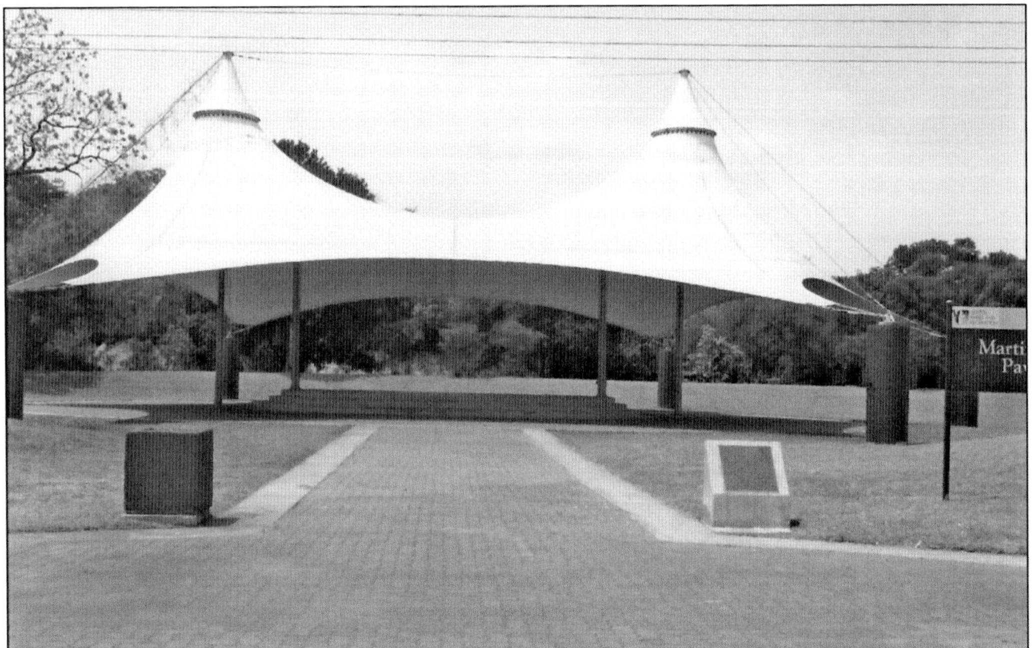

Martin Banks was an Austin musician who graduated from Anderson High school, moved to California in 1953 to study music, and performed with many great artists, including Ray Charles, Duke Ellington, James Brown, Dizzy Gillespie, and the Sun Ra Arkestra. This pavilion in Givens Park was named in honor of Mr. Banks.

Author Gilberto Rivera recalls that when he was growing up in the late 1950s, the current site of the city maintenance yard at 2600 Webberville Road (just south of the Rosewood-Zaragosa Neighborhood Center) served as the local health clinic. In the 1980s, when Mr. Rivera's children were small, Chestnut House (located at 1183 Chestnut, just north of the Rosewood Recreation Center) housed a health clinic. In 2010, the city replaced Chestnut House with a new facility.

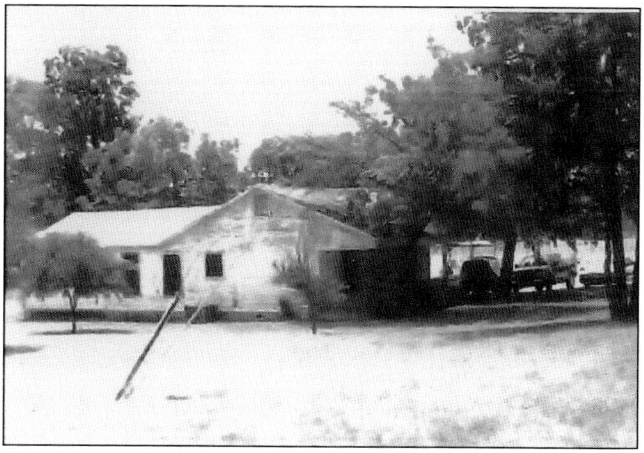

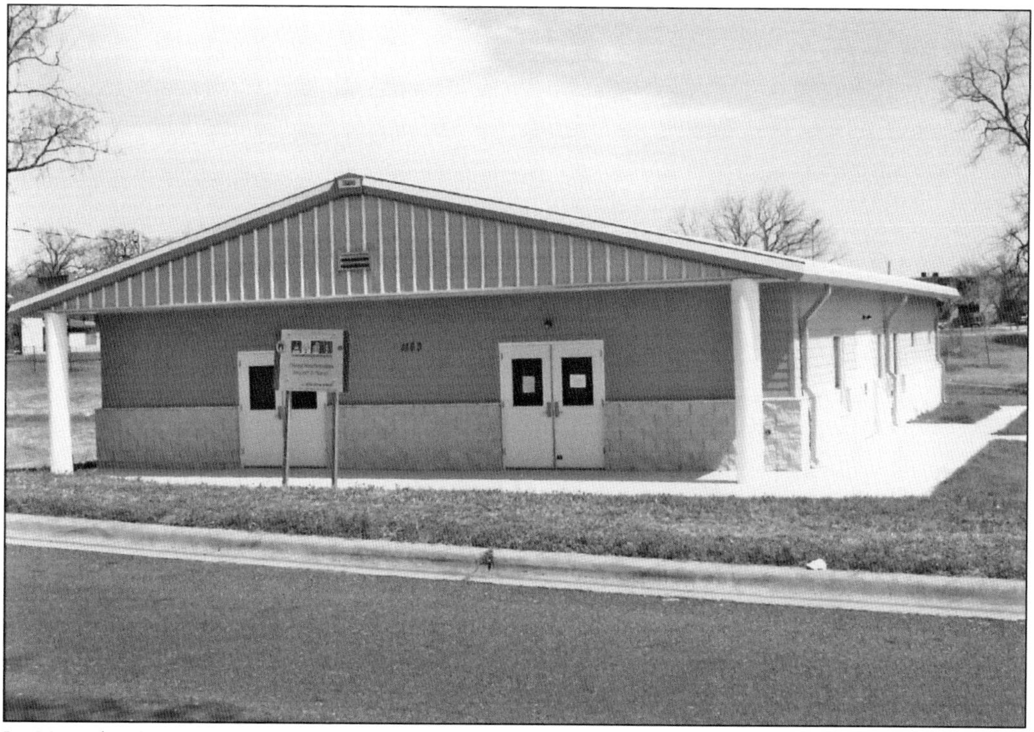

In 2011, the Austin City Council named the new Chestnut House the Britton, Durst, Howard and Spence Building in honor of Lawrence M. Britton Sr., Rev. Albert Lavada Durst, James Howard, and Donald Joseph Spence.

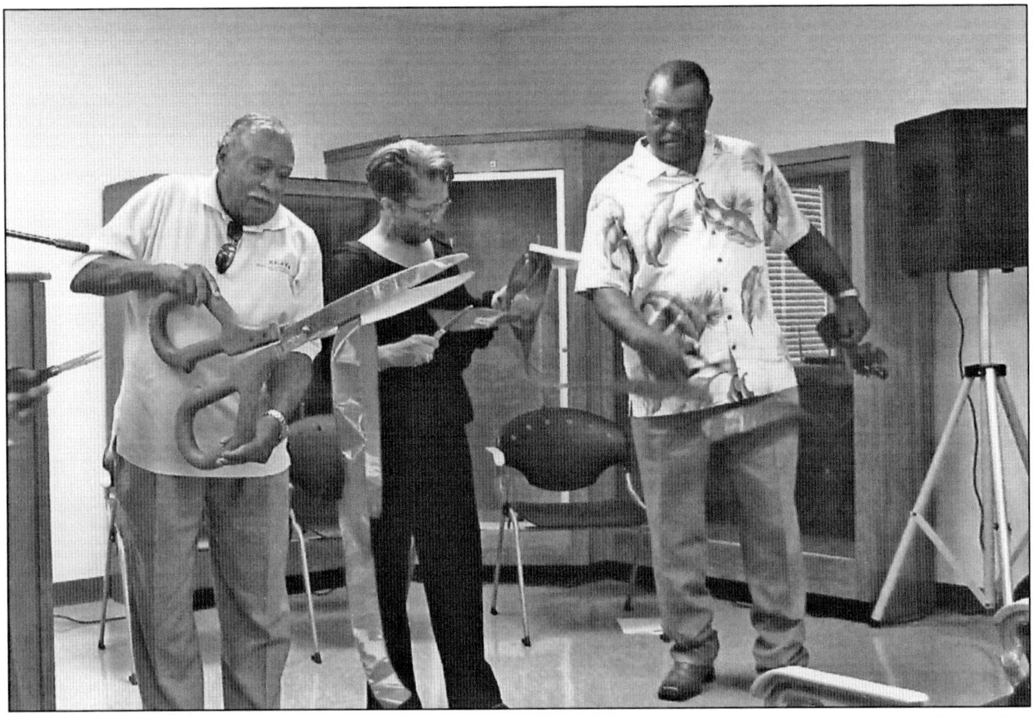

Lawrence Britton Jr. is pictured at the right in this ribbon-cutting ceremony image from the opening of the Britton, Durst, Howard and Spence Building held on August 6, 2011. Mr. Britton Sr. taught 29 years in AISD, first at the old L.C. Anderson High School. He was also assistant coach in football, head coach in track and field, and head coach in basketball. Under his leadership, Anderson won four state championships. Mr. Britton Sr. was one of the founders of the East Austin Youth Foundation. James Howard (left), another cofounder of the East Austin Youth Foundation, was also founder of the Greater East Austin Youth Association (GEAYA) and still coaches at GEAYA. Mr. Howard's wife is in the center of the photograph.

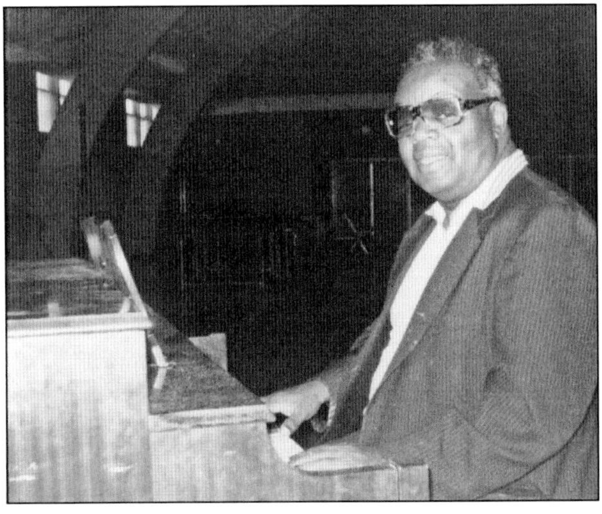

The Durst family has been in the Austin area for over 120 years. Rev. Albert Lavada Durst served as athletic director of the Doris Miller Auditorium, bringing in famous musical guests such as Duke Ellington, Lionel Hampton, and Ella Fitzgerald. He retired from the city's parks department in 1979. Reverend Durst was also an announcer for the Austin Senators, an African American Negro League baseball team that played at Downs Field. Reverend Durst became a pastor after he retired from the parks department. (Courtesy of AHC, PICB 12153.)

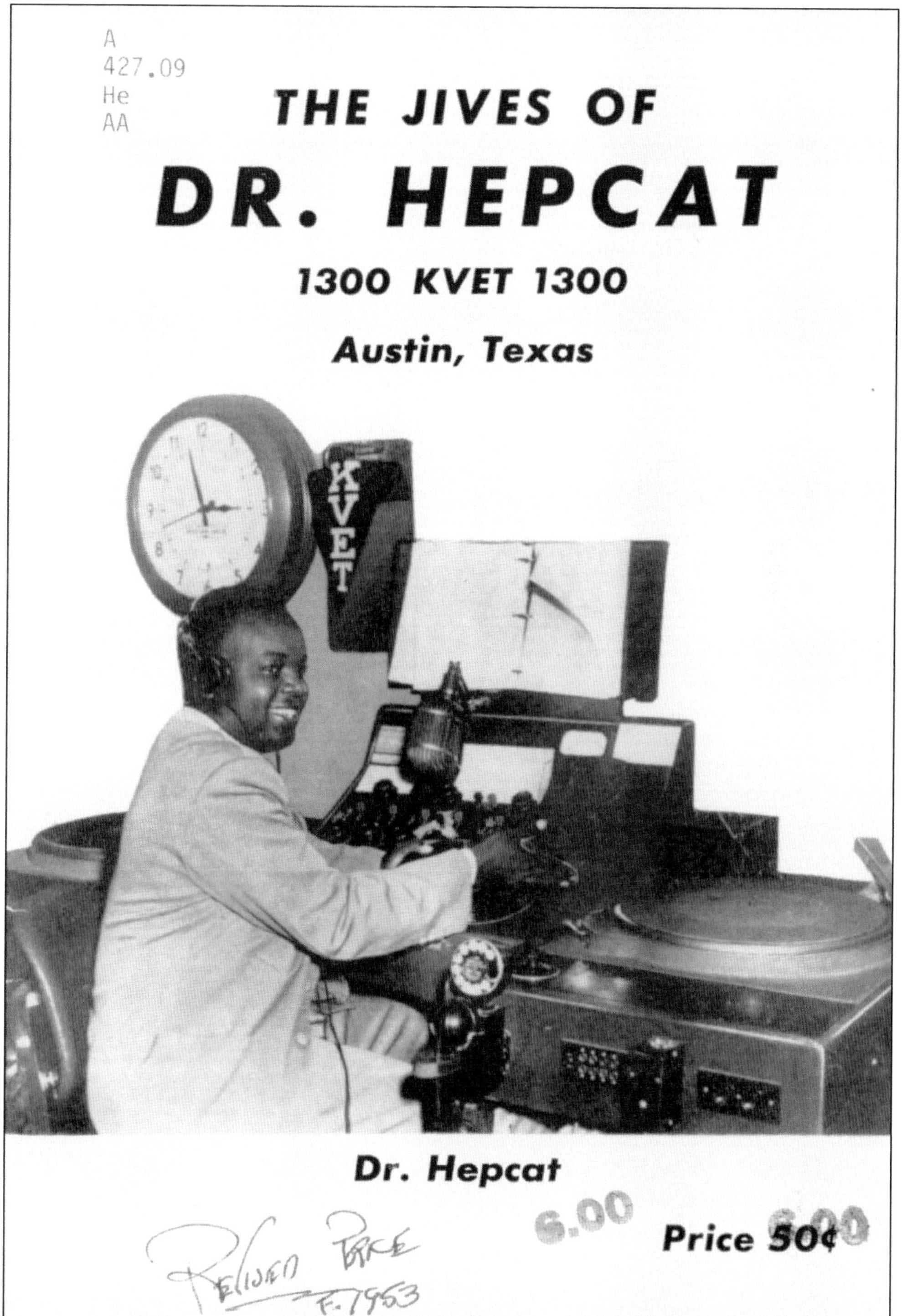

Rev. Albert Lavada Durst was also one of the first African American deejays in America and was a pianist and recorded singer as well. This is the cover of a booklet for his evening radio show, for which Reverend Durst assumed the name Dr. Hepcat. (Courtesy of the AHC, A427.09HeAA.)

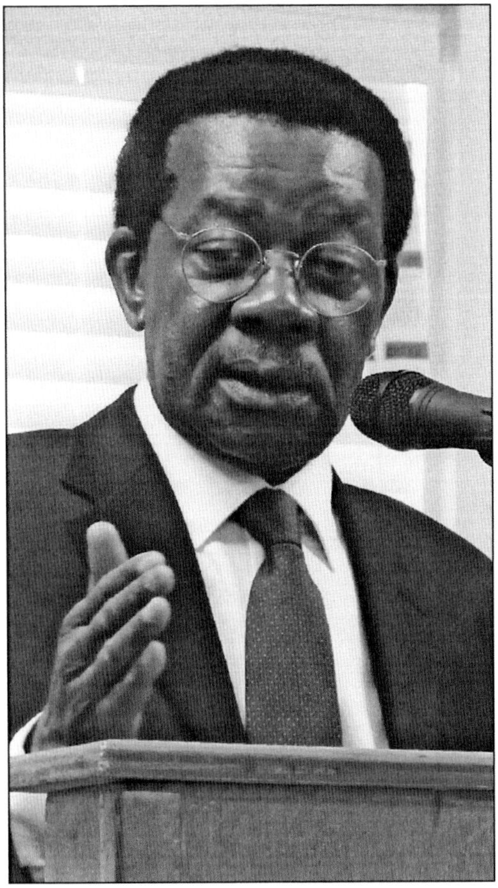

Charles Durst, son of Rev. Albert Lavada Durst, is shown here at the grand-opening ceremony of the Britton, Durst, Howard and Spence Building.

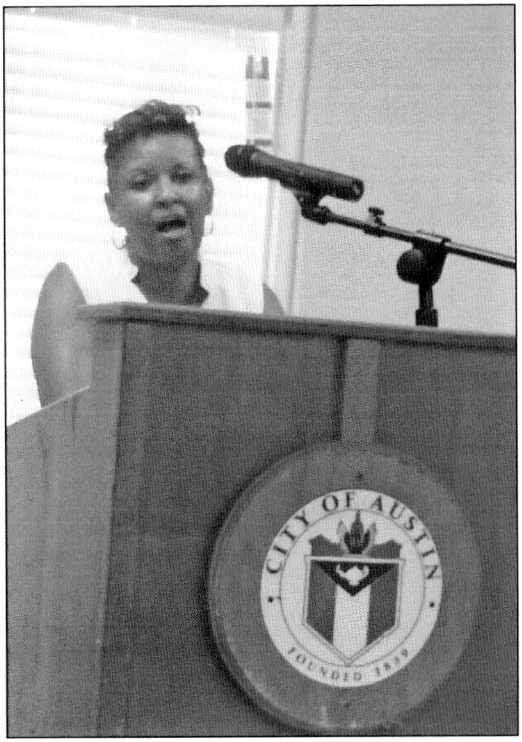

Carla Scales, niece of Donald Joseph Spence, is shown here at the grand-opening ceremony of the building named in honor of her uncle. Mr. Spence graduated from Anderson High School and Huston-Tillotson College. After teaching in Elgin, Texas, and Oakland, California, he went to work with the Austin Parks and Recreation Department, serving in various positions including East Austin program manager. After retiring, he became commissioner for the Greater East Austin Youth Association.

Shown here, from left to right, are James L. Stewart, his son Anthony Stewart, and his wife, Annie F. Stewart. Mr. Stewart graduated from Anderson High School, Huston-Tillotson College, Tyler Barber College, Prairie View A&M University, and several professional seminars. Ms. Stewart graduated from Emile High School in Bastrop, Texas, Nixon Clay Business College, Modern Barber College of Austin, and various professional seminars. (Courtesy of Annie F. Stewart.)

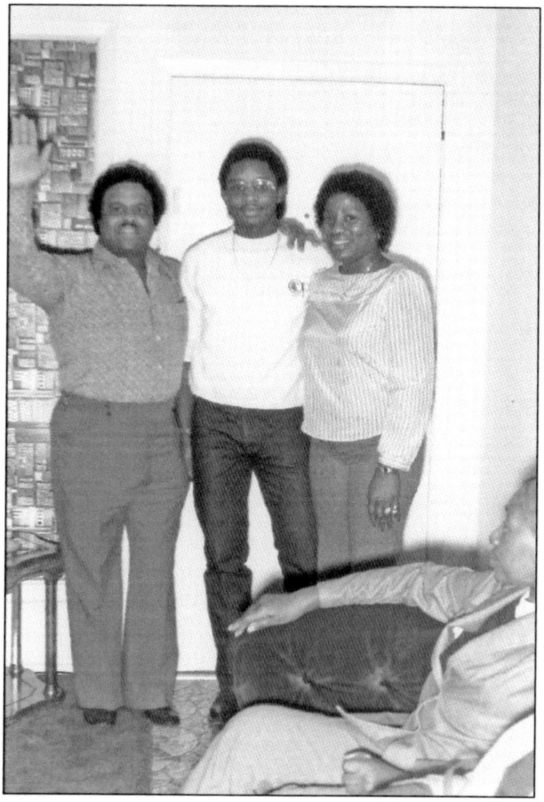

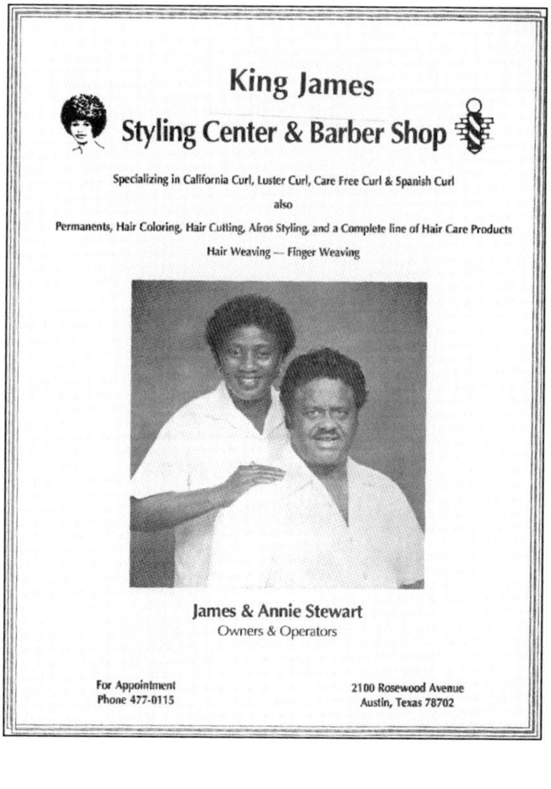

Mr. Stewart owned and operated four barbershops for 38 years in Rosewood, including the King James Styling Center and Barber Shop at 2100 Rosewood. For 10 years, he served as president of the Texas Association of Tonsorial Artists (TAOTA). Mrs. Stewart was active not only in the shop but also served with the Texas Agricultural Extension Service for 21 years and was assistant secretary of TAOTA and was its Austin chapter's secretary. She was a founding member of the Rosewood–Glen Oaks Neighborhood Association and remains an active member, today serving as treasurer. (Courtesy of Annie F. Stewart.)

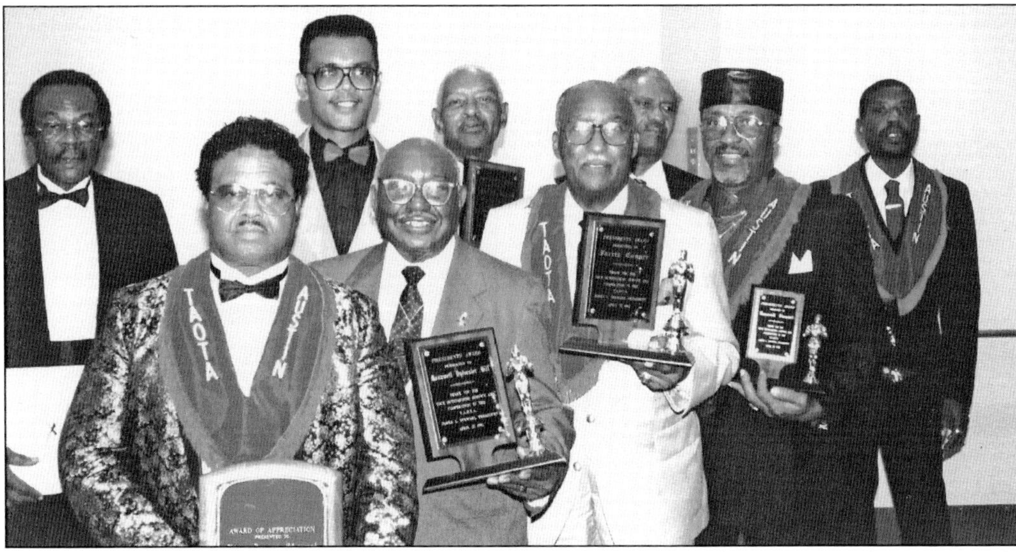

Pictured here is an award of appreciation presented to members for 10 years of service to the Texas Association of Tonsorial Artists on April 27, 1992. The recipients are, from left to right, as follows: Sylvester Hill (member), James L. Stewart (president), Farris Conner (business manager), Roosevelt Stewart (chairman of entertainment), Charles Hardeman (parliamentarian), George Walker (state president), Harold White (treasurer), Rev. David Dukes (chaplain), and Leonard Hill (member). (Courtesy of Annie F. Stewart.)

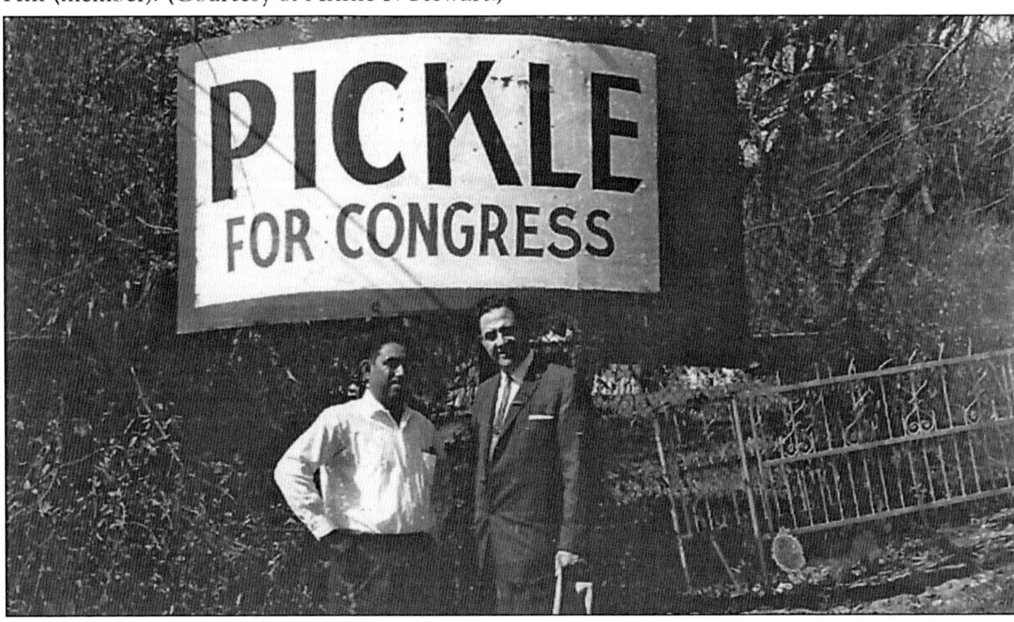

Louis Herrera Sr. founded Herrera Ornamental Iron Works in the late 1940s. A local business leader, Herrera is shown with US congressman Jake Pickle in front of Herrera's business in the 1960s. Congressman Pickle was considered a real friend to the East Side, setting aside funding for the US Army Corps of Engineers to channelize Boggy Creek, which runs north-south straight through Rosewood, thereby eliminating regular, costly flooding to residents and businesses. Longtime Rosewood residents recall that, before the channelizing, many citizens would have to be rescued from their homes by rowboats during major storms. (Courtesy of Louis Herrera Jr.)

Louis Herrera Sr. was well known in the Austin area for his artistic ironwork. Seen here is Mr. Herrera's business truck, with his daughter Sylvia inside. Dr. Sylvia Herrera is a founding member of People Organized in Defense of Earth and Her Resources (PODER) and now works to bring about social and environmental justice. (Courtesy of Louis Herrera Jr.)

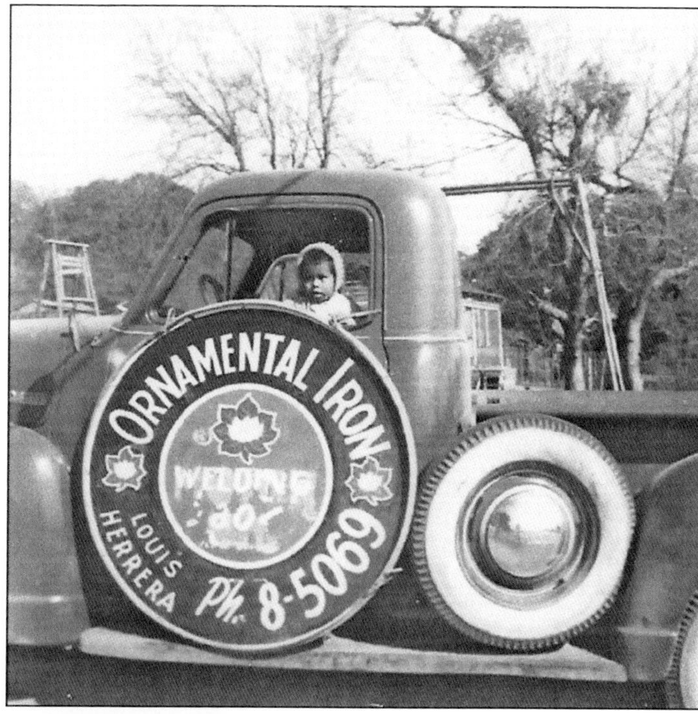

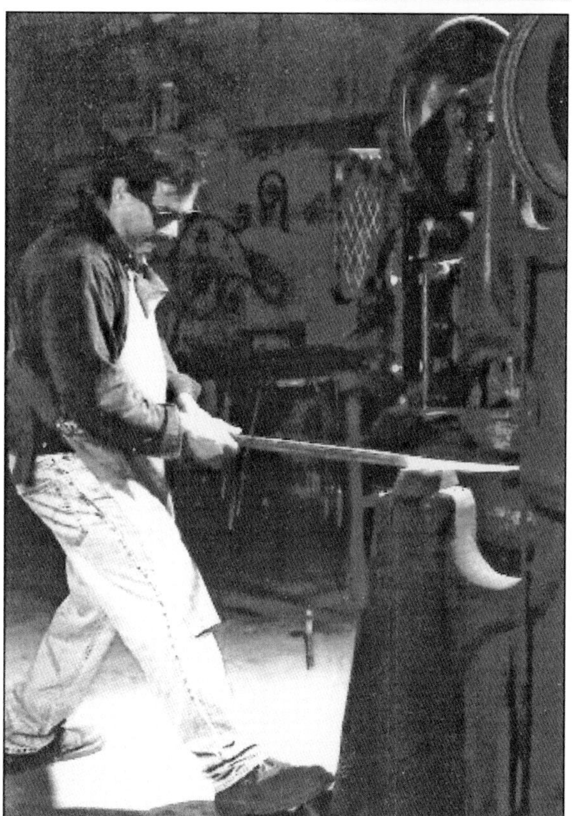

At left, Louis Herrera Jr. is at work in his shop and studio on Oak Springs Drive in Rosewood. He learned the value of hard work from his father, Louis Herrera Sr., who taught his son blacksmithing skills as well as day-to-day operation of the shop. Mr. Herrera Jr. enhanced his skills by studying blacksmithing and metalsmithing under master blacksmith Frank Turley of Santa Fe, New Mexico. Mr. Herrera Jr. has not only continued his father's business, but is himself an established artist recognized statewide and nationally. (Courtesy of Louis Herrera Jr.)

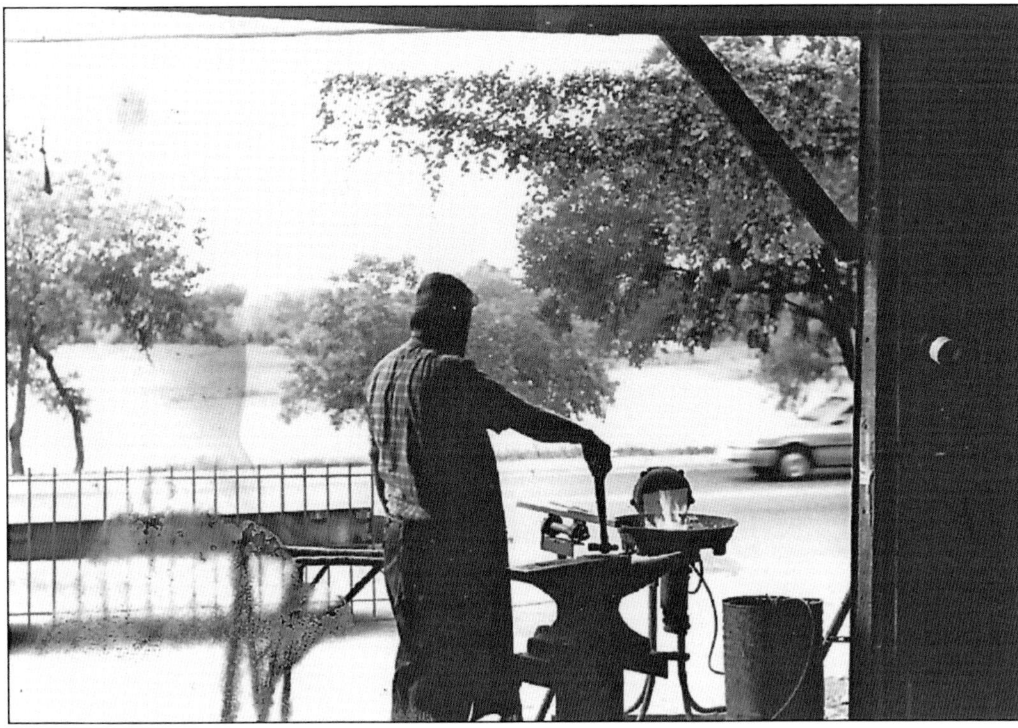

Mr. Herrera Jr. and his work have been featured in a number of magazines, including *Texas Architecture* and *Home and Garden*, and he was featured on television's *Modern Masters* series. Mr. Herrera also served as a member of the board of directors of Texas Folklife Resources and was an active founding member of the Rosewood Neighborhood Contact Team. (Courtesy of Louis Herrera Jr.)

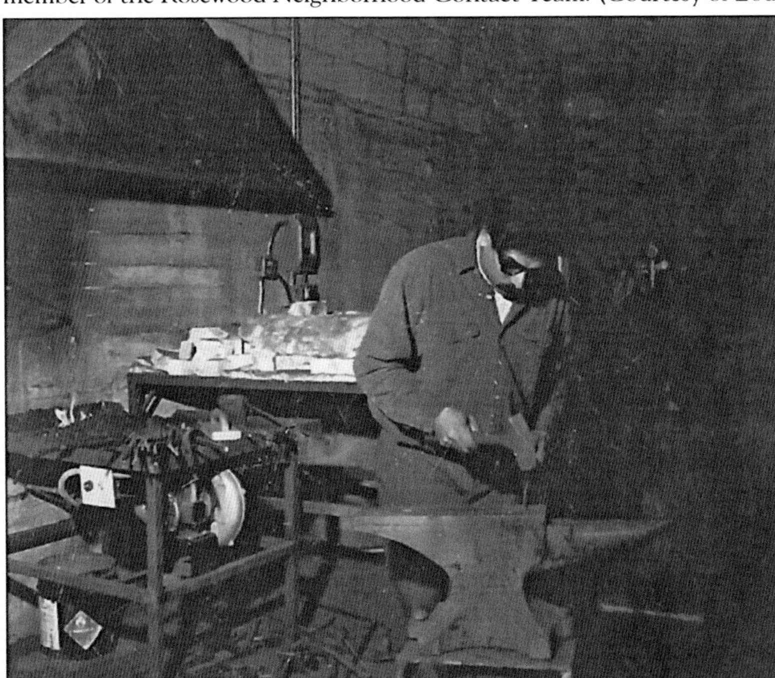

Mr. Herrera is shown here at work on a conceptual design for the artwork for a public installation to be developed along the East Seventh Street corridor. The art will speak to the community's historical roots and will also reflect a modern approach, to transition the corridor back to the heart of the city. (Courtesy of Louis Herrera Jr.)

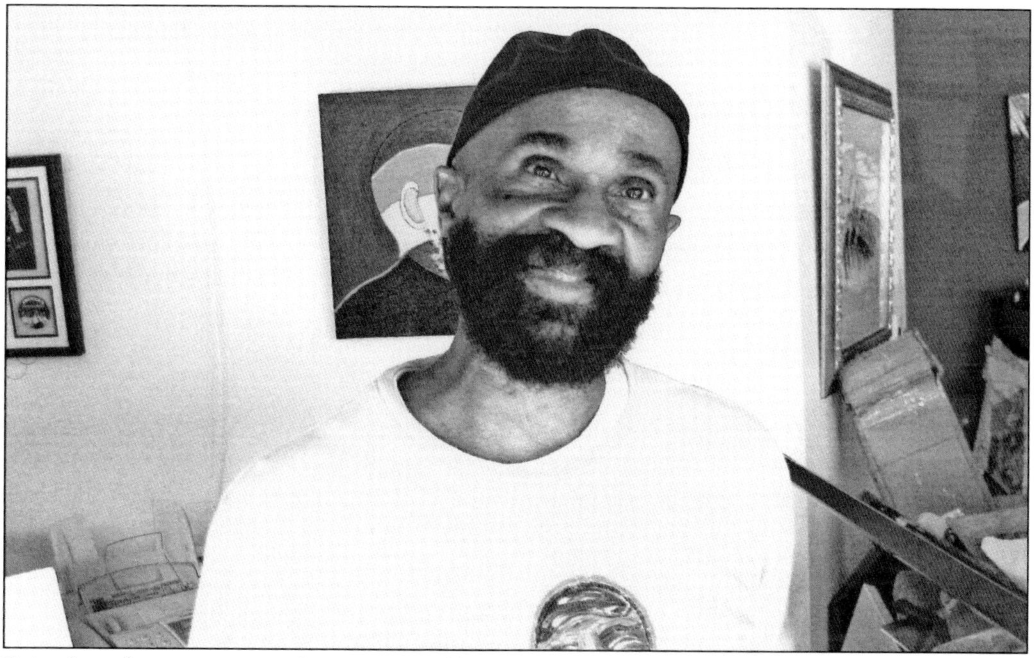

Brian Joseph is an artist and proprietor of BYDEE Art Gallery. Mr. Joseph was born in Trinidad but has lived in the United States for 42 years, including 27 in Austin. He first worked for the City of Austin Parks and Recreation Department but resigned in 1986. Mr. Joseph had viewed art exhibits and remembered that the colors always made him happy, so he decided to start painting. Mr. Joseph has no formal art training, but he started painting Bydee People. Bydee stands for "Bringing You Delightful Entertaining Experiences."

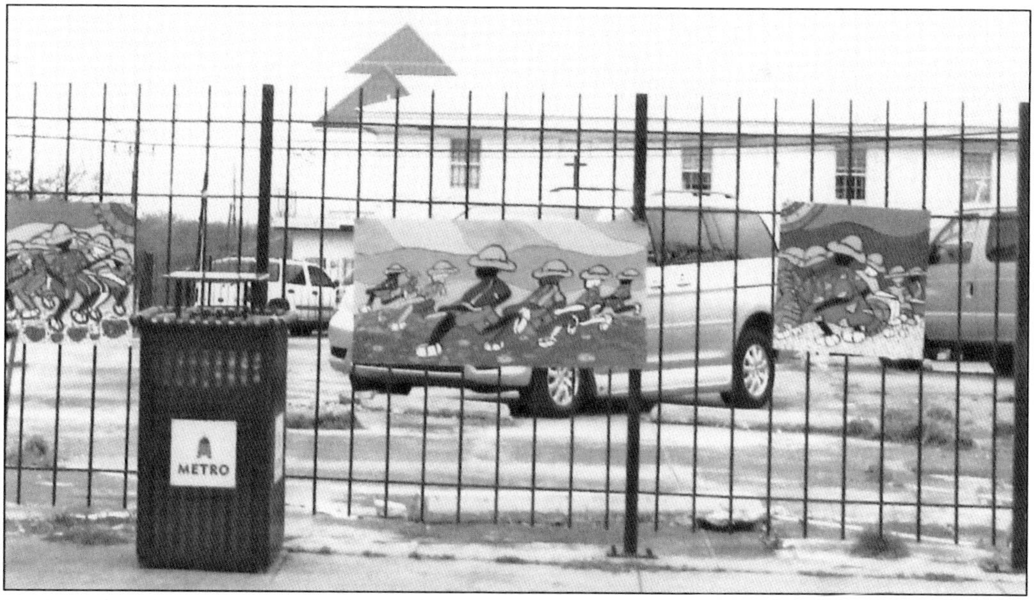

Mr. Joseph paints the colors the Bydee People tell him to paint, which are bright yellows, greens, and reds. The more colors, the more happiness. Shown here is an example of the work, on display on the fence at Twelfth and Chicon Streets. Mr. Joseph decided to help beautify the area and make people happy. He says the neighbors have taken ownership of the murals and protect them.

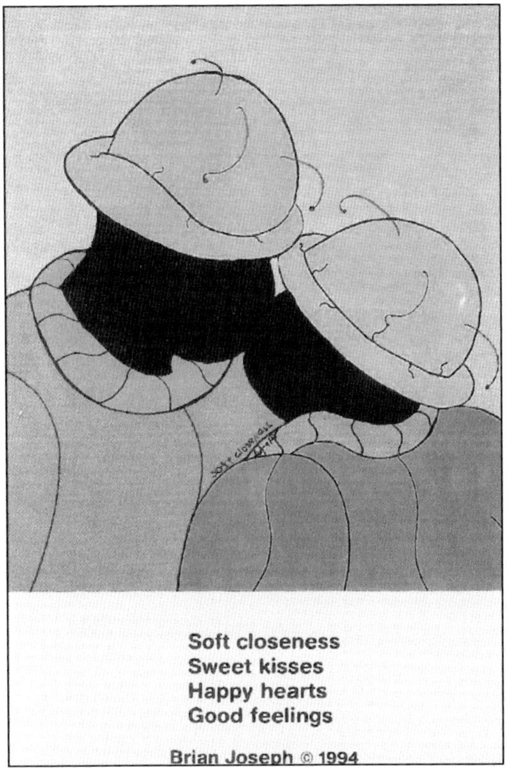

This example of Mr. Joseph's work shows soft closeness, sweet kisses, happy hearts, and good feelings. (Courtesy of Brian Joseph.)

Sam's BBQ, located at 2000 East Twelfth Street, has been a Rosewood-serving business site for 100 years, according to Willie Mays, current owner and operator. Before becoming Sam's, the location was a grocery store and service station. Sam's BBQ was founded 65 years ago by Sam Tasbe, who sold it to Sam Campbell. Mr. Campbell subsequently sold it to Dan Mays, who decided to keep the original name. All of the owners have been related to each other.

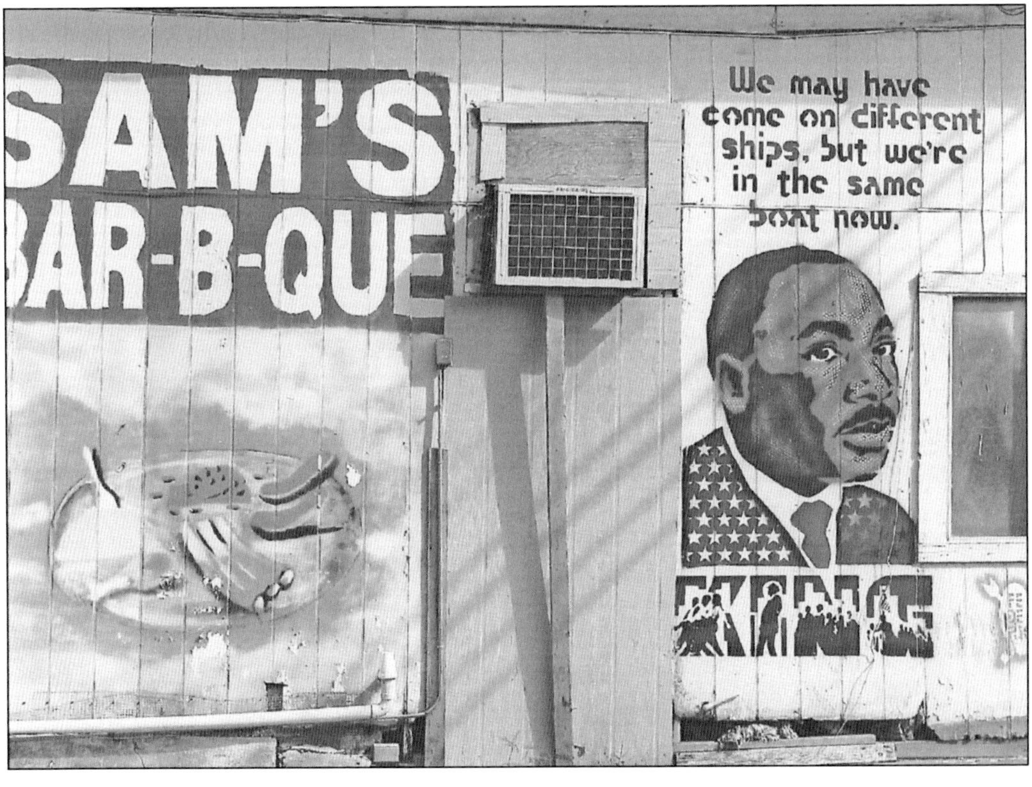

In 1992, the original building burned down, which was a tragic event for the whole community. People from Rosewood and throughout Austin came together to rebuild the iconic business. Since its rebirth, Sam's has received numerous awards, including three "Best of Austin" awards and seven "Restaurant Poll" awards.

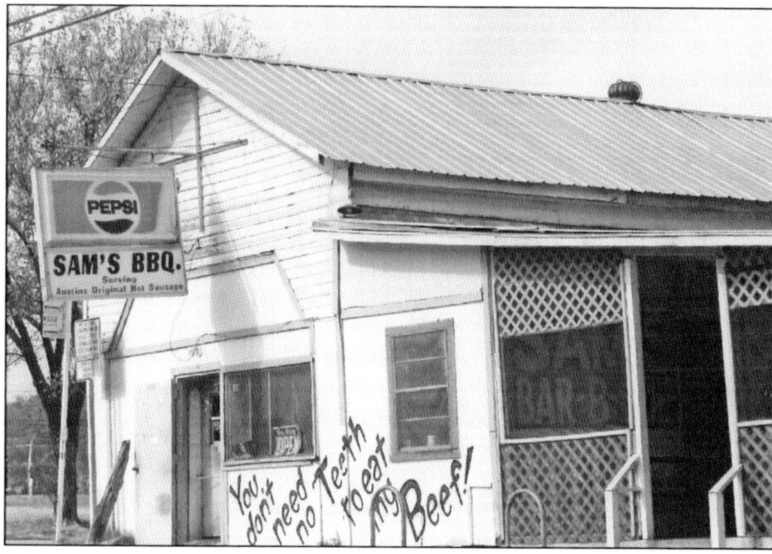

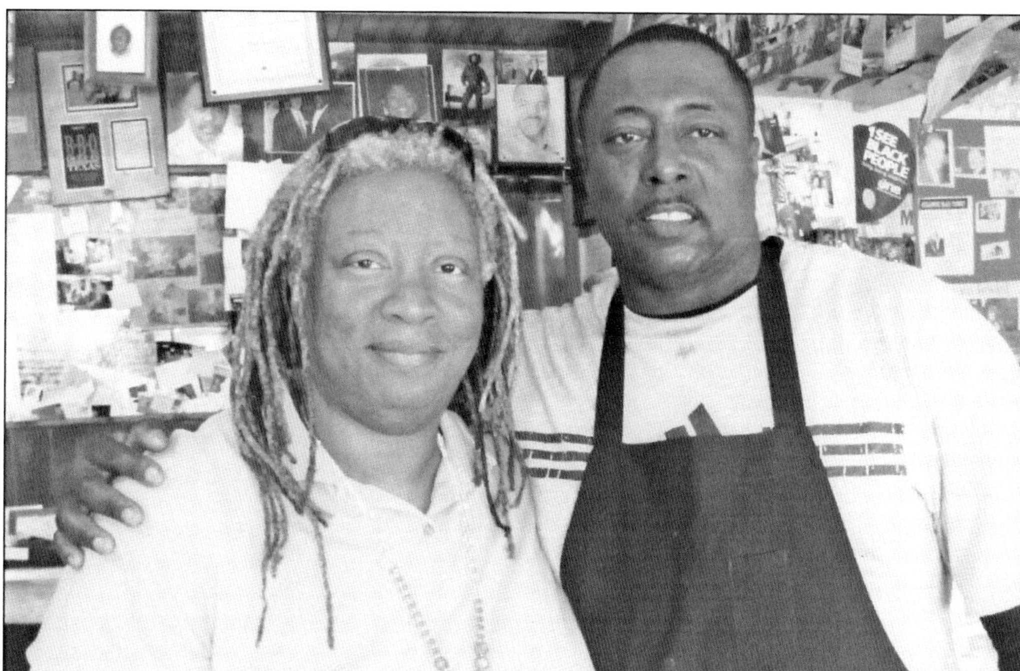

Willie Mays (right), Sam's BBQ proprietor, played baseball with several farm clubs, including the Giants, Phillies, and Rockies, before taking over Sam's. Mr. Mays says that Sam's has a long tradition of providing comfortable, down-home, family-style food and service. Cynthia Brown (left), a longtime customer, says that Sam's represents what the neighborhood is—respectful and familiar. Mr. Mays's customers over the years have included Pres. Bill Clinton, Stevie Ray Vaughan, Ray Benson (of Asleep at the Wheel), Los Lonely Boys, Bruce Springsteen, and Debbie Allen. Mr. Vaughan was such a fan of the restaurant that he had Sam's barbecue flown to him when he was recording outside of Austin.

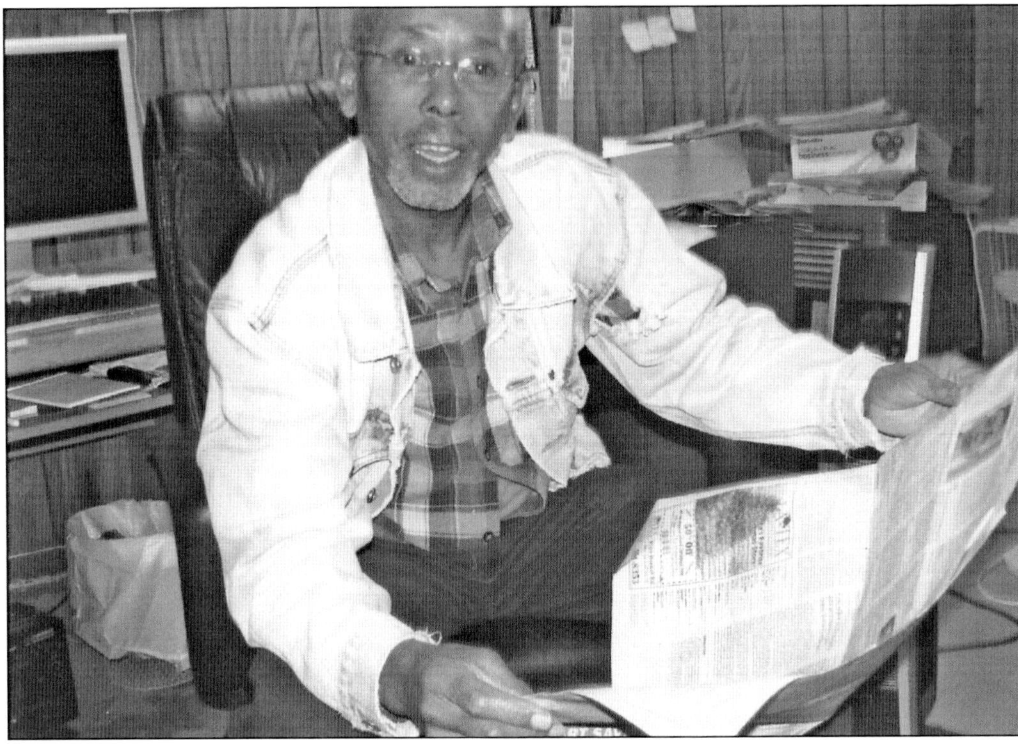

Akwasi Evans, owner, editor-in-chief, and publisher of *Nokoa: The Observer*, is shown here in his office. Mr. Evans moved to Austin in 1978, and initially worked for the *Austin American-Statesman*. He worked with numerous civil rights struggles, supporting author Gilberto Rivera and the Brown Berets in the boat race protests and Dorothy Turner and Velma Roberts and the Black Citizens Task Force protests of the killing of African American Will Cough by Austin police. Through these struggles, Mr. Evans came to realize there was no newspaper for the progressive community. He therefore opened *Nokoa: The Observer* as a weekly newspaper in an office on Rosewood Avenue in 1987. *Nokoa* is Swahili for "the observer."

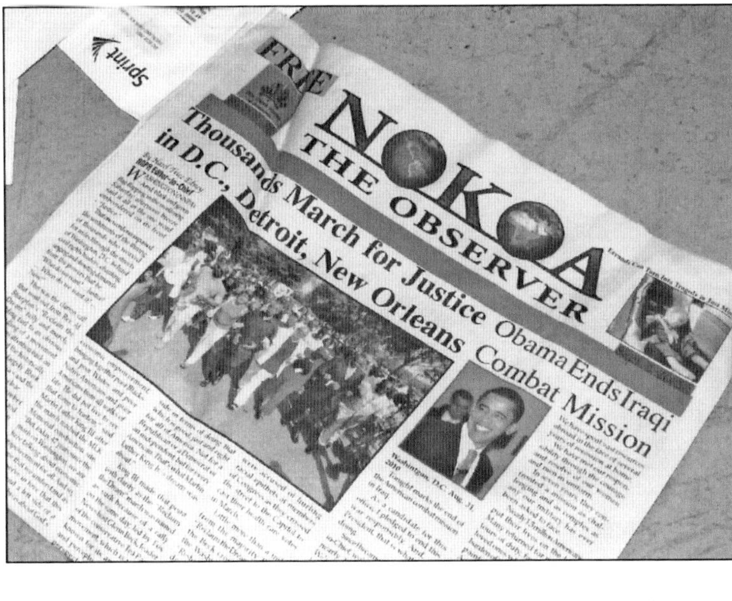

This is the September 2010 issue of *Nokoa: The Observer*. Mr. Evans notes that corporations have not wanted to advertise with *Nokoa*. He feared that he would have to close *Nokoa* in 2011 as gentrification had reduced the number and success of the African American businesses in the Rosewood area that were his main advertisers. *Nokoa* is still in publication.

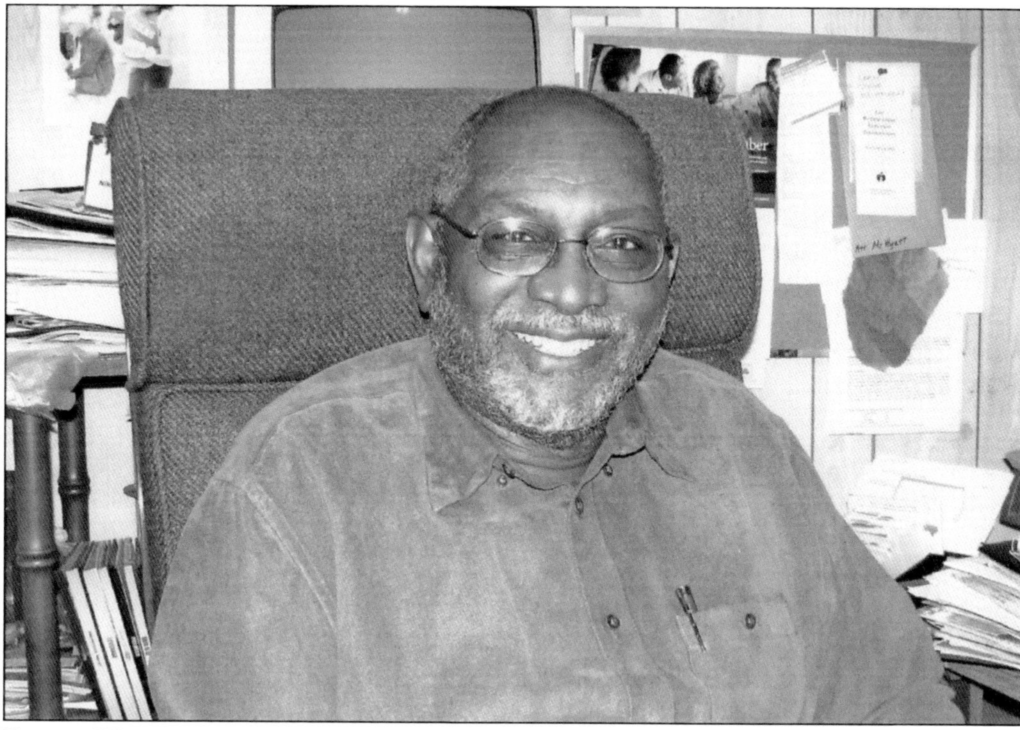

Tommy Wyatt came to Rosewood in 1962 from Lubbock after serving in the US Army and working for several insurance companies. In 1969, he started his own insurance agency. In 1970, his wife was publishing the *Black Business Registry*, an annual publication. Mr. Wyatt notes this registry was the first publication in which African American businesses could readily advertise. It was very popular because members of the community could pick it up and find where to go for whatever they needed.

The *Villager*—a weekly publication—grew out of the annual *Black Business Directory*. Most of the readership lived within an area bounded by Martin Luther King Jr. Boulevard (East Nineteenth Street), IH-35, East Sixth Street, and an indefinite eastern boundary. The newspaper was started because the area's black businesspeople had no affordable options in which to advertise. With their steady support, the paper was published regularly, generally weekly or biweekly.

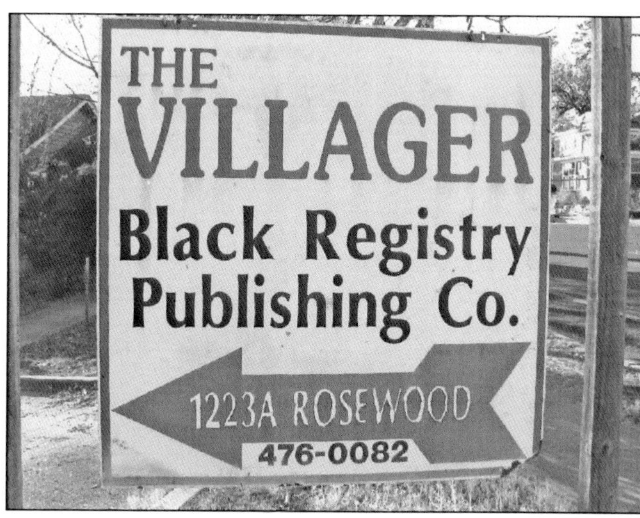

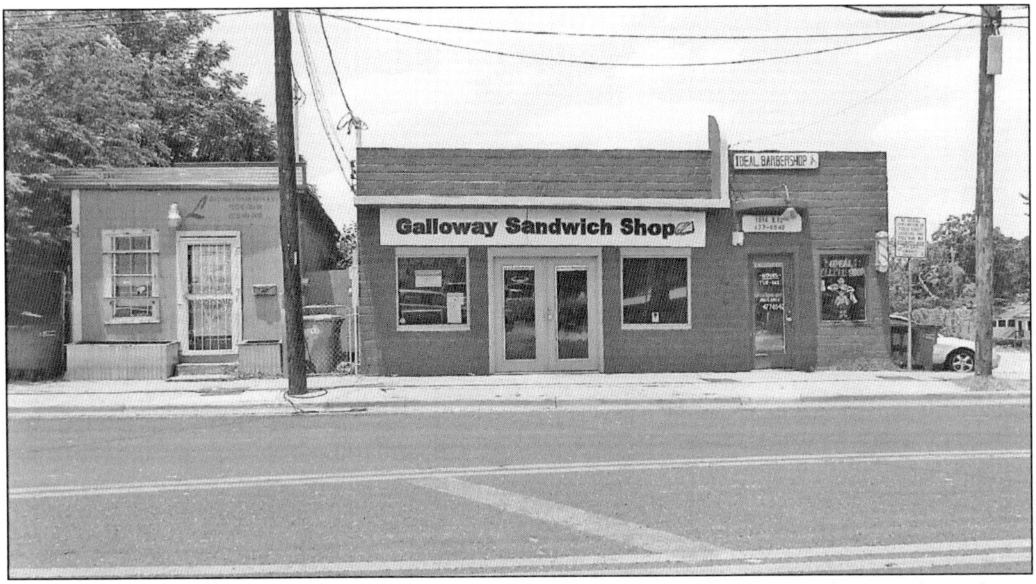

Galloway Sandwich Shop, at 1914 East Twelfth Street, serves down-home, Southern-style cooking. The establishment is run by Stephen Galloway, with the help of his mother, Laverne Galloway. The shop has been open since 1998.

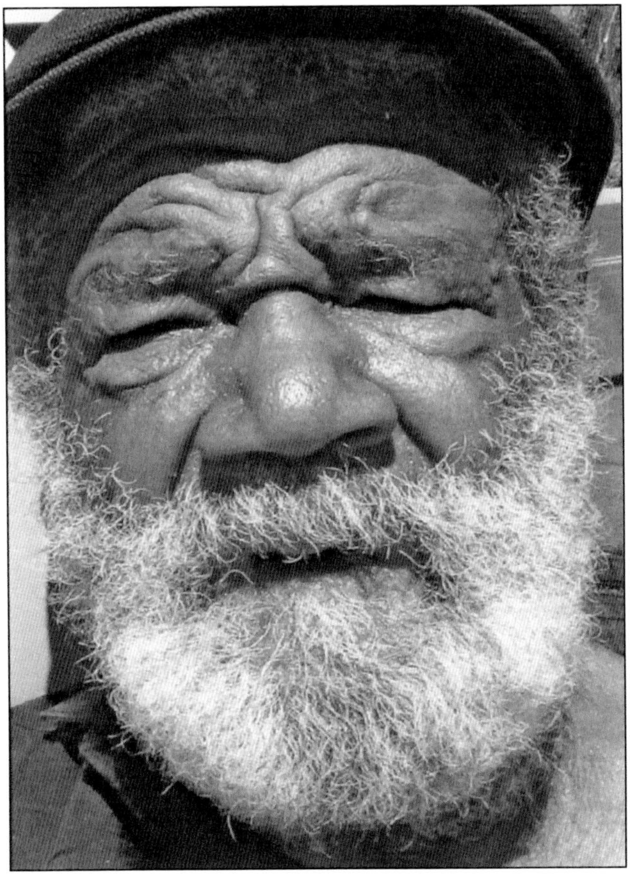

Little Daddy, also known as Short Daddy, also known as longtime Rosewood businessman Gilbert S. Alexander, is seen here in a photograph taken some years ago. Mr. Alexander owned a shoeshine parlor on Rosewood Avenue across from the *Villager* newspaper office. For over 20 years, he also worked nights at the shoeshine stand at Austin's historic blues club Antone's, located on West Fifth Street downtown. He shined the boots of many famous performers at Antone's, including Willie Nelson, Stevie Ray Vaughn, Waylon Jennings, and Joel Guzman.

Four

COMMUNITY

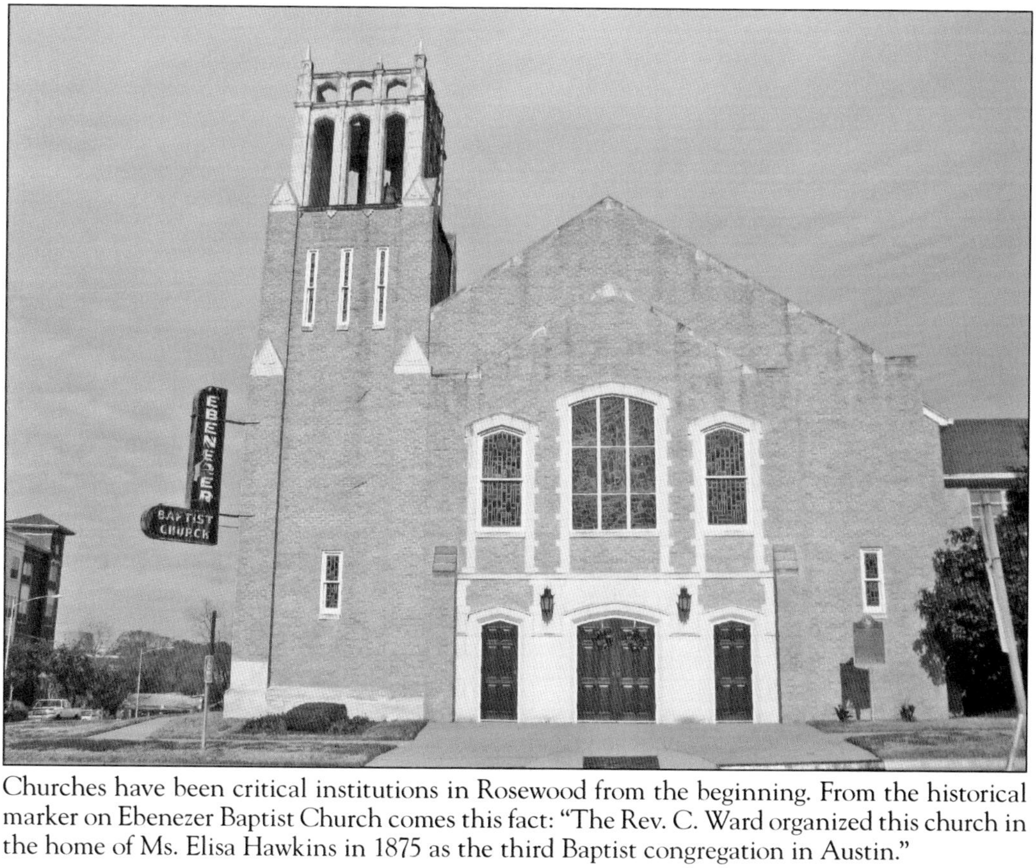

Churches have been critical institutions in Rosewood from the beginning. From the historical marker on Ebenezer Baptist Church comes this fact: "The Rev. C. Ward organized this church in the home of Ms. Elisa Hawkins in 1875 as the third Baptist congregation in Austin."

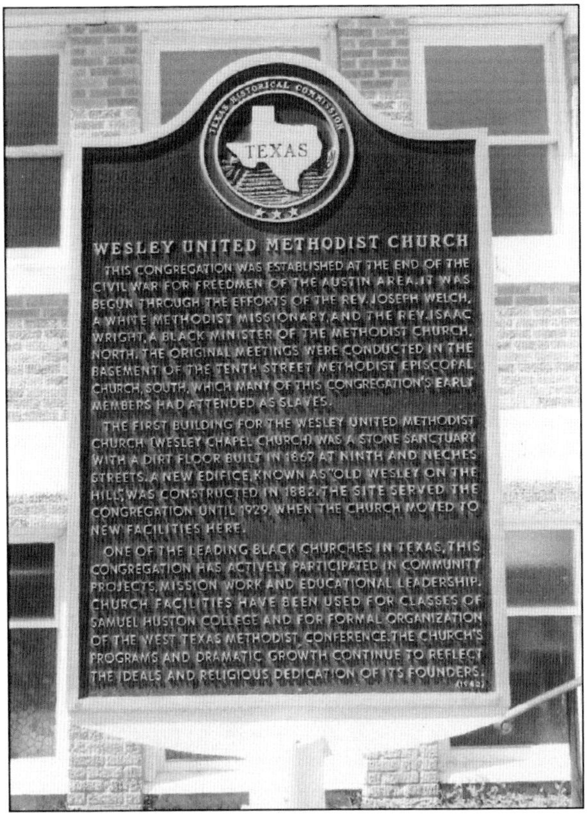

The historic plaque at Wesley United Methodist Church gives the following information: "One of the leading Black churches in Texas, this congregation has actively participated in community projects, mission work and educational leadership. Church facilities have been used for classes of Samuel Huston College and for formal organization of the West Texas Methodist conference. The Church's programs and dramatic growth continue to reflect the ideals and religious dedication of its founders."

Dr. William Charles Akins, a 60-plus-year member of the Wesley United Methodist Church congregation, notes that the church has reached out, and continues to reach out, to new residents of the surrounding neighborhoods, welcoming them to join.

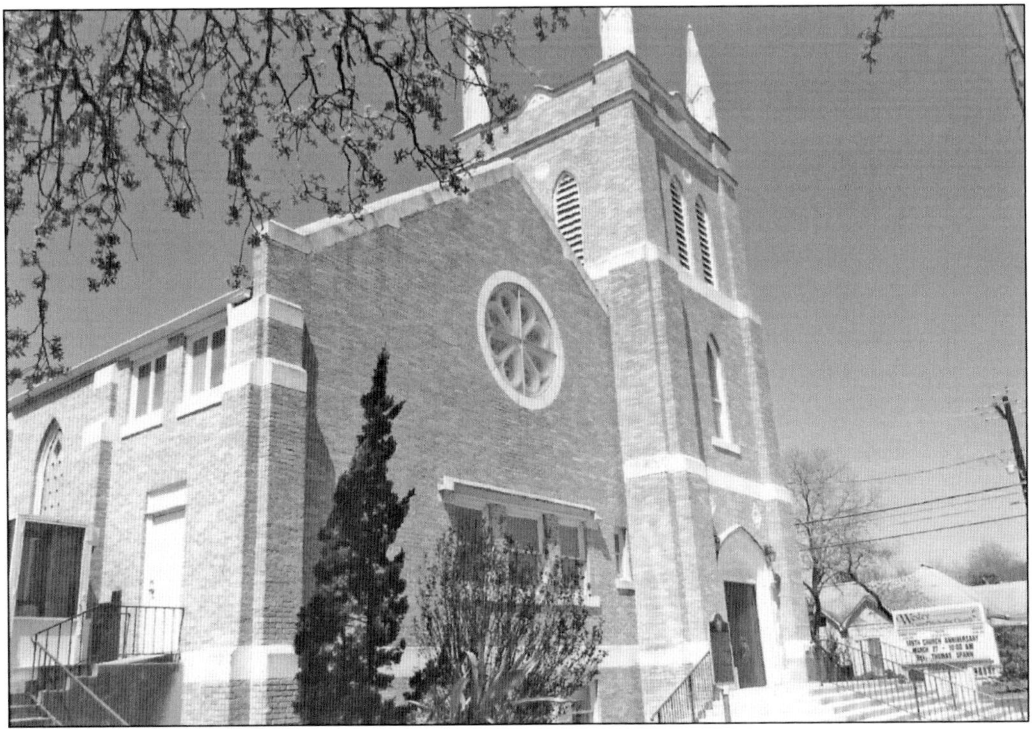

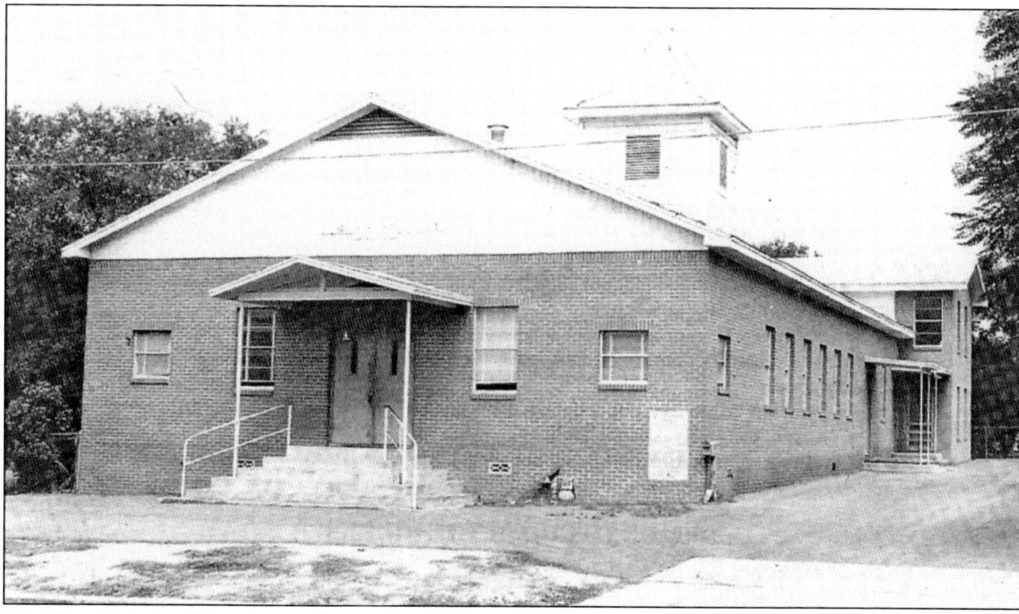

Mt. Zion Baptist Church was formed in 1873 in Williamson Creek. In 1948, the walls of Mt. Zion Williamson Creek were torn down and reconstructed at 2942 East Thirteenth Street, assuming its present name. (Courtesy of Mt. Zion Baptist Church.)

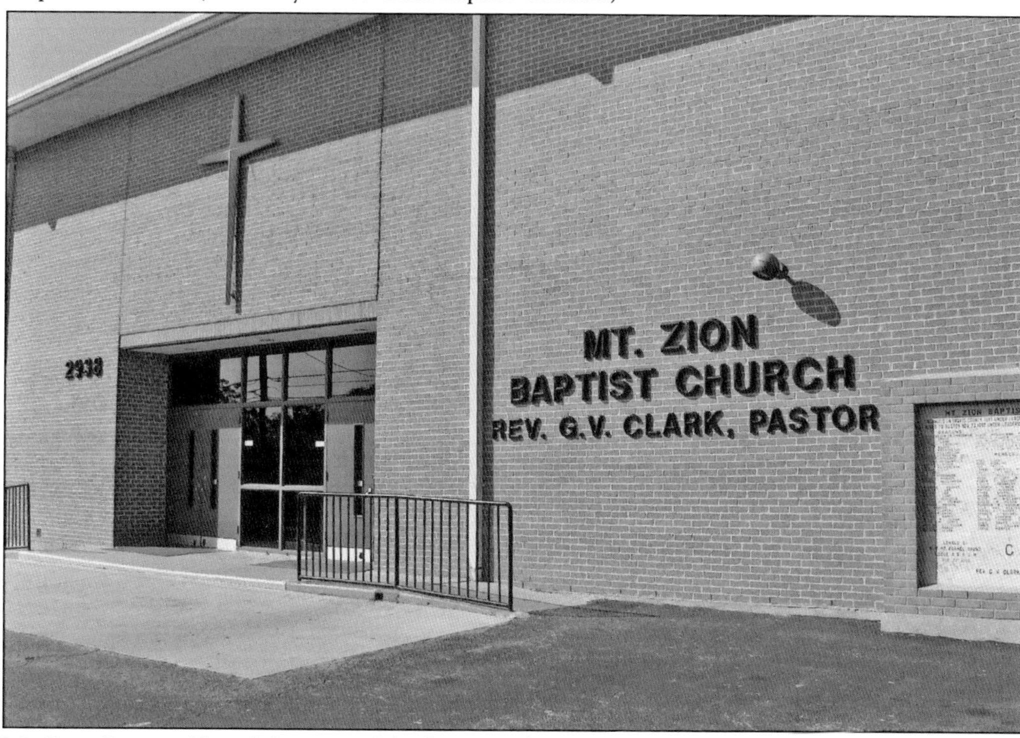

Mt. Zion Baptist Church has one of the larger and more active congregations in Rosewood today. Mt. Zion hosts numerous community-oriented events, including regular meetings of the Rosewood Neighborhood Contact Team. In addition to the church properties, Mt. Zion owns 10 single-family units for senior citizens in Rosewood. (Courtesy of Mt. Zion Baptist Church.)

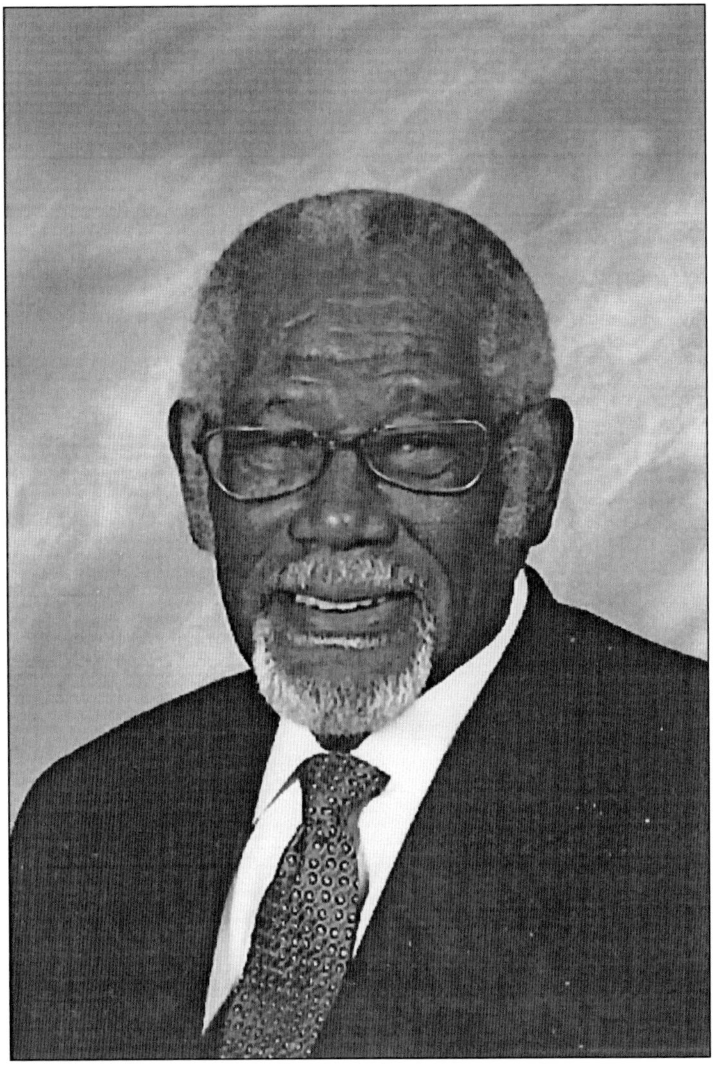

The Reverend G.V. Clark became leader and pastor of Mt. Zion Baptist Church in 1970. Reverend Clark was born in Webberville, Texas, and served in several professional positions prior to his service at Mt. Zion, including as teacher in the Round Rock public school district, chaplain of Terrell State Hospital, coordinator of equal opportunity and later director of the Office of Civil Rights for the Texas Rehabilitation Commission, and pastor of St. Mary's Baptist Church in Pflugerville and Sweet Home Baptist Church in Round Rock. (Courtesy of Mt. Zion Baptist Church.)

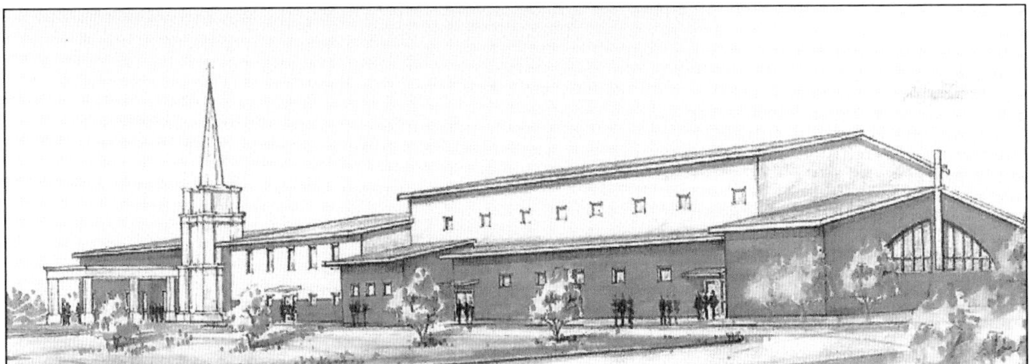

Mt. Zion Baptist Church is in the process of replacing the original structure with a new community building and Family Life Center to better serve the needs of the growing congregation and the surrounding neighborhoods. (Courtesy of Mt. Zion Baptist Church.)

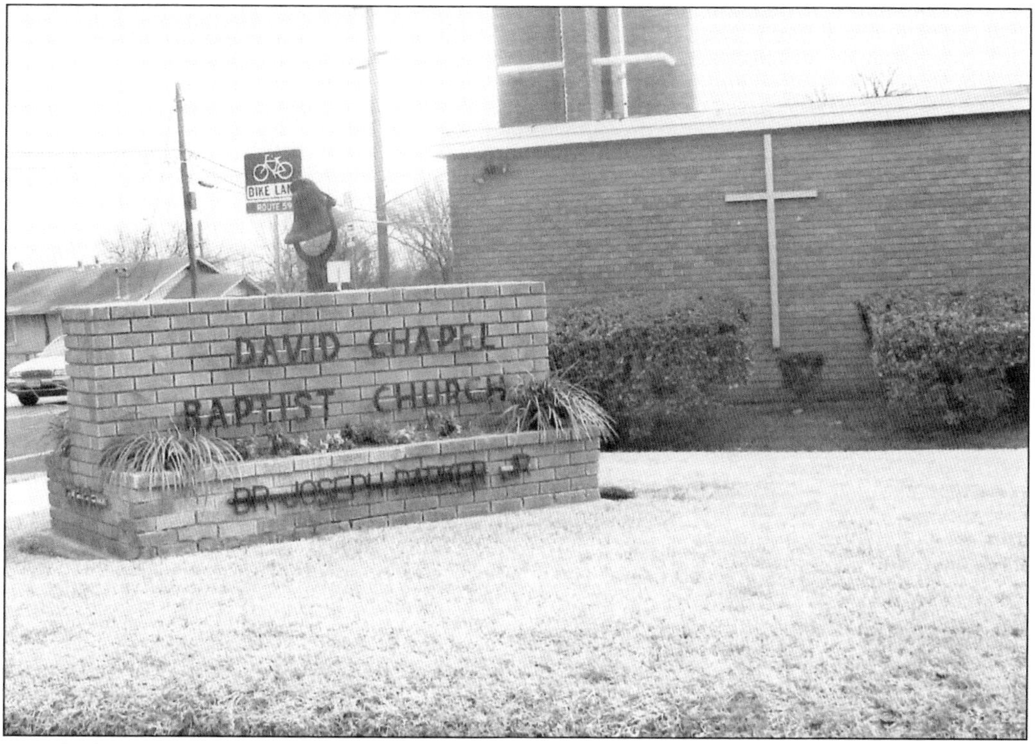

David Chapel Missionary Baptist Church was formed in 1924 at a former blacksmith shop. The church was named Davis Chapel in honor of the Horace Davis family, on whose farm it was organized. The name of the church was changed to David Chapel in 1926, when the congregation moved from the Ceiling Hills community to a new tabernacle in downtown Austin.

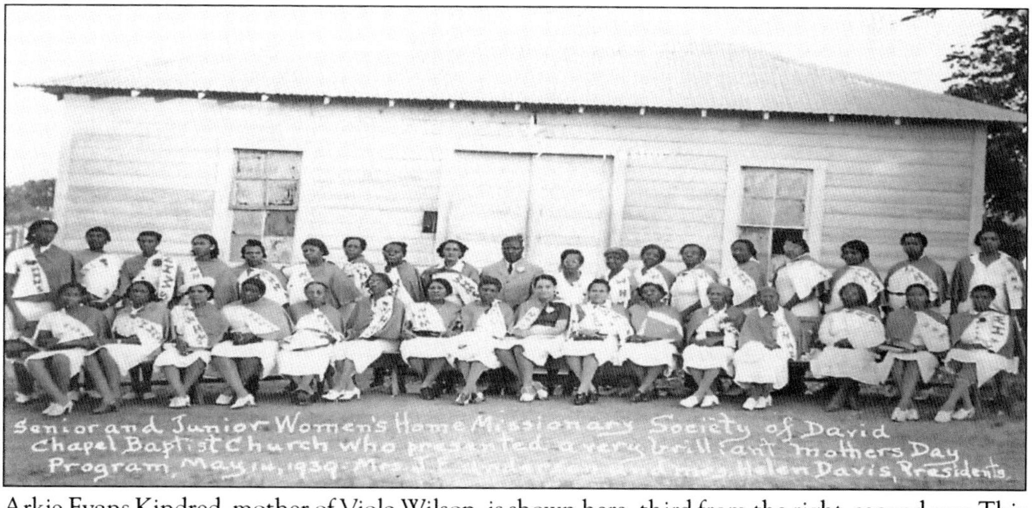

Arkie Evans Kindred, mother of Viola Wilson, is shown here, third from the right, second row. This photograph was taken on Mother's Day 1939 at the David Chapel Baptist Church. At the time, this church was located at Fourteenth Street and Chestnut Avenue. (Courtesy of Viola Wilson.)

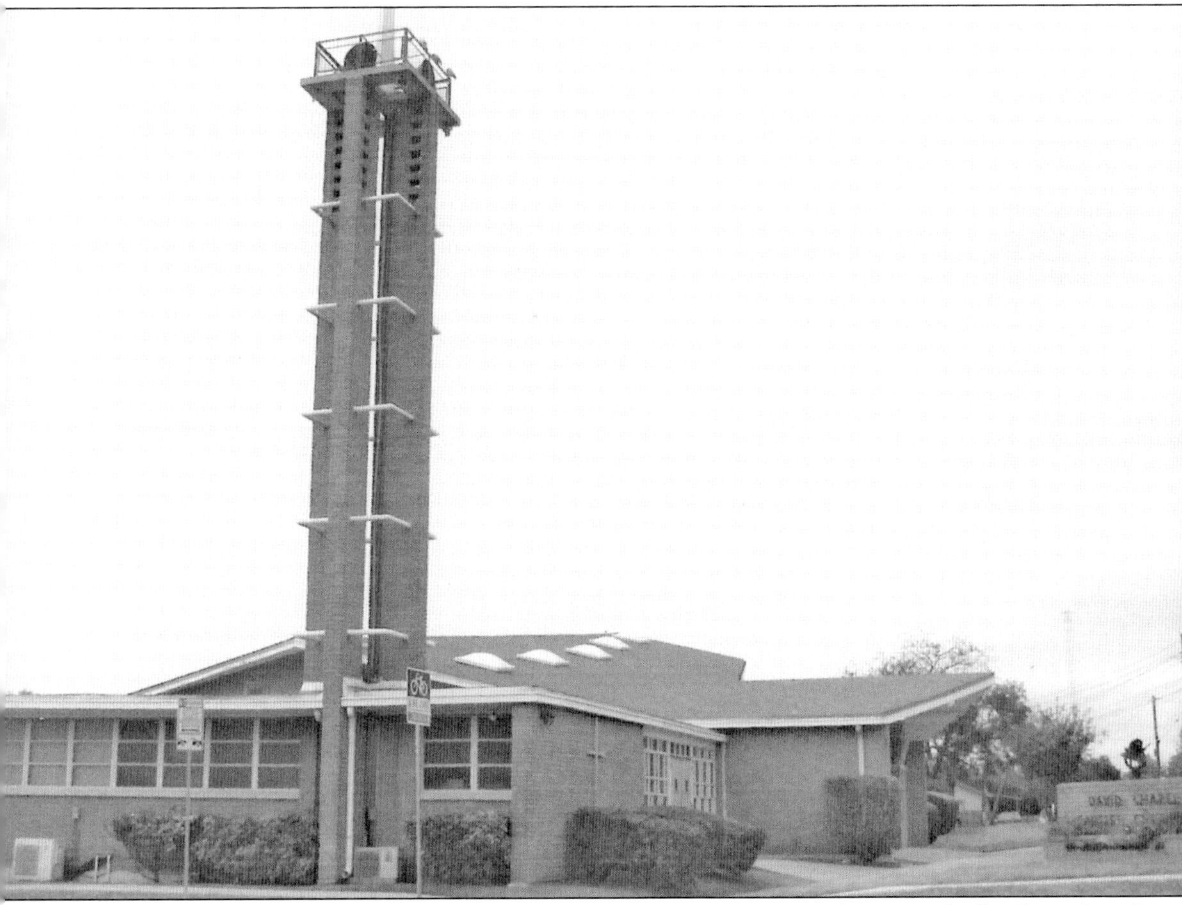

The current David Chapel Church is located at East Martin Luther King Jr. Boulevard and Chestnut Avenue. The Reverend James E. Obey Sr. became pastor in 1964. God called Pastor Obey home in 1992, and the Reverend Joseph C. Parker Jr. became senior pastor. Reverend Parker is an author, a Texas attorney, and a teacher as well. David Chapel has expanded over the years and has sponsored a low-income housing project. The church has hosted community-serving organizations such as the Chestnut Neighborhood Planning Team and a wide variety of neighborhood meetings and continues to be a focal point in the community.

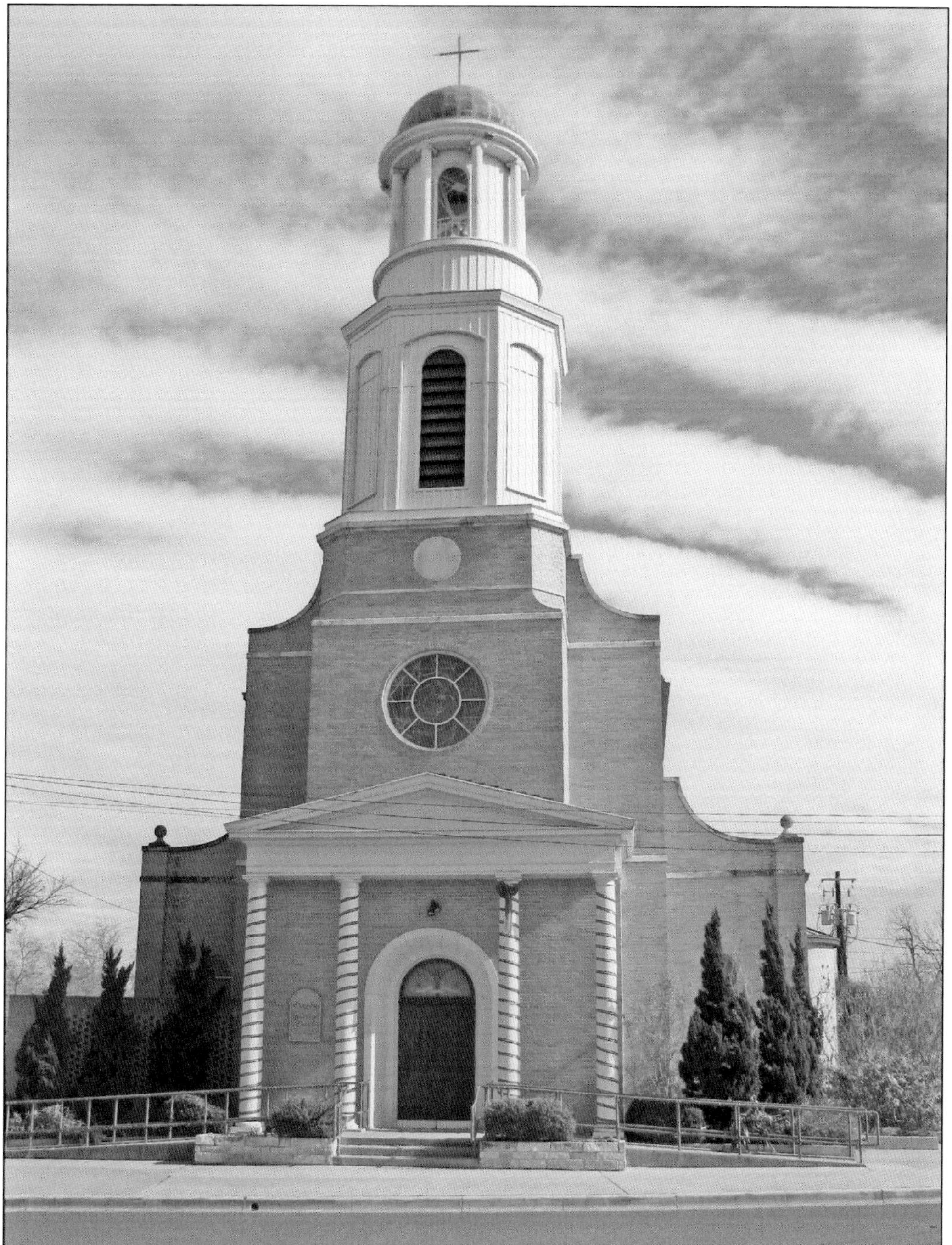

Shortly after the time of the 1928 Master Plan, the Catholic Diocese of Austin relocated the Mexican parish, which offered mass in Spanish, from its downtown location to an area of East Austin later known as the Guadalupe Neighborhood, located just west of Rosewood. This photograph shows the current main building and chapel of Our Lady of Guadalupe Church. Our Lady of Guadalupe was later joined by St. Julia's and Cristo Rey as Catholic churches serving the predominantly Mexican Catholic population of East Austin.

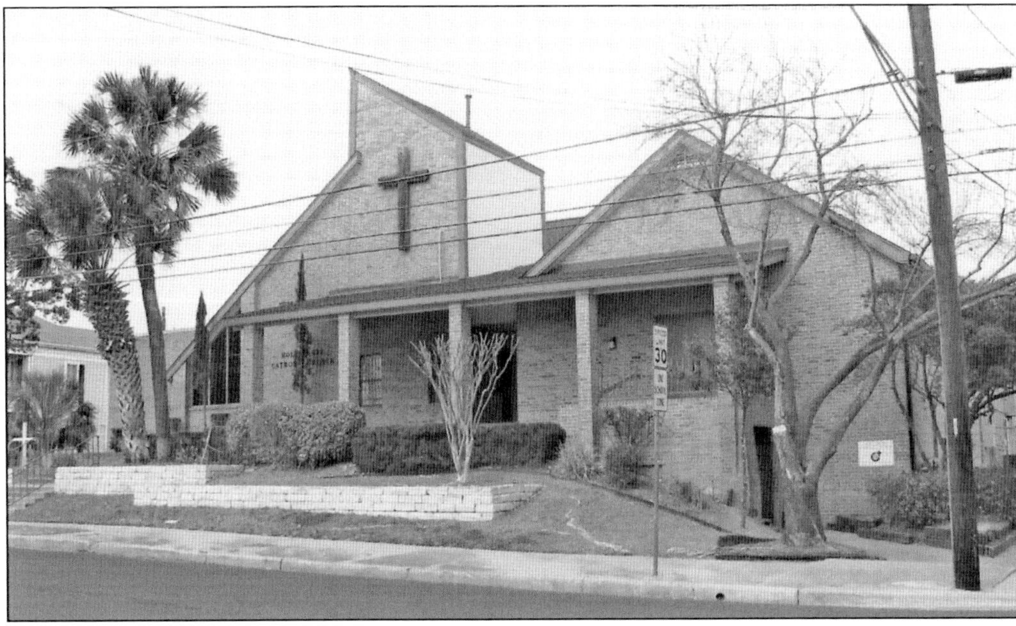

Holy Cross Catholic Church was founded in 1936 by the Reverend Francis R. Weber. Those African American Catholics already baptized in the faith met in the living room of William M. Tears's family home at 1203 East Twelfth Street for mass. The first church building was constructed in 1937. In 1972, Meals on Wheels and More was founded at Holy Cross. The volunteers used the kitchen in the church basement and the kitchen at another East Austin church to prepare meals for those in need, delivering the meals three times a week.

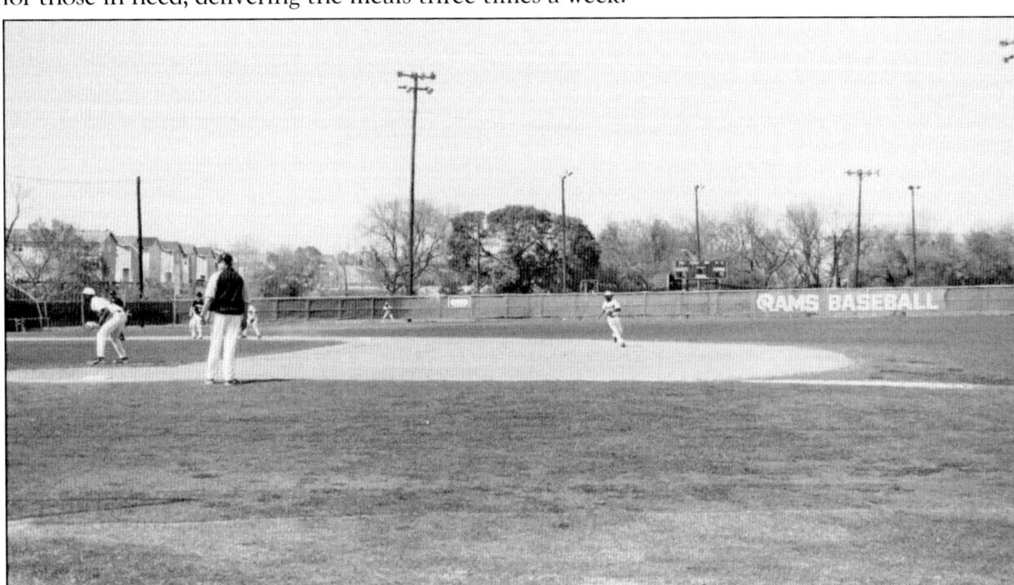

Historic Downs Field, a baseball diamond located in the heart of Rosewood, hosted the Negro League baseball teams beginning in the 1920s and 1930s, with such greats as Jackie Robinson, Satchel Paige, and Willie Wells. Once owned by Huston-Tillotson, Downs Field is currently owned by the City of Austin, while Huston-Tillotson maintains it and uses it as its home field for college baseball games.

Sheryl Cole became the first African American woman elected to the Austin City Council in 2006 and the first African American woman mayor pro tem in 2011. The Honorable Ms. Cole, an Austin resident for over 25 years, earned a juris doctorate from the University of Texas Law School. As a member of the city council, Ms. Cole championed upgrades to Downs Field that included Americans with Disabilities Act (ADA) parking and needed repairs to the facilities. Mayor Pro Tem Cole notes: "I have three boys, and I know you must have a dynamic entertaining place for children outside the house that centers on some sort of ball." Ms. Cole, a strong supporter of parks, is the council sponsor of the Waller Creek flood control and parks improvement initiative. (Courtesy of Mayor Pro Tem Sheryl Cole.)

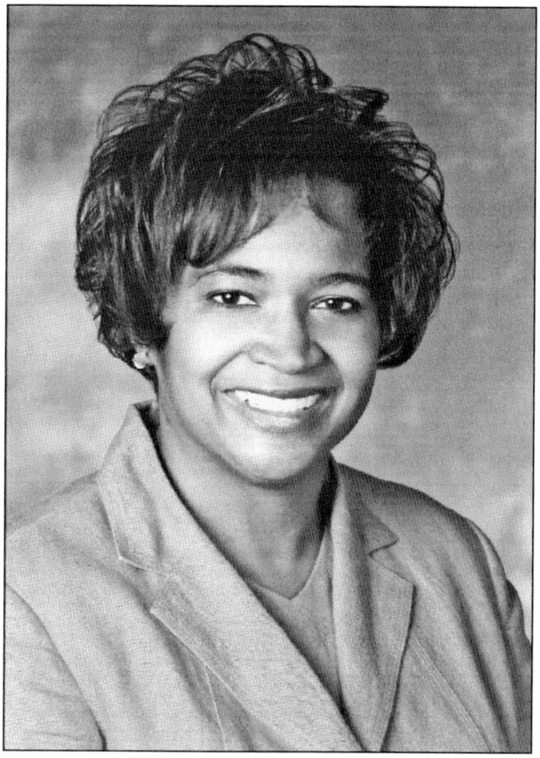

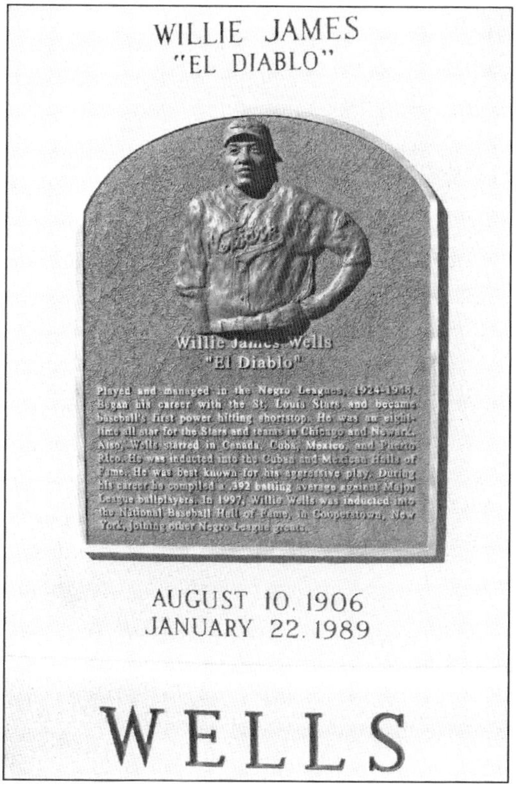

This is the gravestone of Willie James Wells, also known as El Diablo ("the devil") due to his notoriety for speed on the ball field in Mexico and Central America, where he played. Wells was a native of Rosewood who attended Anderson High School and Huston College. He was one of the best shortstops in African American baseball in the 1920s and 1930s, playing first for the San Antonio Black Aces in 1923 and ending his career in 1954 with the Birmingham Black Barons. He was posthumously inducted into the National Baseball Hall of Fame in 1997. Wells was originally buried in Evergreen Cemetery, but is now buried in the Texas State Cemetery. The state cemetery is a neighbor of Huston-Tillotson and is located directly across the street from Our Lady of Guadalupe Church.

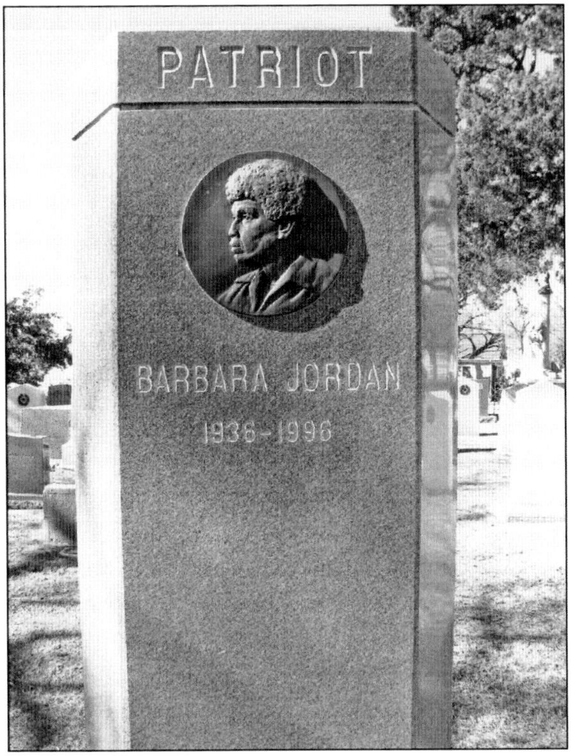

The Texas State Cemetery is the final resting place of most state legislators, including Sen. Barbara Jordan. Born in Houston's Fifth Ward, a historically African American community somewhat like Rosewood, Senator Jordan, in 1966, became the first African American woman elected to the Texas Senate since 1883. She was the first African American woman elected to the US Congress, in 1972. In both bodies, Senator Jordan sponsored bills that championed the poor, African Americans, and disadvantaged people.

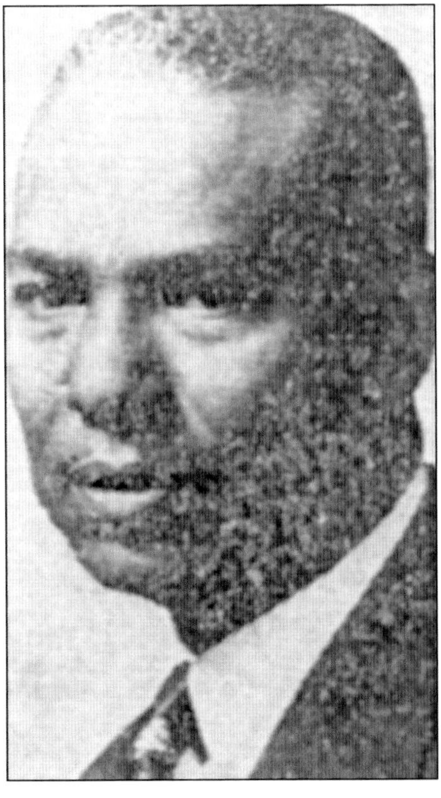

In 1951, community activist and journalist Arthur B. DeWitty was nearly the first African American elected to the Austin City Council. Election to the council was then changed to all at-large, making it more difficult for an African American or Latino candidate to win. Repeated efforts to return city council elections to single-member district representation have failed, and the council operates on what is often called a "gentlemen's agreement" that Place 5 is for a Latino and Place 6 is for an African American. (Courtesy of AHC, PICB 19327.)

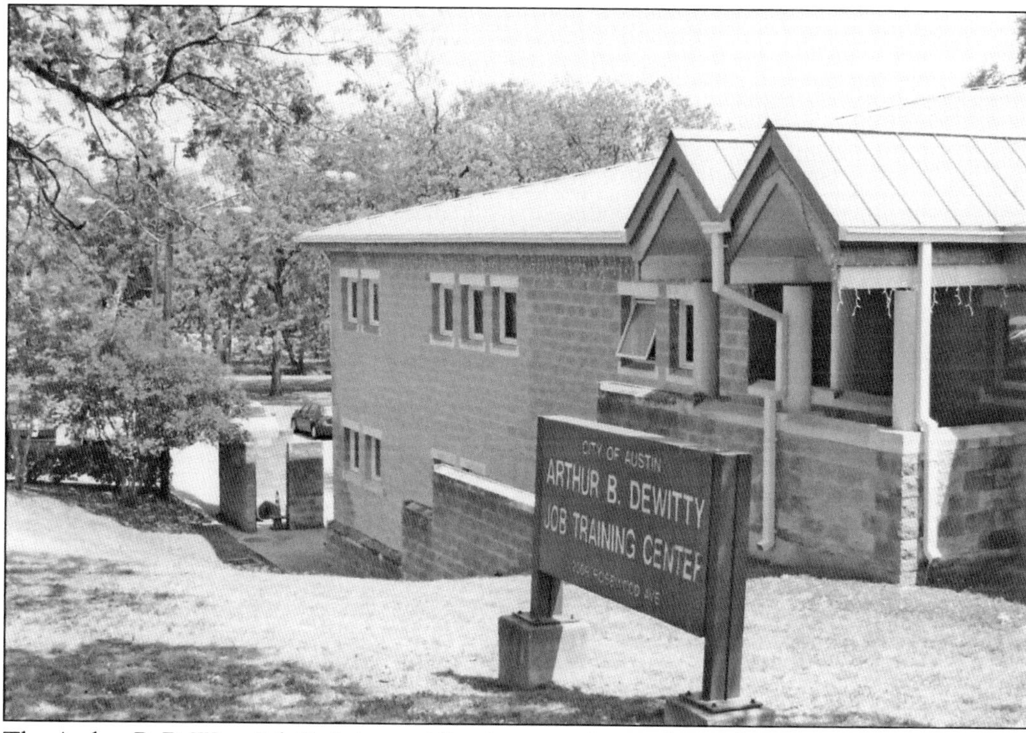

The Arthur B. DeWitty Job Training and Employment Center, located at 2209 Rosewood Avenue, was created with grants from the City of Austin, H.E.B. foods, the Lola Wright Foundation, Microsoft, IBM, and numerous volunteers and individual contributors. It was named in honor of activist and journalist Arthur B. DeWitty.

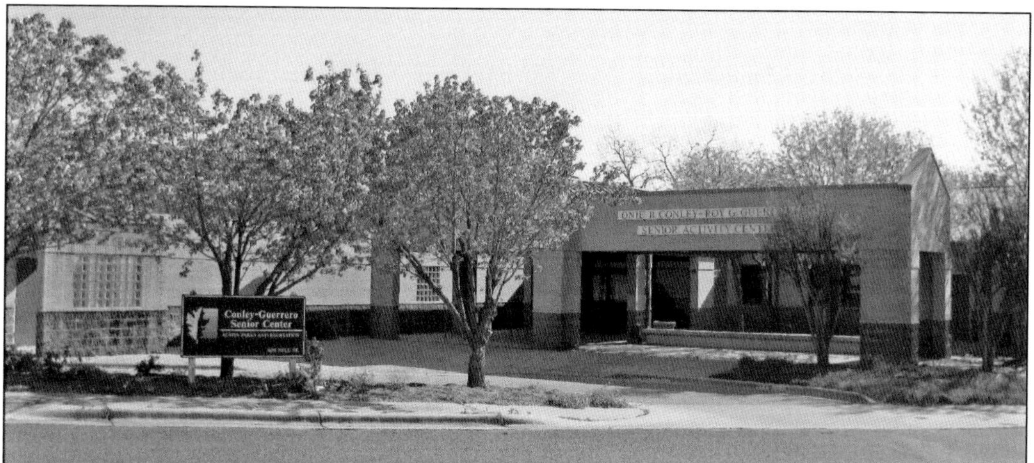

The Onie B. Conley–Roy G. Guerrero Senior Activity Center was dedicated in March 1988 by an Austin City Council that included Mayor Pro Tem John Trevino Jr., the first Latino elected to the city council, and Dr. Charles Urdy, then a professor at Huston-Tillotson College. The building was named in honor of educator Onie Conley and Roy G. Guerrero, a 30-year employee of the City Parks and Recreation Department and community leader. In 2001, the city further honored Mr. Guerrero by adding his name to the Colorado River Park. In 2007, Ms. Conley was again honored by the city, which named the second pavilion in the Boggy Creek greenbelt for her.

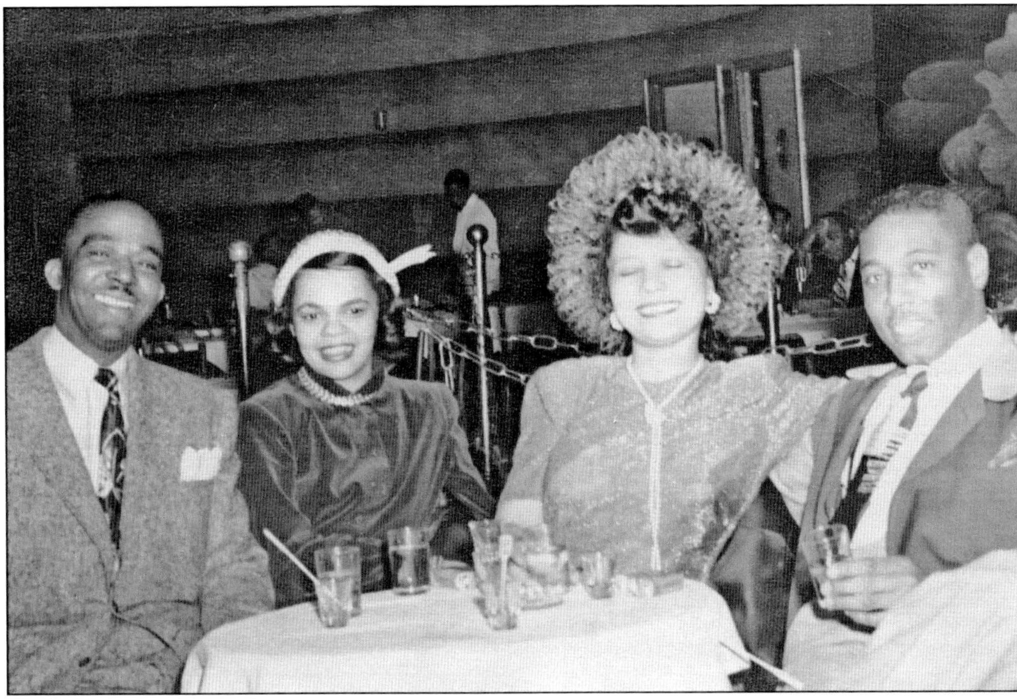

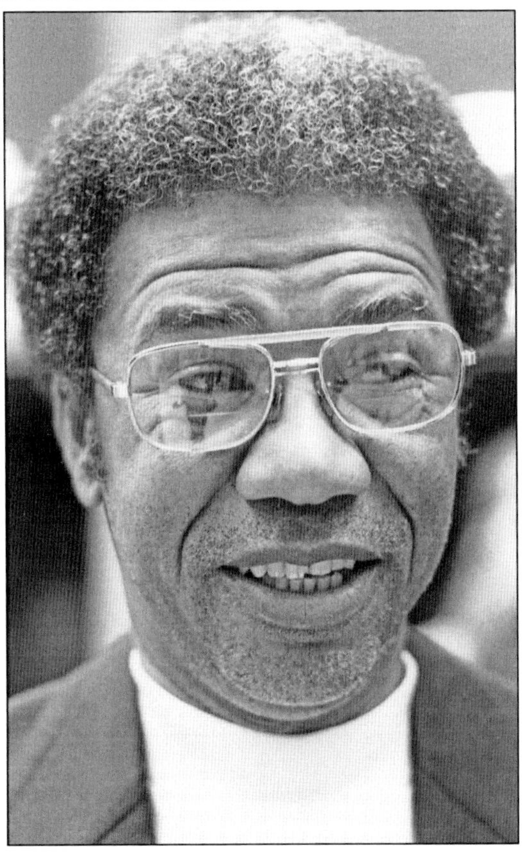

Thelma Mitchell Elliott was born in San Antonio, Texas, and became one of the first African Americans to complete a master's in social work at the University of Texas–Austin. Ms. Elliott was married to O.H. Elliott, and the couple had two daughters, Ora Anne Elliott Houston and Thelma Karen Elliott Charleston. Thelma served with many local organizations. The Elliotts are at right in the above image; the other couple is unidentified. (Courtesy of AHC, AR 2007.017[1-27-Front].)

Volma Overton graduated from Huston-Tillotson. In 1947, Mr. Overton was asked to give up his seat on a bus in downtown Austin so that a white commuter could sit down. When he returned to Austin as a World War II veteran, he purchased a home in the Cedar Valley subdivision. Returning black veterans were restricted to East Austin and soon bought all the Cedar Valley homes. Mr. Overton joined the NAACP in 1958 and became president of the Austin chapter in 1962. In 1968, the Austin chapter of the NAACP presented him with the DeWitty Award for his service. (Courtesy of AHC, PICB 17167.)

Nelson Linder, a 1984 alumnus of Huston-Tillotson, is current chair of the local chapter of the NAACP. The local chapter offices are at this facility, which serves multiple local functions.

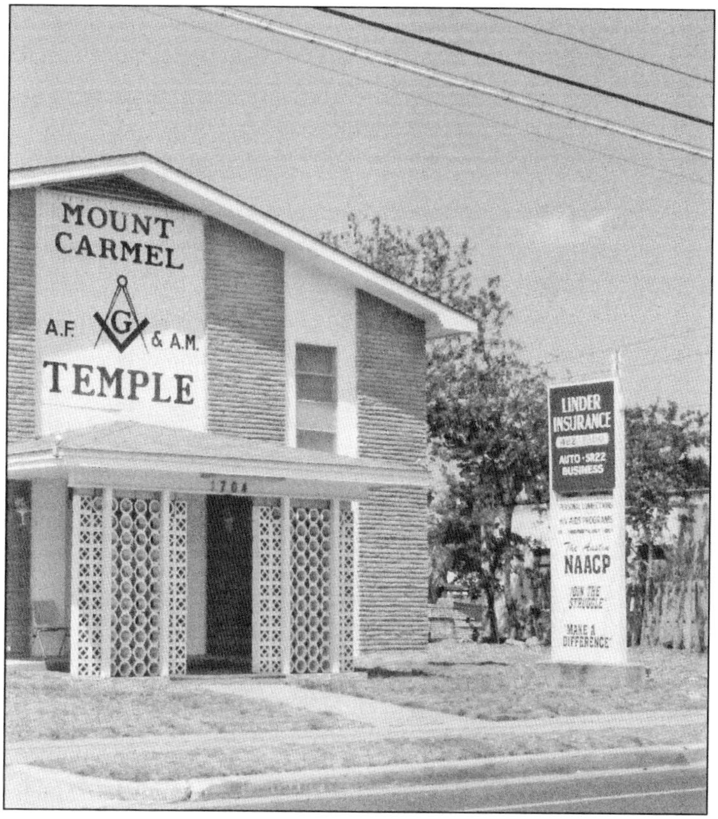

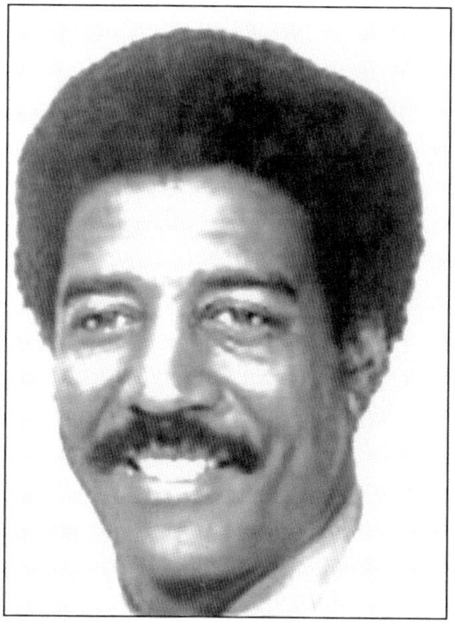

Berl L. Handcox, the highest-ranking African American employee at IBM at the time, ran for Austin City Council in 1971. He lived in Northwest Austin, not Rosewood, but he was someone the entire community could respect, essential in a city where all city council seats are at-large. The *Villager* strongly endorsed his candidacy, and Mr. Handcox won, becoming the first African American elected to the Austin City Council since the at-large system was adopted in the 1950s. He was reelected in 1973. Ever since Mr. Handcox served in Place 6, that position has been filled by African Americans Jimmy Snell, Dr. Charles E. Urdy (elected to a record five terms), Eric Mitchell, Danny Thomas, Willie Lewis, and Sheryl Cole. (Courtesy of the *Villager*.)

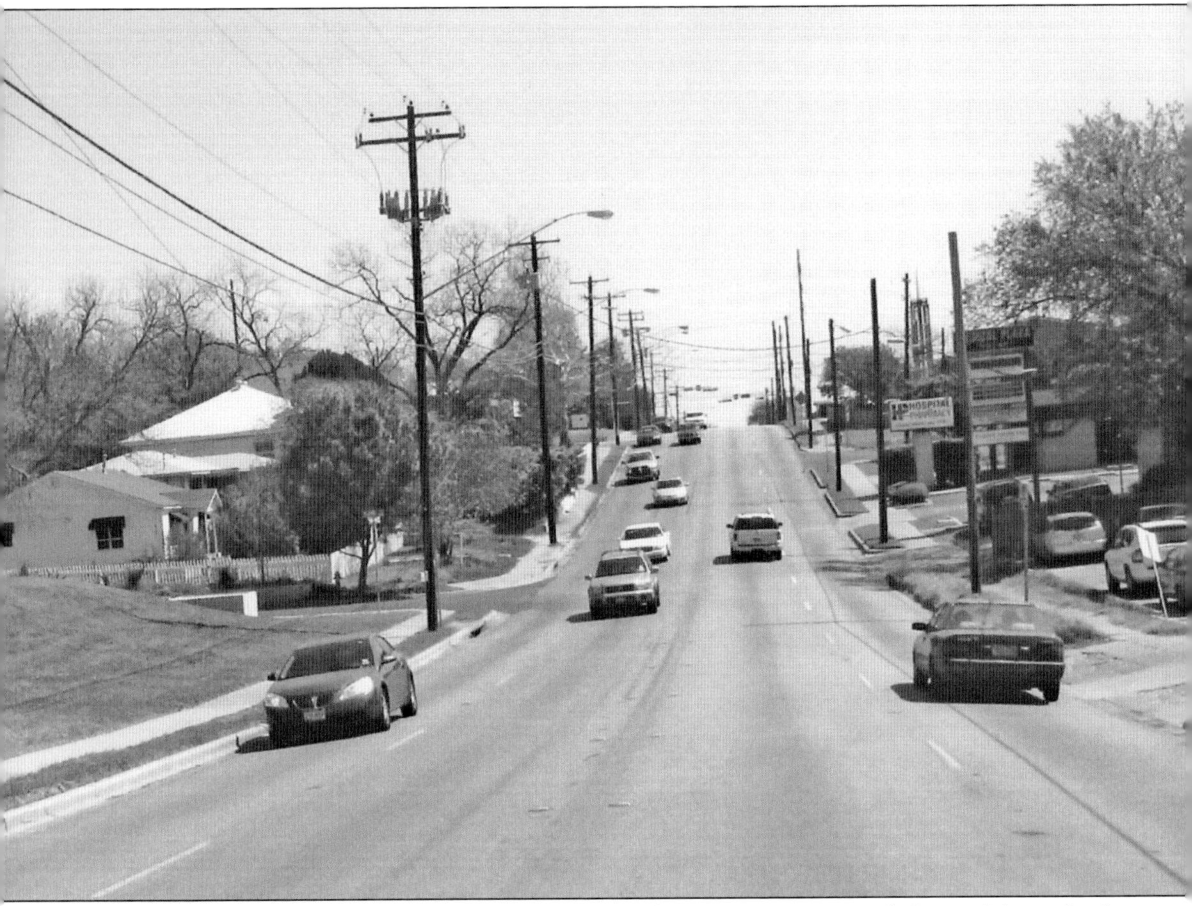

In 1975, a majority of the Austin City Council voted to rename Nineteenth Street, Martin Luther King Jr. Boulevard. The vote changed the name of the street, beginning at its starting point at Lamar Boulevard on the west, to the city limit on the east. The previous week, the council had voted to rename only that portion from IH-35 east to Ed Bluestein Boulevard, but numerous speakers at the public hearing about the renaming protested the patronizing gesture of dedicating only that section of the boulevard that runs through predominantly black neighborhoods. There was an appeals court challenge of the revised name change, but the court held the change to be legal in April 1976.

Dr. Charles E. Urdy was born in Georgetown, Texas, to a large family of sharecroppers. He moved with his family to Austin following World War II. He earned a bachelor of science in chemistry from Huston-Tillotson. While a student there, he participated in early efforts to achieve racial equality after collecting poll taxes in East Austin. Dr. Urdy served in the US Army Chemical Corps, then earned a PhD from the University of Texas, attending along with Dr. William Charles Akins. Dr. Urdy was elected to a record five terms on the Austin City Council. (Courtesy of AHC, PICB 17221.)

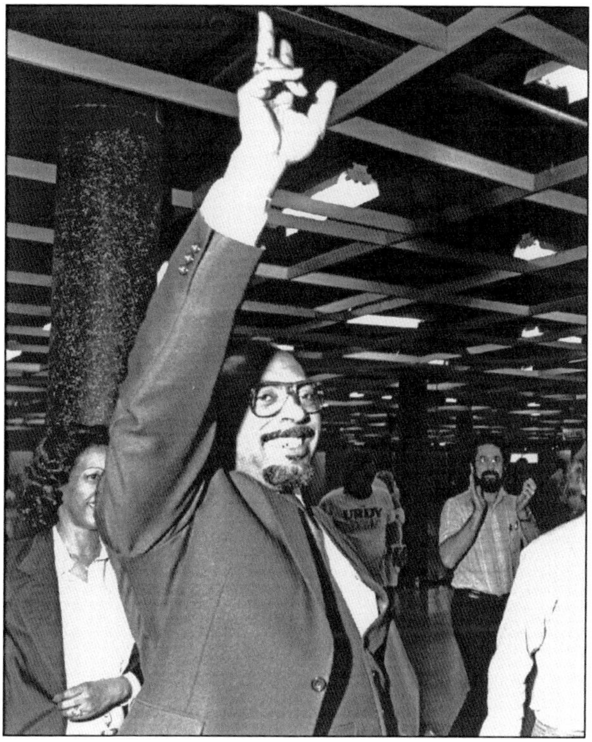

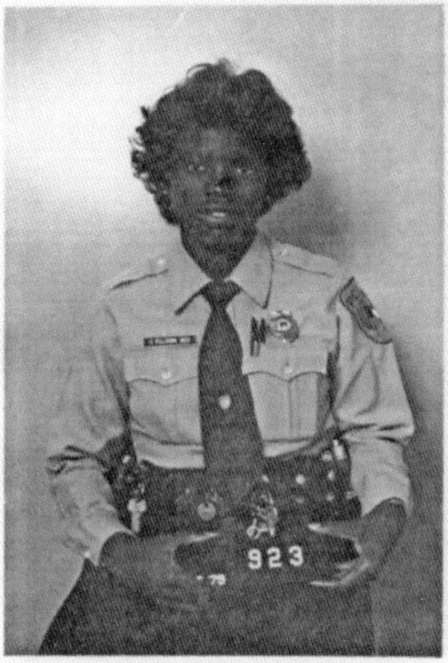

POLICE OFFICER CATHY ELLISON
1978

Born May 25, 1956
Dale, Texas

Attended High School in Lockhart, Texas, and S.W.T.S.U. in San Marcos, Texas.

According to Louie White, cited in the bibliography, in 1871, Henry G. Madison was not only appointed to the city's governing body, he was also appointed to serve on the city police force, becoming the first African American to do so. Henry B. Willis was appointed the second African American police officer. It was not until the 1960s that Officer Freddie Maxwell was promoted to sergeant that the city had its first African American sergeant. Then, in 1978, Cathy Ellison, shown here, became the first African American female police officer in the city of Austin. Officer Ellison was named acting chief of the Austin Police Department in May 2006, thus becoming the first African American in that position. She remained acting chief until a final selection for the position was made. (Courtesy of AHC, 352.2WhAA-Ellison.)

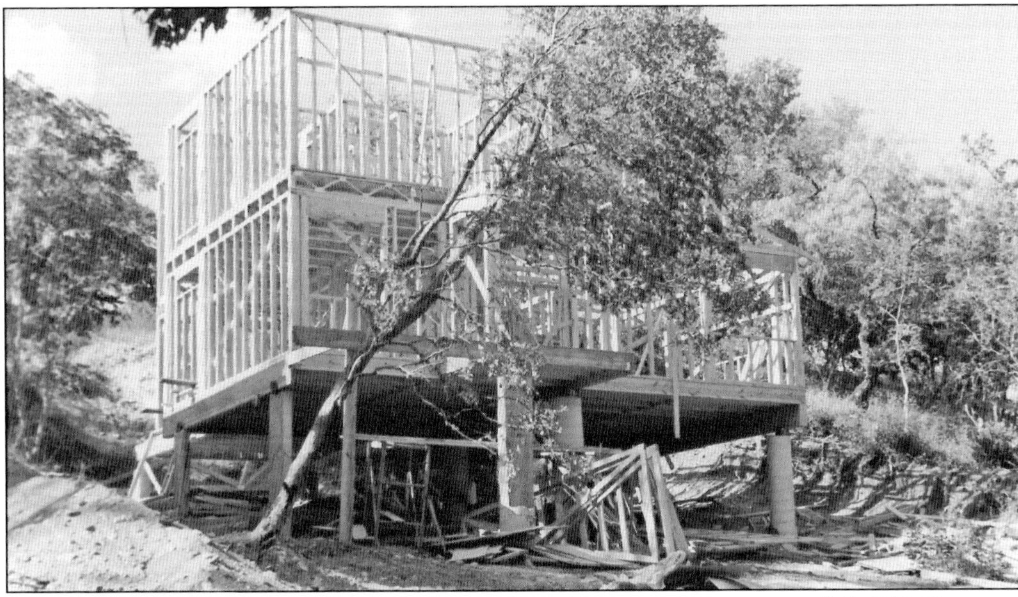

In 1982, the East Austin Chicano Economic Development Corporation (EACEDC), one of several community development organizations funded by the city at that time, built nine new single-family homes just east of Rosewood on Oak Springs Drive in a development called Nueva Vida (New Life). This is one of the Nueva Vida houses under construction.

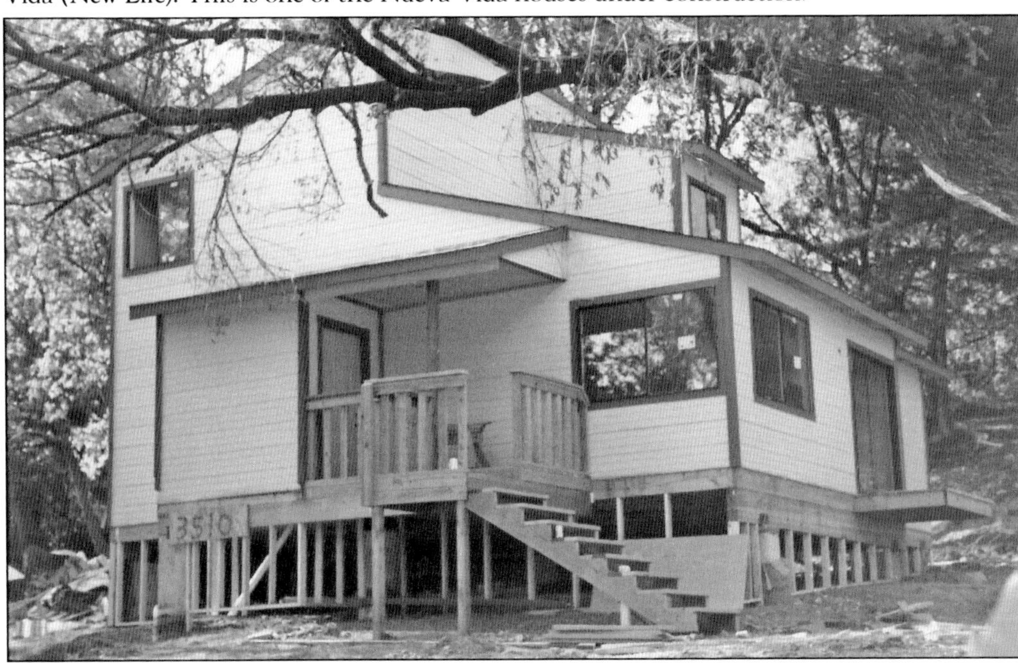

Nueva Vida was the area's first new development of single-family residences in over 20 years. EACEDC took applications from prospective first-time home buyers and pre-qualified them for loans that were extended by University Savings, a local savings and loan association. The builder financed the development himself, with assistance from a city grant, to ensure the pier and beam foundations were adequate for the location, which included some natural springs, for which the street was named.

Author Dr. Jane H. Rivera is standing in front of the Nueva Vida project office. The authors were the EACEDC Nueva Vida project managers.

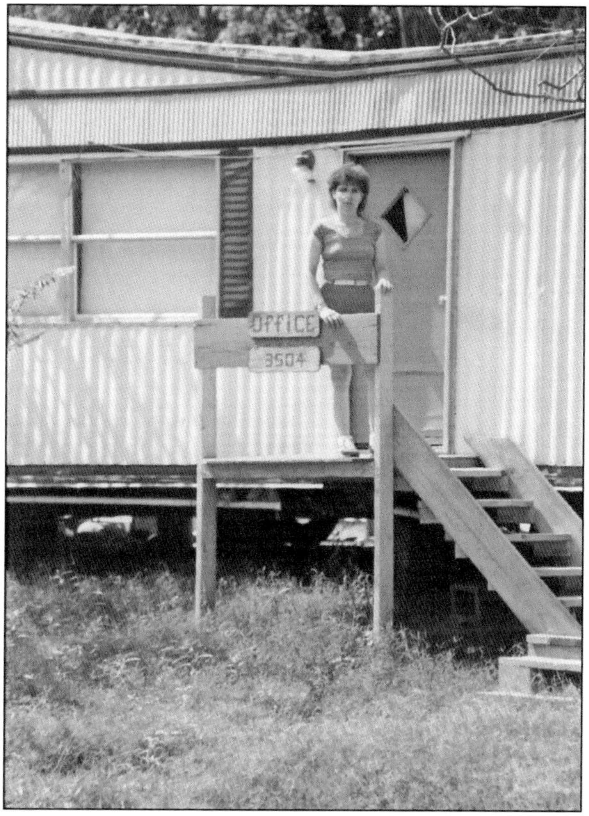

James and Annie Stewart began construction of their home on Nile Street in 1988, completing it in 1991, and holding an open house on September 22, 1991. Most new construction in Rosewood at the time was done by the owners; Mr. Stewart built the house with help from his family. This photograph shows Mr. Stewart and his son Anthony as they started the framing. The Stewarts became one of the first new homeowners in the Rosewood Glen Oaks area following urban renewal. The style was very modern and split-level, and the house remains a landmark in the neighborhood. (Courtesy of Annie F. Stewart.)

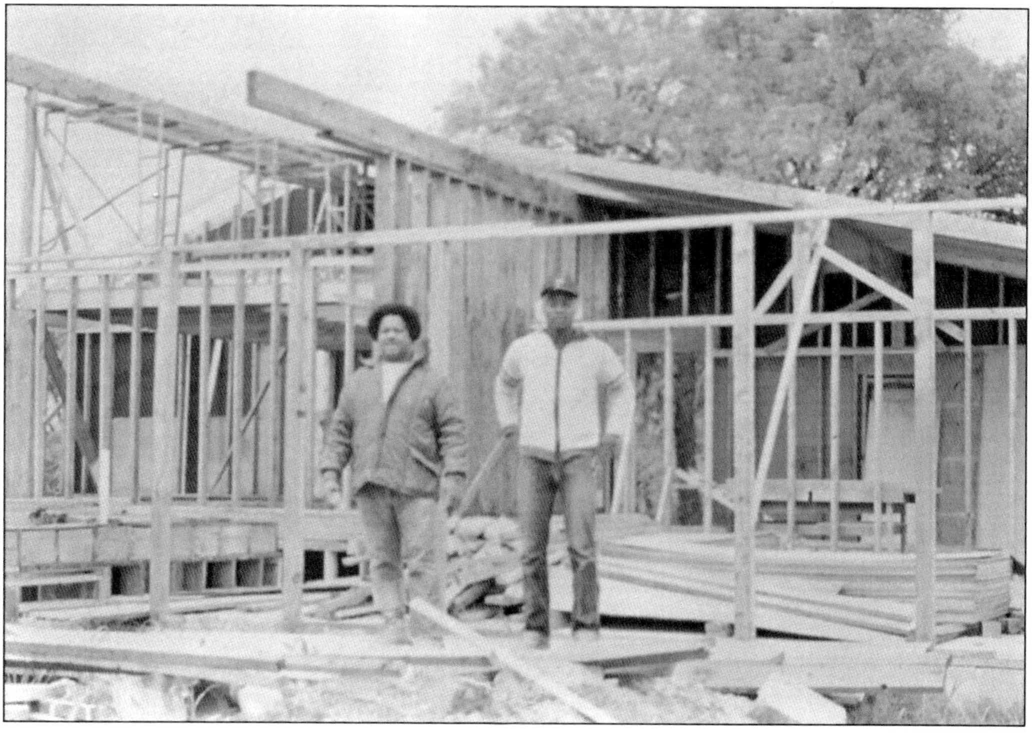

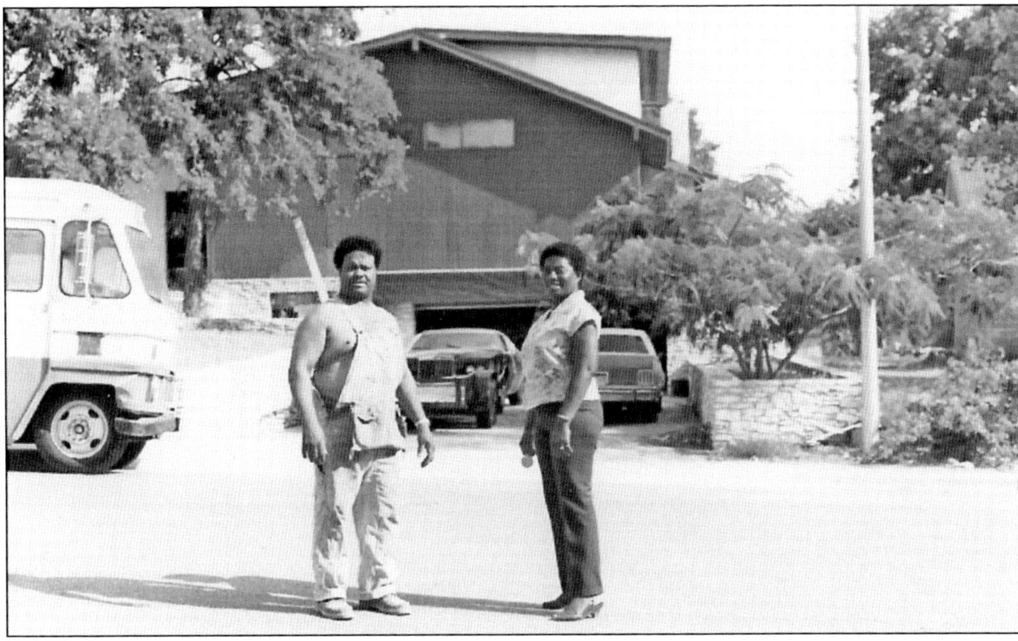

James and Annie Stewart stand in front of their completed home. The Stewarts owned and operated a barbershop on Rosewood Avenue and were active in the Rosewood–Glen Oaks Neighborhood Association and the Metropolitan A.M.E Church. (Courtesy of Annie F. Stewart.)

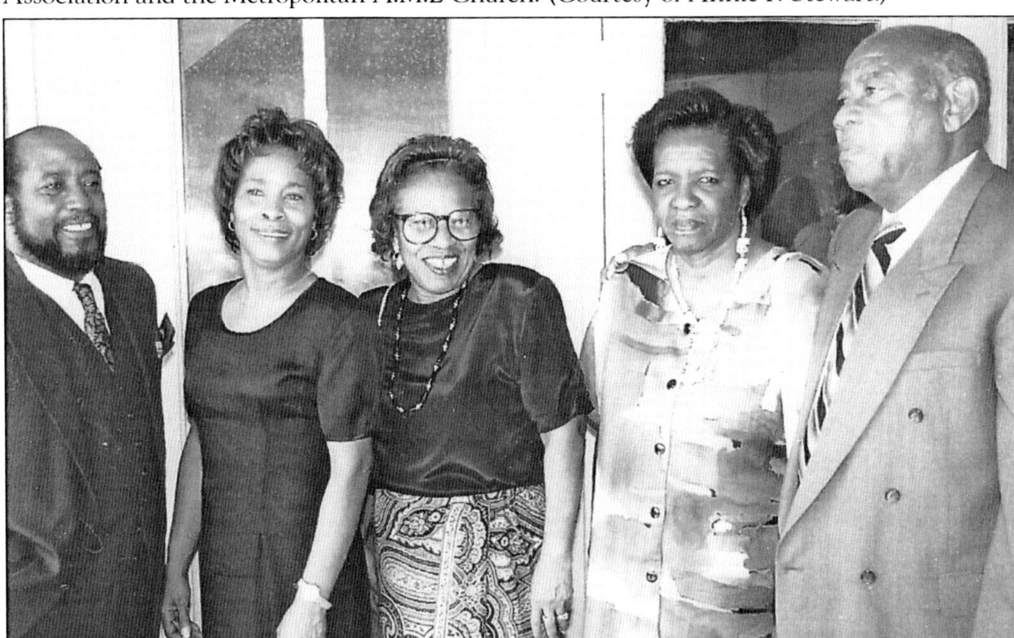

The siblings shown here are, from left to right, William Earl Carter, Carlean Johnson (who managed human resources for the DeWitty Center), Mattie Callins, Velma Roberts, and Blake Y. Sterling. They were born in Austin, raised in East Austin, attended AISD schools, and graduated from Anderson High School. Mattie assisted her sister Velma with many of her community activities. (Courtesy of Mattie Callins.)

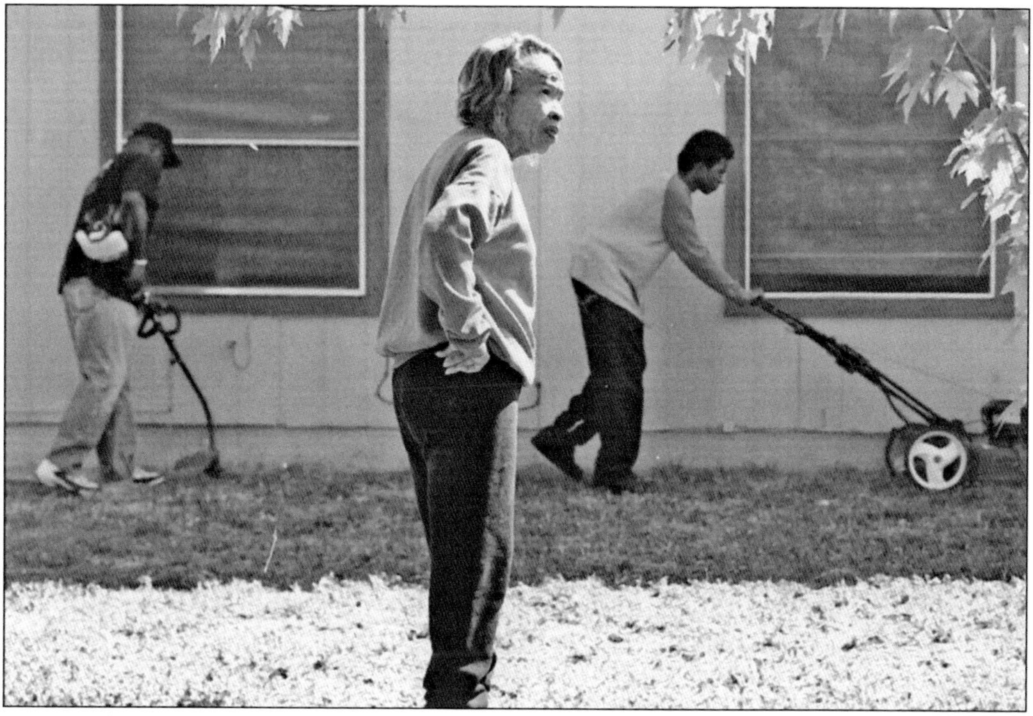

In 1984, the city provided partial funding for private builders to construct five new single-family homes on Glen Oaks Drive in the southern part of Rosewood. In 1985, the city helped fund a collaboration between developer Gary Bradley and Clark Wilson Homes to build 10 single-family homes on Glen Oaks Court. Financially qualified first-time homebuyers were eligible to purchase the homes. Here, longtime neighbors help Mattie Callins with yard work. (Courtesy of Julia Robinson.)

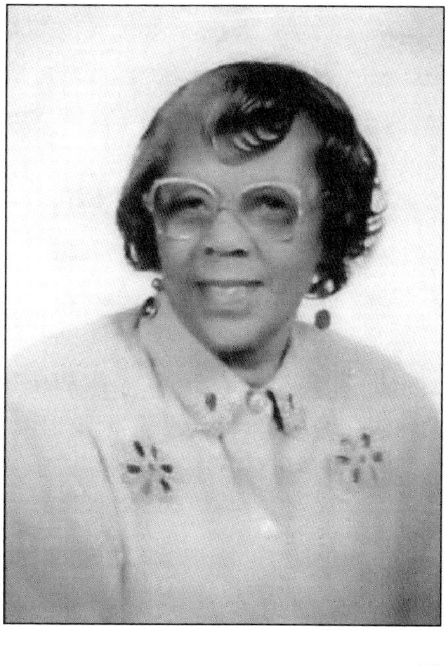

Elizabeth Snipes (known to her neighbors as "Liz") was born in Harlingen, Texas, but moved to Austin as a child and attended East Side schools. Ms. Snipes served under missionary E.B. Scott and remained a proud member of the E.B. Scott Missionary Society. After moving to Rosewood in 1984, Ms. Snipes and her neighbors formed the Rosewood–Glen Oaks Neighborhood Association. She became the third president of the association, with Alta Ochiltree as vice president. Ms. Snipes remained president until illness forced her to retire in 2006. She moved to Bowie, Maryland, to live with her daughter Wilma Snipes-Persaud, son-in-law Kris Persaud, grandchildren, and great-grandchildren. (Courtesy of Wilma Snipes-Persaud.)

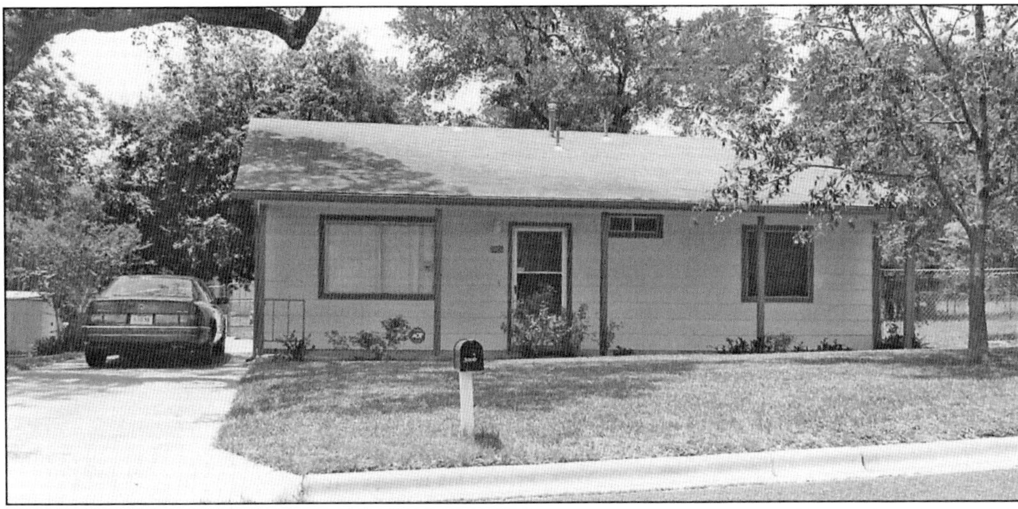

Elizabeth Snipes's home was central command for community activism. Under her leadership, Rosewood–Glen Oaks helped residents paint privacy fences, mowed the yards of the ill and elderly and vacant properties, created a tool lending library, set up Neighborhood Watch, provided input and assistance to the city regarding plans for the Conley-Guerrero Senior Activity Center and the Lyons Gardens Senior Residences, dealt with a drug house that occurred when an elderly owner's relatives began to misuse her home, successfully fought efforts to place a facility for state felons who were also substance abusers in the neighborhood, and provided input and assistance to Austin Community College regarding its Eastview Campus.

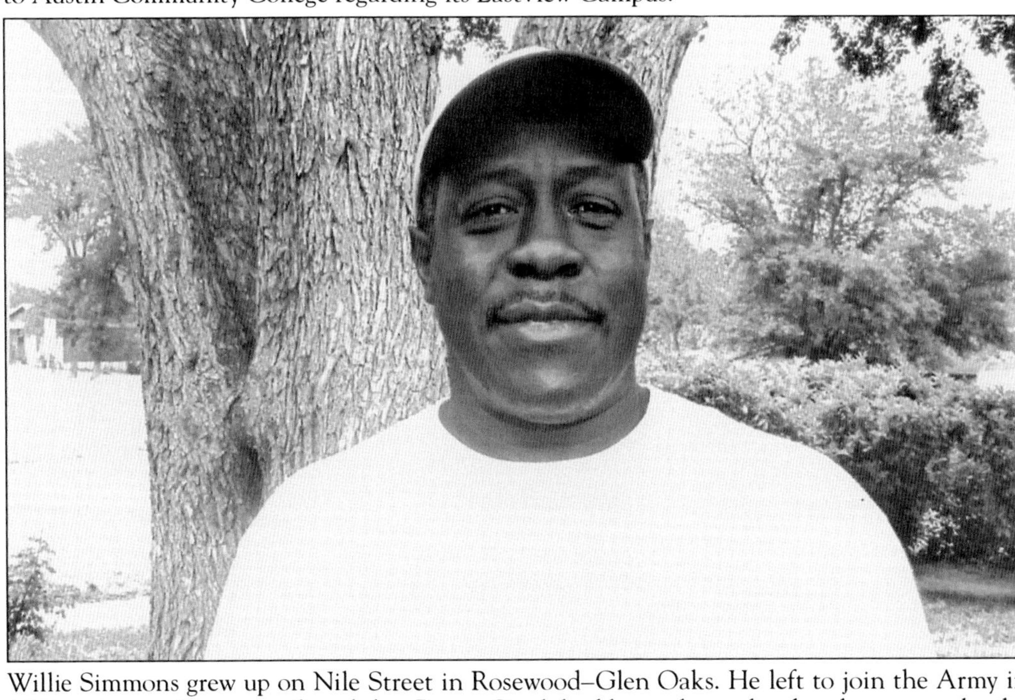

Willie Simmons grew up on Nile Street in Rosewood–Glen Oaks. He left to join the Army in 1973, and upon his return, found that Boggy Creek had been channelized with concrete by the US Army Corps of Engineers. He returned to Rosewood again in 2003, when the original owner of the house on Glen Oaks where he now lives sold it to him. He likes the way the neighborhood is currently integrated, and intends to spend the rest of his life here.

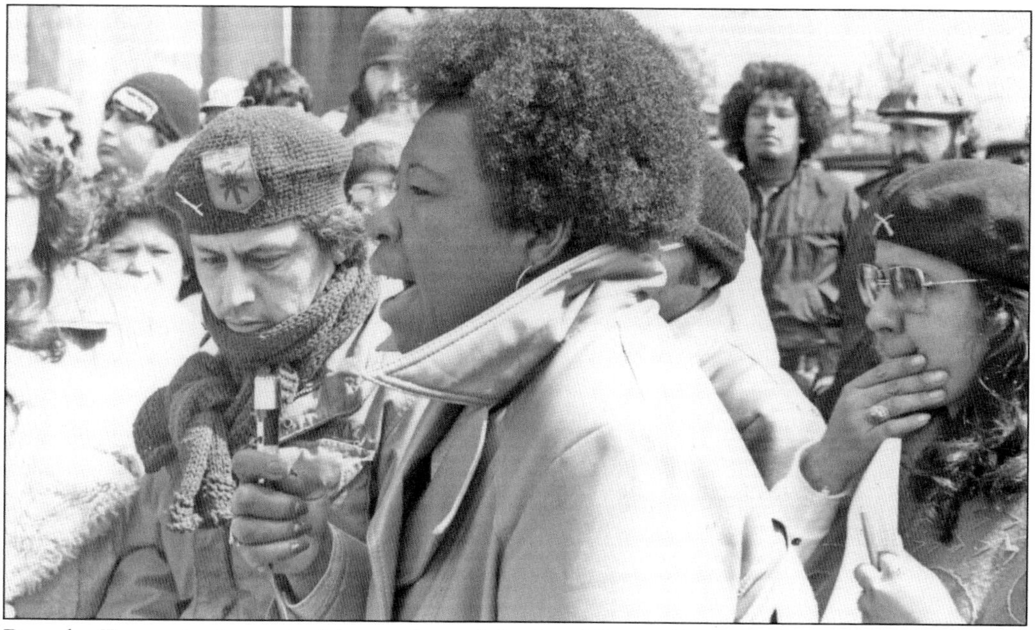

Dorothy Turner is pictured with members of the local Brown Berets organization in the 1970s. Ms. Turner cofounded the Black Citizens Task Force (BCTF) in 1974, becoming president in 1977. Ms. Turner was involved in getting a library for northeast Austin, The Millennium Youth Entertainment Complex in Rosewood, and creating KAZI-FM, a radio station that features programming for the African American community. Rev. Sterling Lands II, pastor of the Greater Calvary Baptist Church, was quoted in the *Austin American-Statesman* of April 8, 2005, as saying, "Dorothy was a self-motivated freedom fighter. Her focus was always on how to help her people." (Courtesy of AHC, AR.2001.002[T-1].)

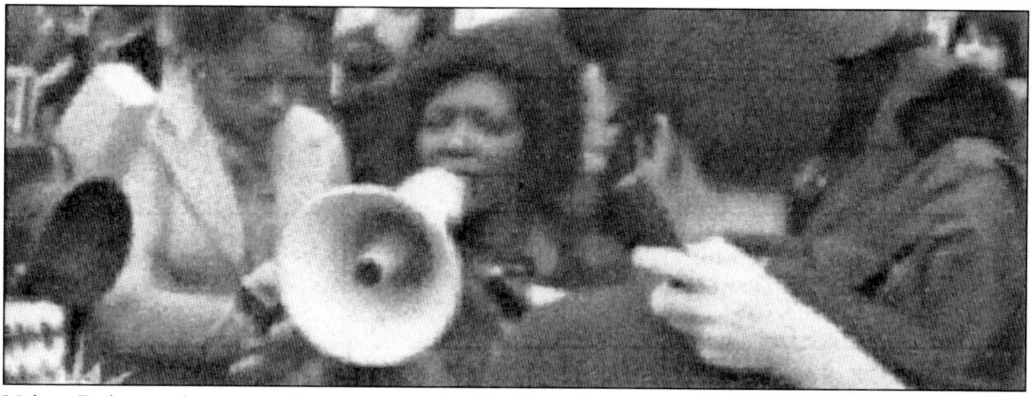

Velma Roberts, shown speaking against the Ku Klux Klan at its rally in Austin in 1983, founded the Austin Welfare Rights Organization, the local chapter of the National Welfare Rights Organization, in 1969. Two of her children were plaintiffs in *Overton vs. AISD*, the case that finally led to the desegregation of Austin schools. Ms. Roberts organized a boycott of AISD schools, founding an alternative school funded by donations for neighborhood children. Ms. Roberts also became the first president of the Black Citizens Task Force. Akwasi Evans wrote in his eulogy article of November 16, 2000, "One African superstition holds that whenever it rains on the day someone is buried it is a sign that the soul has ascended to heaven. At 8:25 a.m. Wednesday morning a single cloud burst. . . . I smiled at the thought of this brief shower on the morning of Velma Roberts's home going."

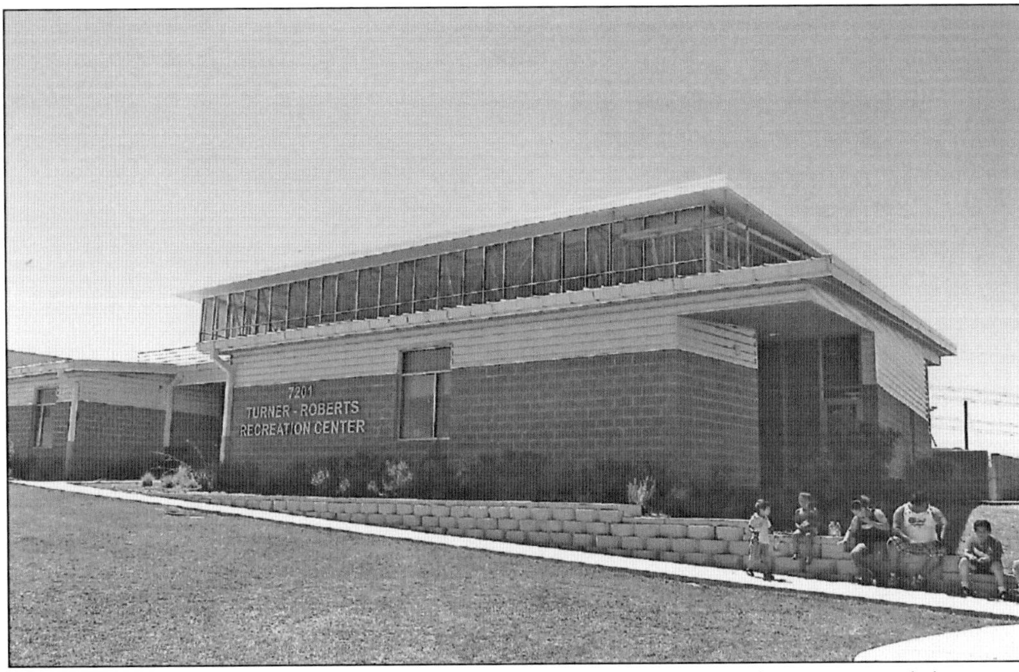

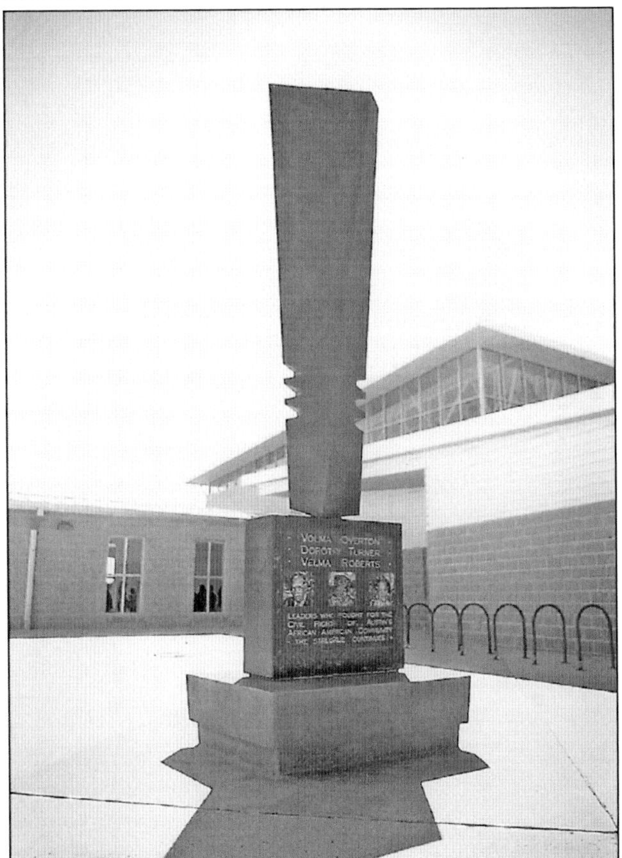

In 2008, the city opened the Turner-Roberts Recreation Center in the Colony Park neighborhood of northeast Austin, named in honor of Dorothy Turner and Velma Roberts. In addition to the naming of this facility, in 1981, Ms. Roberts received the Friends of VISTA Award, and in 1992, Ms. Turner was awarded the Arthur L. Green Civil and Human Rights Award.

This sculpture, by artist John Christensen, is located between Overton Elementary School and Turner-Roberts Recreation Center in a shared complex on Colony Loop Drive in far northeast Austin. (Courtesy of Ryah Christensen.)

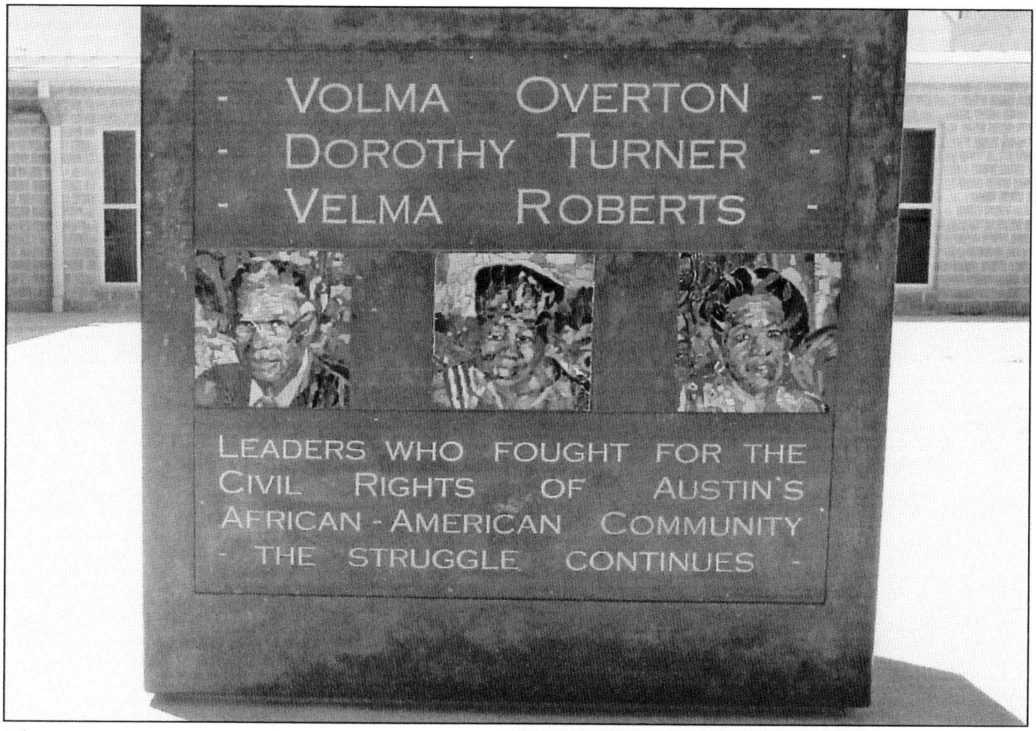

These mosaic portraits of Volma Overton, Dorothy Turner, and Velma Roberts by Rosewood artist Ryah Christensen appear on the base of the sculpture by her father, John Christensen. (Courtesy of Ryah Christensen.)

Rep. Dawnna Dukes is currently a nine-term, 17-year tenured member of the Texas House of Representatives and a third-generation native of District 46—East Austin and Northeast Travis County. She reflects on her childhood: "I grew up in Austin and three generations of my family lived at the northwest corner of Olive and Waller. In my formative years, I attended Saint Mary's Catholic School on Tenth Street, Pearce Junior High and Reagan High School. I also attended Holy Cross Catholic Church on East Eleventh Street where my great grandmother was one of the two founding members of Holy Cross." Representative Dukes has traveled extensively as an ambassador for the State of Texas and the United States. (Courtesy of Rep. Dawnna Dukes.)

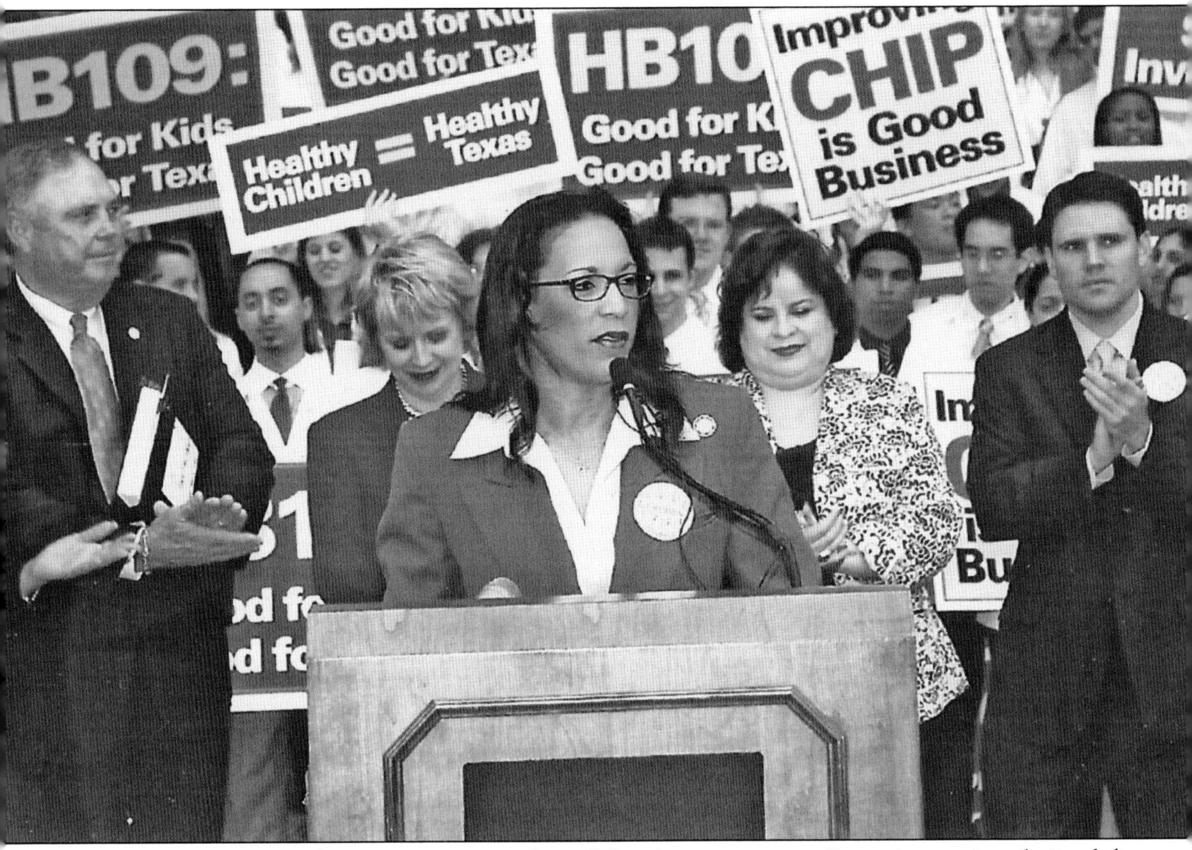

Representative Dukes serves as a member of the Appropriations Committee, vice chair of the Health and Human Services Subcommittee on Appropriations, and a member of the Culture, Recreation and Tourism Committee. She has received many awards and titles, including the 1999 Outstanding Human Rights Advocate title by the Human Rights Campaign; the 1999 State Legislator of the Year by the National Association of Small Disadvantaged Businesses; the 2002 YWCA Woman of the Year Award; the 2010 National Foundation of Black Public Administrators Distinguished Public Servant Award; and the 2011 Women Who Do Award by the City of Austin. Her many accomplishments include her 2009 success in creating jobs and stimulating the economy by creating the Texas Moving Image Industry Incentive Program and securing $60 million to bring Texas into the forefront of the competitive film industry. (Courtesy of Rep. Dawnna Dukes.)

Five

TRANSFORMATION

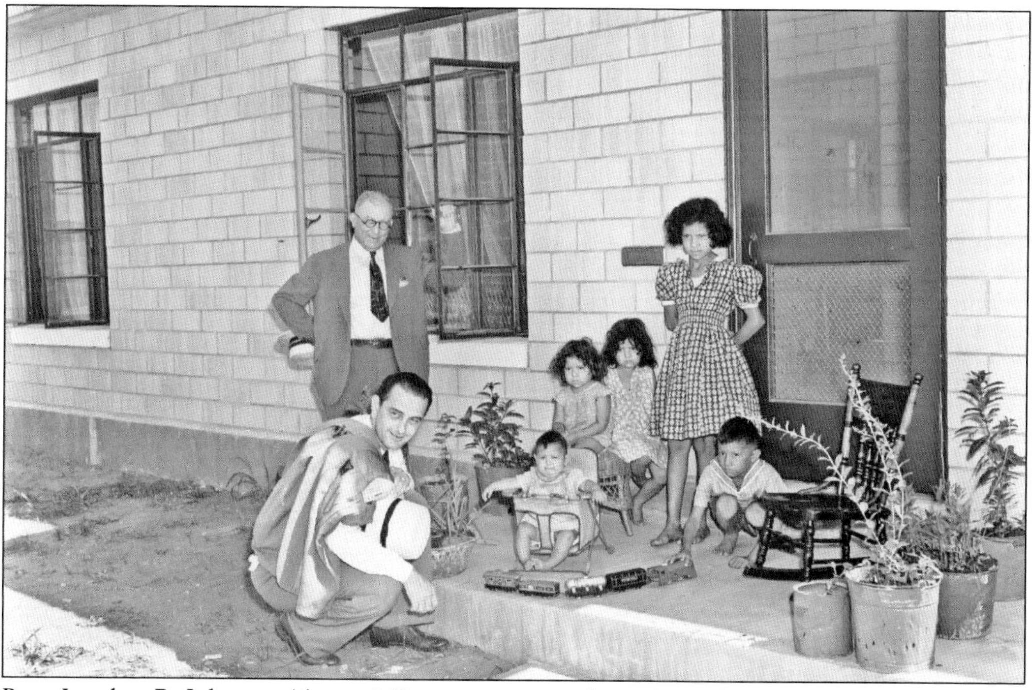

Pres. Lyndon B. Johnson (then a US representative from Austin) is pictured at the opening of Santa Rita, an Austin low-income housing project completed under the federal 1937 Slum Clearance Housing Project Act. The three Austin projects were first in the nation to be built under this act. Santa Rita was built for Mexican Americans, Chalmers for whites, and Rosewood for African Americans. The Rosewood project is the site that some longtime residents recall was once Emancipation Park. President Johnson entered into the Congressional Record his deep feelings about the need for the projects, noting to private developers opposed to the project, "Yes, sir: it is true. The Government is competing with shacks and hovels and hog sties and all the other foul holes in which the underprivileged have had to live." (Courtesy of the Lyndon Baines Johnson Library and Museum, photograph by Neal Douglass/*Austin Statesman*.)

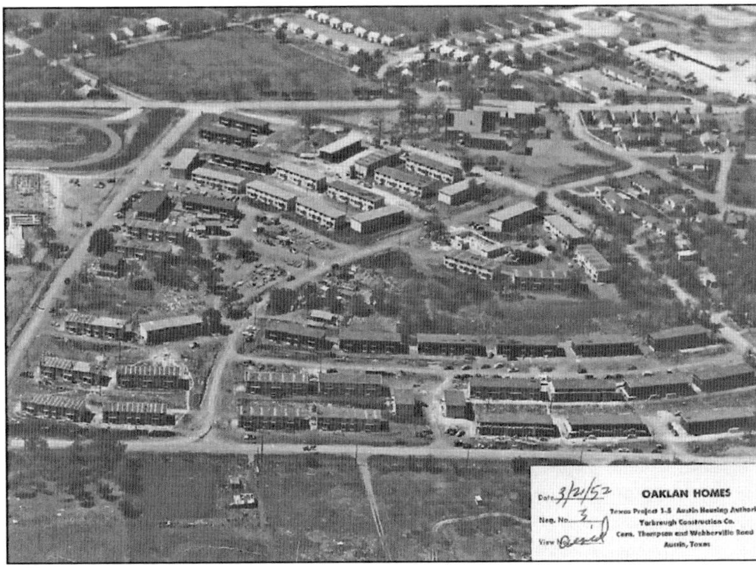

The Booker T. Washington housing project, built and managed by the Housing Authority of the City of Austin, consists of 216 units for income-qualified residents. Construction began in 1951 and was completed in 1952. (Courtesy of the Housing Authority of the City of Austin.)

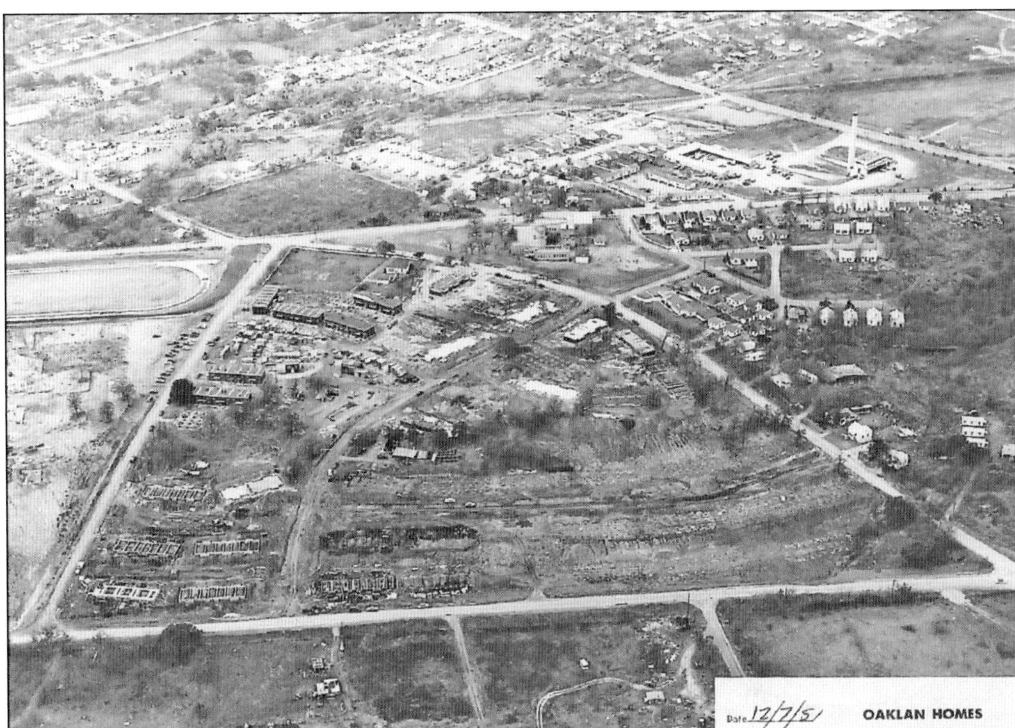

The housing at "Booker T," as it is commonly referred to in Rosewood, was greatly appreciated, but one problem that current Rosewood residents remember from their childhood in the area was the smell of the trash incinerator located at the city's solid waste center on Hargrave Street. The incinerator is the tower at the upper right of this picture, which was still in operation when the Booker T. Washington residences first opened. (Courtesy of the Housing Authority of the City of Austin.)

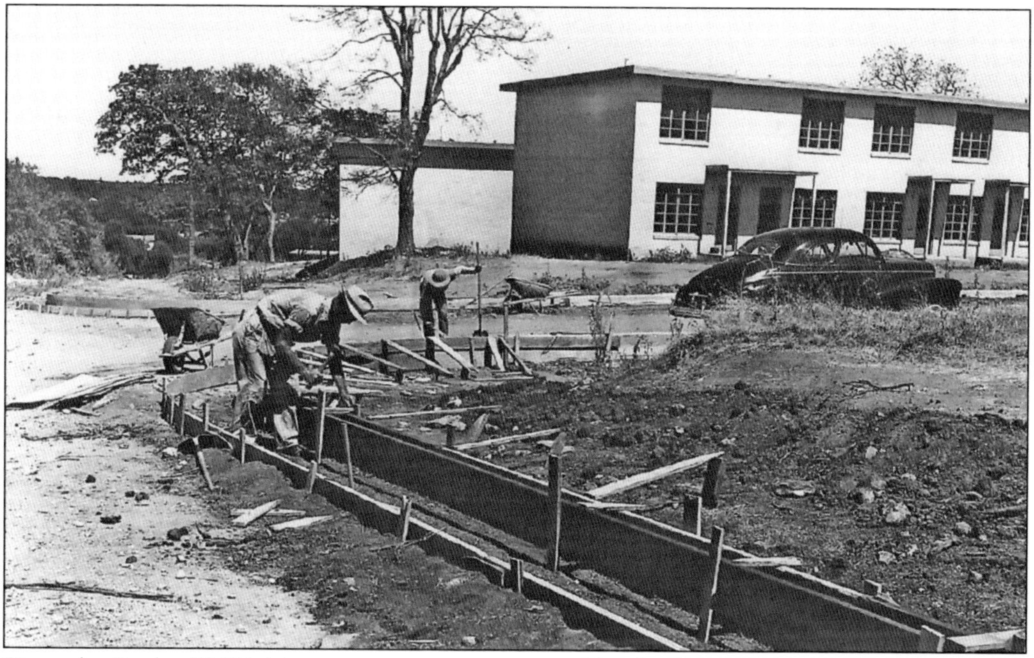

Since the Booker T. Washington apartments, managed by the Austin Housing Authority during the 1950s, had all modern facilities, as opposed to some of the earlier residences they replaced, resident Marvin Douglas recalls that "It was an honor to live there." (Courtesy of the Housing Authority of the City of Austin.)

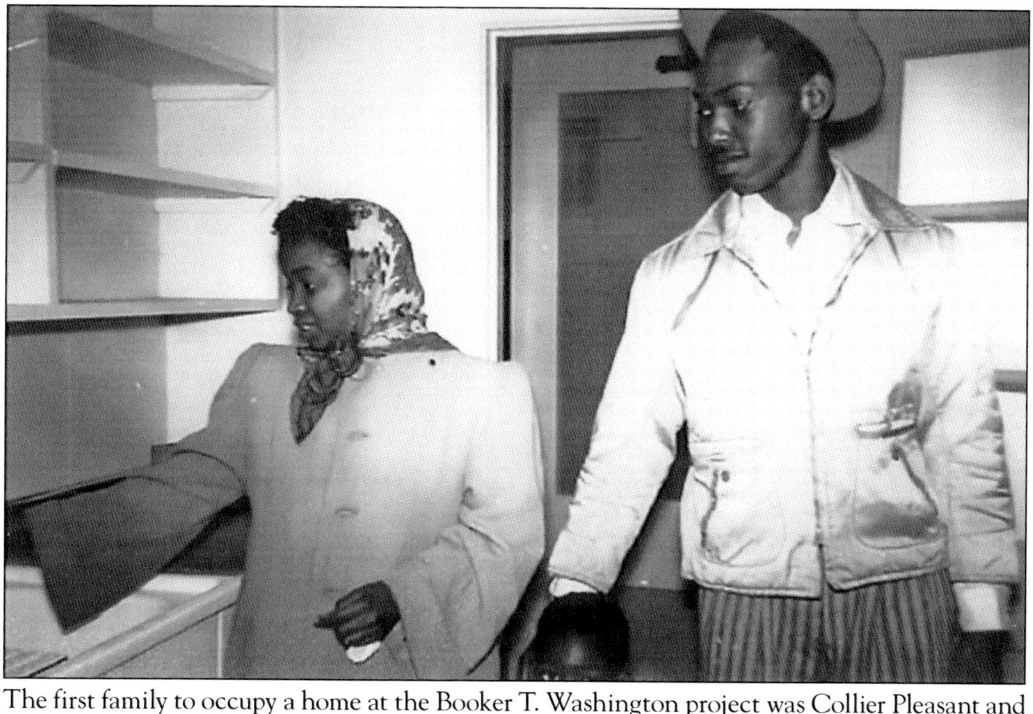

The first family to occupy a home at the Booker T. Washington project was Collier Pleasant and his family, who moved into their home on March 9, 1953. (Courtesy of the Housing Authority of the City of Austin.)

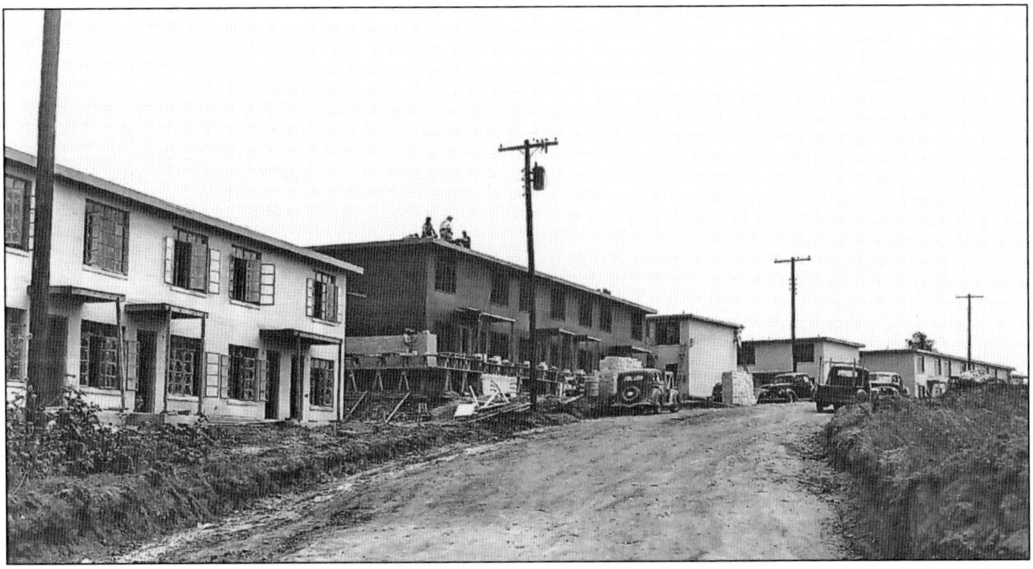

The first units at Booker T. Washington were occupied in 1953. Current Rosewood resident Clara Cobble's family moved into the Booker T. Washington apartments around 1953. She was a child, but recalls that Rosewood Elementary School had been there for many years and that the Booker T. Washington apartment homes were very nice. (Courtesy of the Housing Authority of the City of Austin.)

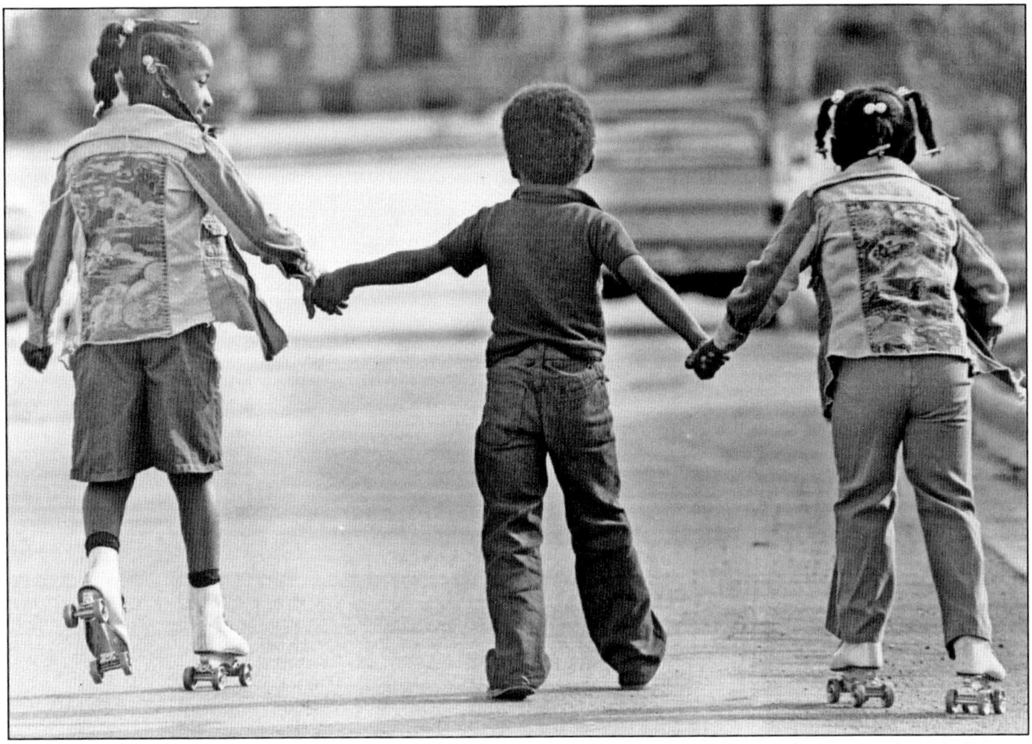

Tonya Allen, age eight, Will Washington, age six, and Niecey Smith, age five, were headed from the Booker T. Washington apartments to the grocery store. (Courtesy of AHC, PICA 12028.)

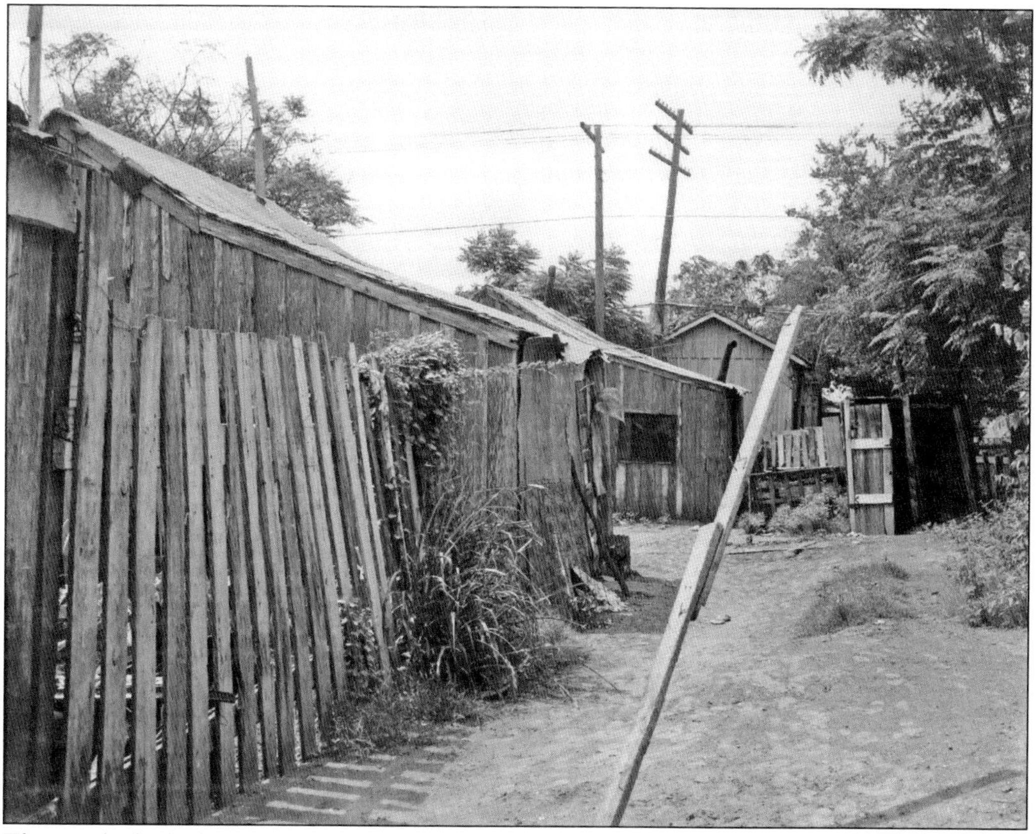

The city kicked off federally funded urban renewal in 1956 with the intent to "clear slums and eliminate urban blight" such as that documented in this photograph. Unfortunately, as an article in the January 24, 1985, *Daily Texan* noted, "City-sponsored urban renewal programs, sometimes called 'urban removal' by east Austin residents, bulldozed hundreds of east Austin homes, which were to be replaced by new structures . . ." but often were not. Urban renewal in Austin lasted over 15 years. In 1975, the City of Austin applied for the first year of Community Development Block Grant (CDBG) funding from the US Housing and Urban Development Department. The city's application noted that the Austin Urban Renewal Agency was to complete projects it had not completed with the earlier funds. (Courtesy of AHC, PICA 34458.)

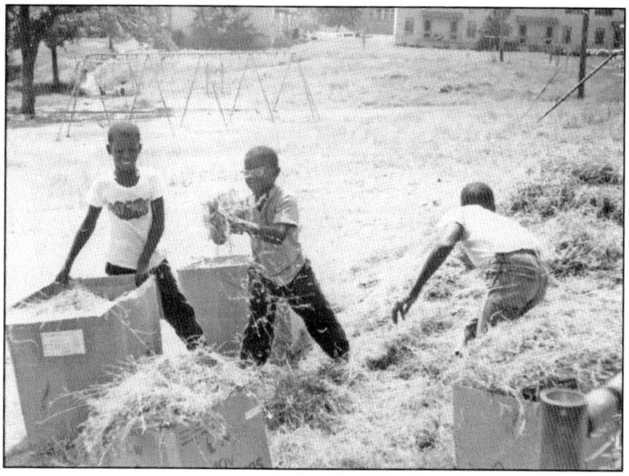

In 1966, a new anti-poverty program titled Project ENABLE (Education and Neighborhood Action for Better Living Environment) was launched in Austin by the United Fund and a US Office of Economic Opportunity grant. Thelma Elliott was the project leader. This photograph shows child resident volunteers helping with Booker T. Washington housing project cleanup through Project ENABLE. (Courtesy of AHC, AR.2000.019[p24-2].)

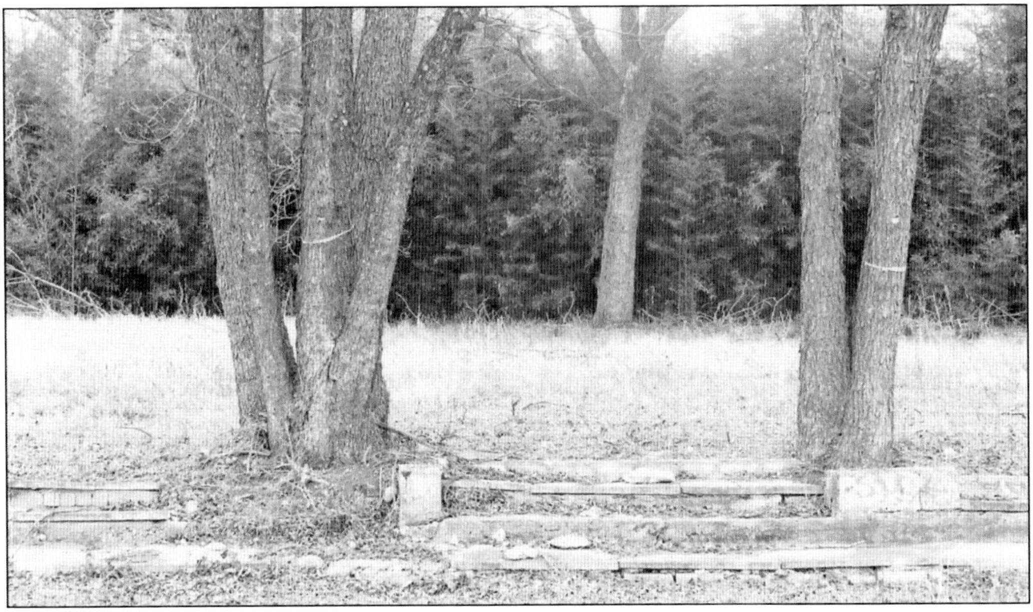

In 1967, the city selected the southern portion of Rosewood as an urban renewal area called the Glen Oaks Project. A total of 360 families and 20 businesses were condemned and the owners relocated within the Glen Oaks Project, including all families owning property on the Boggy Creek side of Nile Street. This photograph shows the remains of a former home in the Boggy Creek greenbelt. Many families did not want to move, and those who were willing to move found the prices offered for their property inadequate for them to relocate. An article in the *Austin American-Statesman* of June 13, 1969, listed total relocation payments received by three Glen Oaks families: $1,650, $2,750, and $4,950. A resident quoted on July 24, 1968, summed up neighborhood concerns: "Rev. R.H. Hawkins of 3005 Hargrave said he wanted an answer to the question: 'If we live in a slum and get paid for slum property, how are we supposed to move into anything better?'"

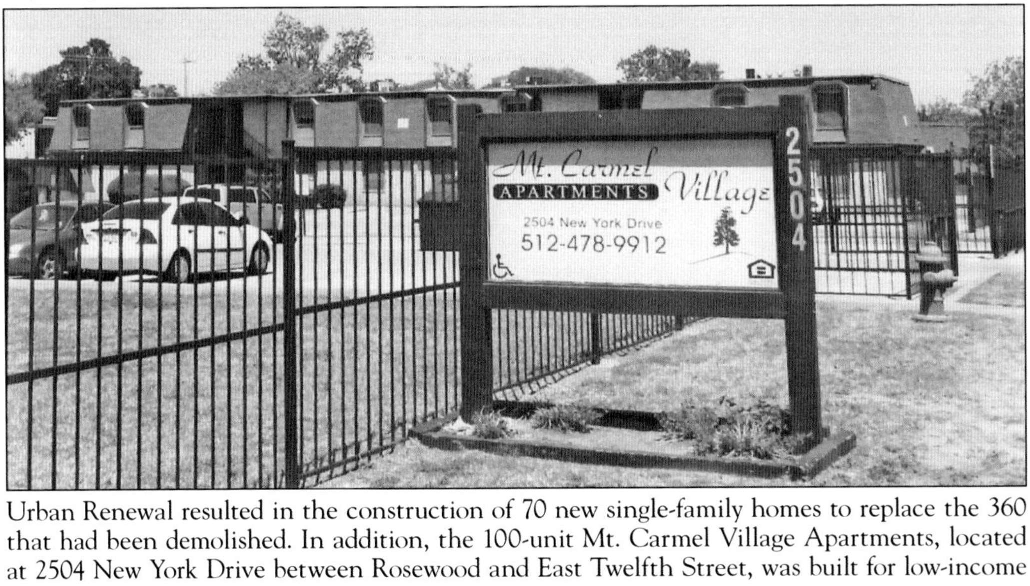

Urban Renewal resulted in the construction of 70 new single-family homes to replace the 360 that had been demolished. In addition, the 100-unit Mt. Carmel Village Apartments, located at 2504 New York Drive between Rosewood and East Twelfth Street, was built for low-income tenants receiving FHA rent supplements.

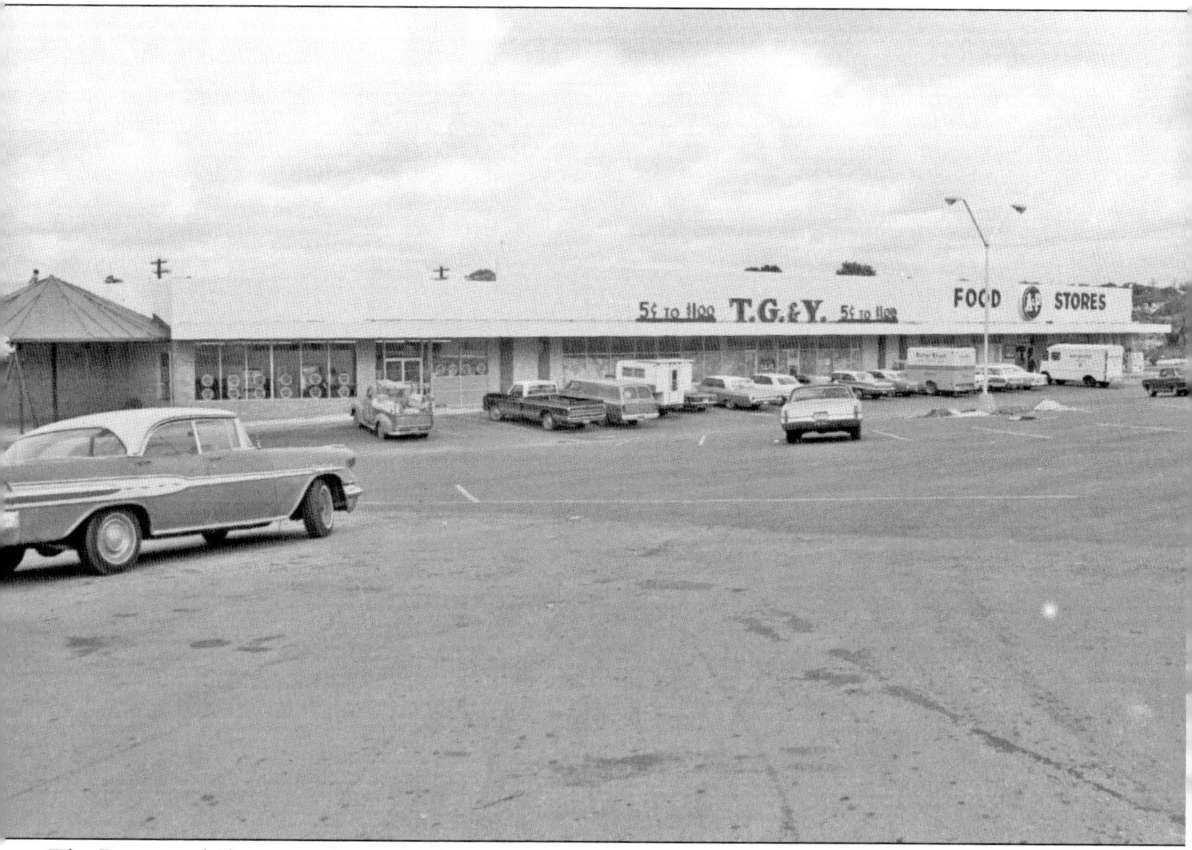

The Rosewood Shopping Center held its grand opening on July 4 and 5, 1969, with Congressman J.J. Jake Pickle cutting the ribbon. The center, located at Rosewood Avenue and Hargrave Street, was the only shopping center in Texas built in an urban renewal project. It was located across the street from Anderson High School and included a grocery store, a variety store, a laundry, a drugstore, a barber and beauty shop, a fried chicken store, and the urban renewal office. The anchor tenant was a TG&Y Store, a variety and convenience store. This shopping center was replaced in 1999 by the Millennium Youth Entertainment Center. (Courtesy of AHC, AS-69-71720-19.)

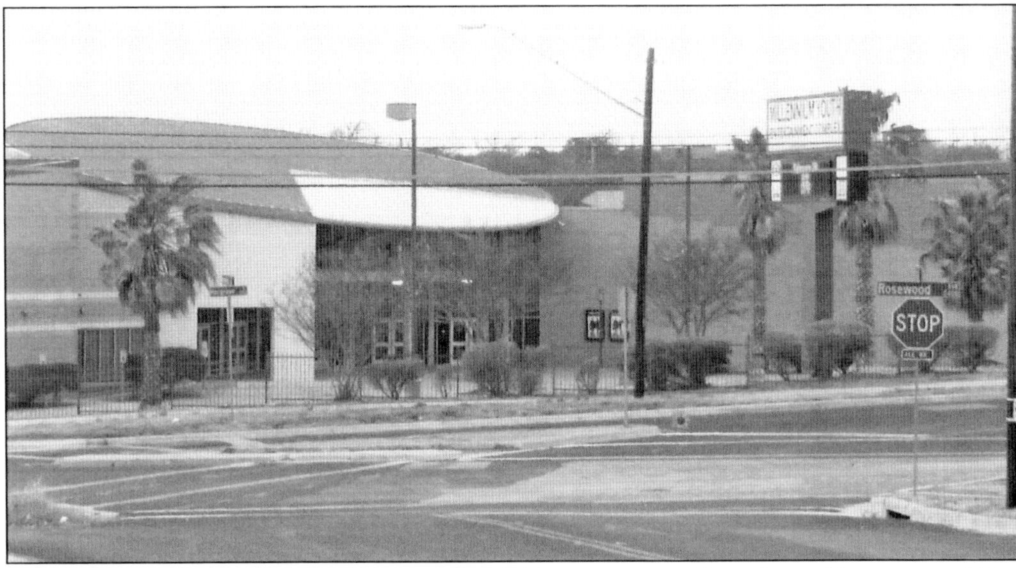

The City of Austin built the Millennium Youth Entertainment Complex at Hargrave and Neal Streets in the former location of the Rosewood Shopping Center and contracted with a private company to run a movie theater, a bowling alley, games, a food court, and a roller-skating rink on the site. The complex was built in response to a drive-by shooting just after Christmas 1992. Tamika Ross, 16, who had obtained her GED certificate and was working toward a career as a hair stylist, died in the shooting. A group of young people supported by former city council member Dr. Charles Urdy asked the city to help. The city determined that the then abandoned Rosewood Shopping Center would be a good place to build an entertainment center for East Austin youth.

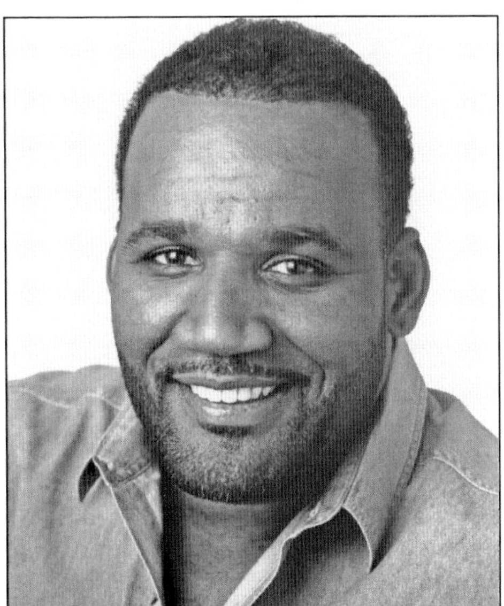

Thomas "Hollywood" Henderson is an Austin native and former member of the Dallas Cowboys of the National Football League. He went on a hunger strike for a week in 1997 to raise money to renovate the old Yellow Jacket Track and Field at 900 Neal Street, the site of the old Anderson High School. His nonprofit group, East Side Youth Services and Street Outreach, built and manage the field. Henderson had been let go from the Cowboys years earlier due to abuse of drugs and alcohol, and later spent some time in prison. Following his release, he turned his life around and became determined to help local youth. In March 2000, he won the Texas Lottery. "Now that track and field will be endowed for the next 100 years," he was quoted as saying in the *Austin American-Statesman*. (Courtesy of AHC, AR 2001-002 7/2.)

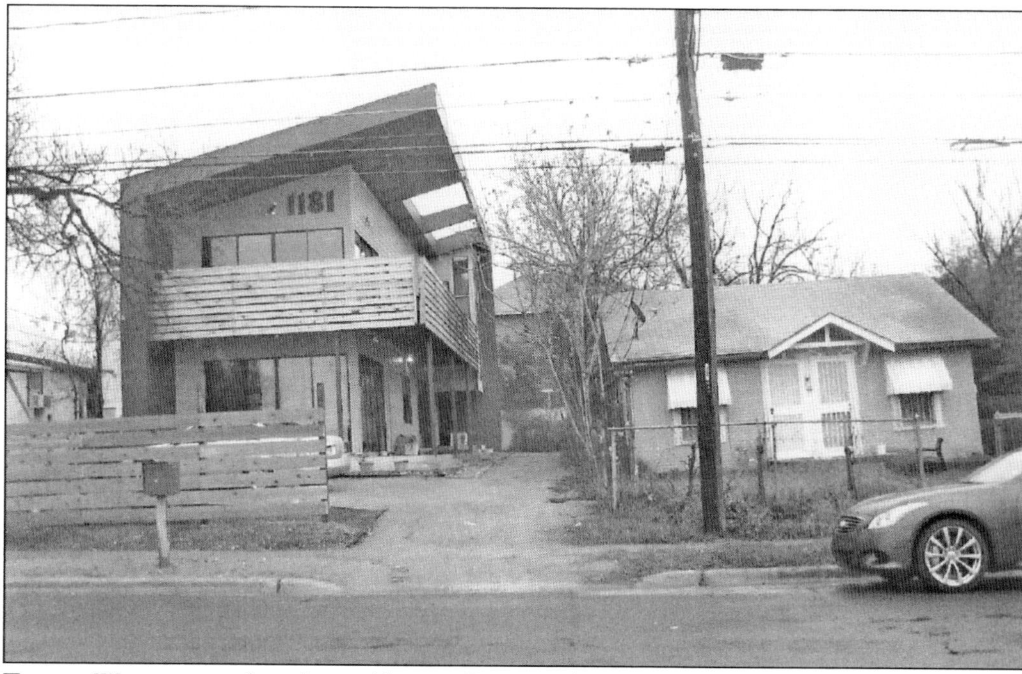

Tommy Wyatt notes that the problem in Rosewood, just as in Blackland and the rest of the African American community, is that it is no longer cohesive. Few Rosewood homeowners were able to get their homes fixed before 1968, so many moved out to be able to buy a better home. As they moved out, new immigrants have purchased those properties, torn down the original homes, and built new homes. These newer homes are generally much larger and more grand than the traditional Rosewood homes, and are valued by the Travis Central Appraisal District at much higher values. This creates a tax burden for remaining longtime residents. Remaining African American homeowners, most of whom are elderly, cannot afford the new property taxes that have escalated as expensive new homes have been built. The city is responding to the new immigrants by providing improved services, sidewalks, and things that the African American community had sought for many years.

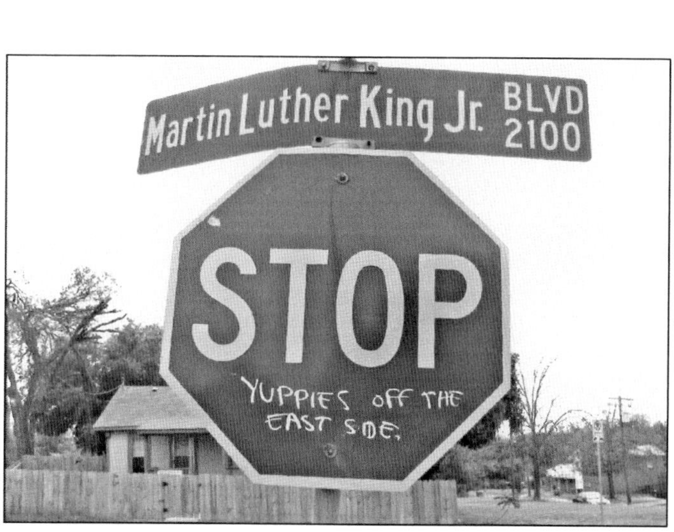

"Gentrification in the 2000s is the functional equivalent of segregation in the 1950s and 1960s," said Max Rameau. The graffiti on this traffic sign expresses the feelings of some residents. As a result of the arrival of new residences and businesses with higher tax values than the older places, East Austin had the highest rate of tax foreclosures in the city according to a study conducted by students at the University of Texas School of Business in the mid 2000s.

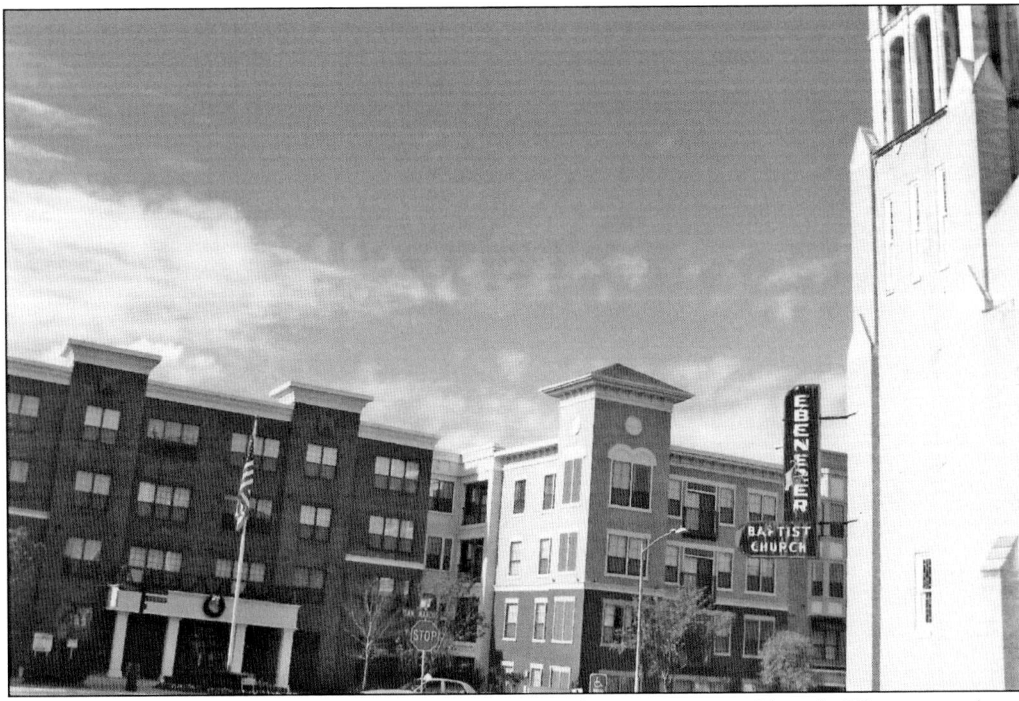

This view is toward downtown Austin from historic Ebenezer Baptist Church. The city replaced old residential and commercial structures with new office and business establishments during the 1990s and 2000s in the East Eleventh and Twelfth Street corridors near Interstate 35 through a grant process that funded projects of the Austin Revitalization Authority (ARA).

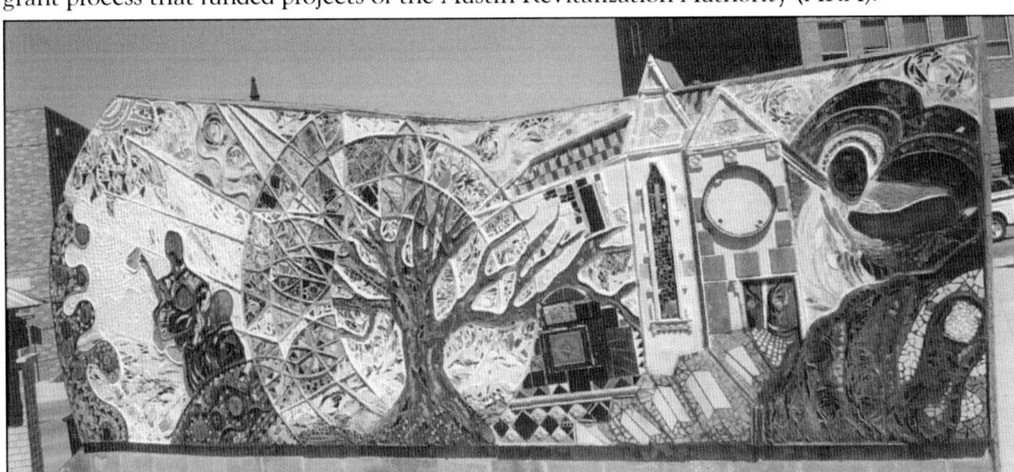

The ARA is a private, nonprofit community development corporation whose mission is to respect the people, institutions, cultures, and history of East Austin; restore a sense of hope and pride in the community; and revitalize the area's commercial, residential, and social components in a manner that promotes diversity, stability, and prosperity. As part of the ARA work on the historic Eleventh and Twelfth Street corridors, a double-sided mural was funded by ARA and created by faculty of the University of Texas at Austin Department of African and African American Studies. This side, "Sankofa," is by Regina Thomas. It is meant to depict the old Rosewood neighborhood character.

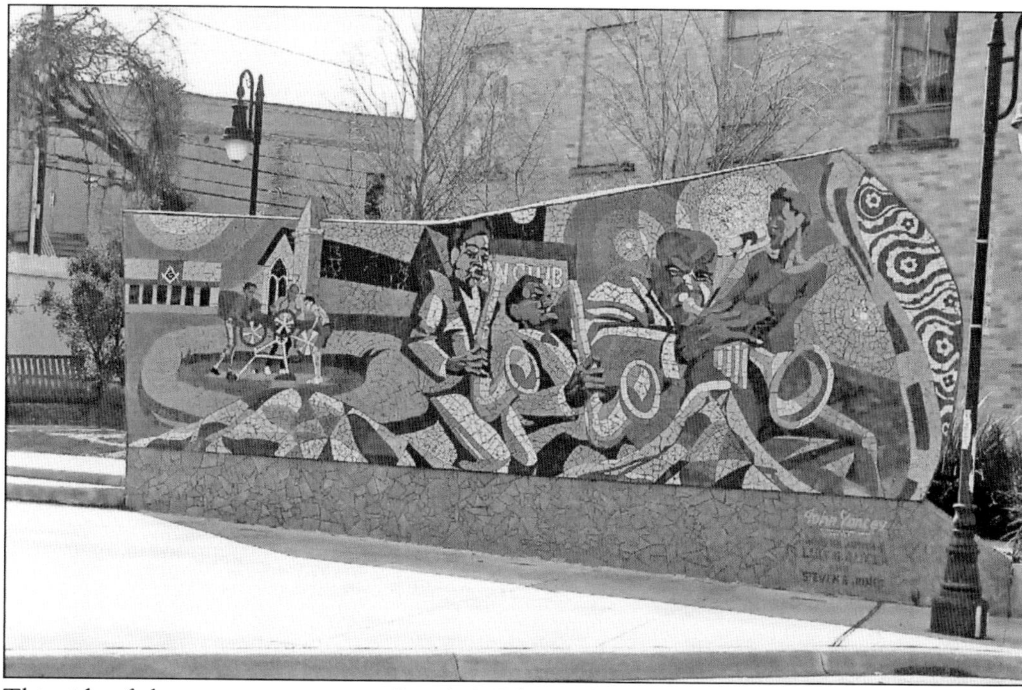

This side of the ceramic mosaic wall, titled "Rhapsody," was created by artist John Yancey. It commemorates and celebrates the jazz center that East Eleventh Street was only 70 years ago. Jazz greats such as Duke Ellington, Count Basie, and Ornette Coleman played at East Side venues like Charlie's Playhouse and the Cotton Club. "Rhapsody" pays homage to the vibrant community of which these clubs were a part.

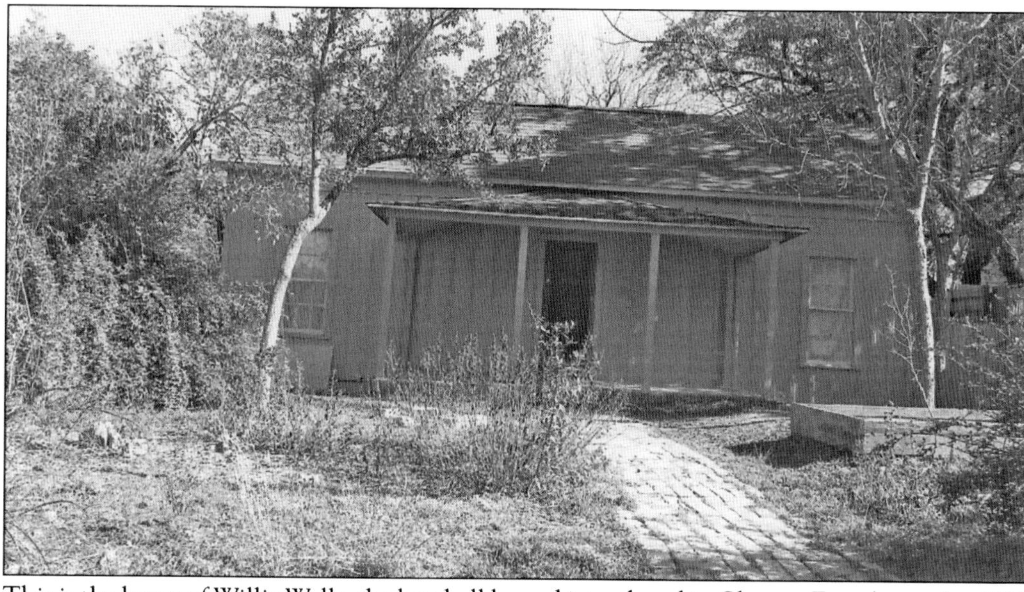

This is the home of Willie Wells, the baseball legend introduced in Chapter Four, located at 1705 Newton Street near South Austin. Current neighbors are well versed in Mr. Wells's accomplishments, including the invention of the baseball helmet.

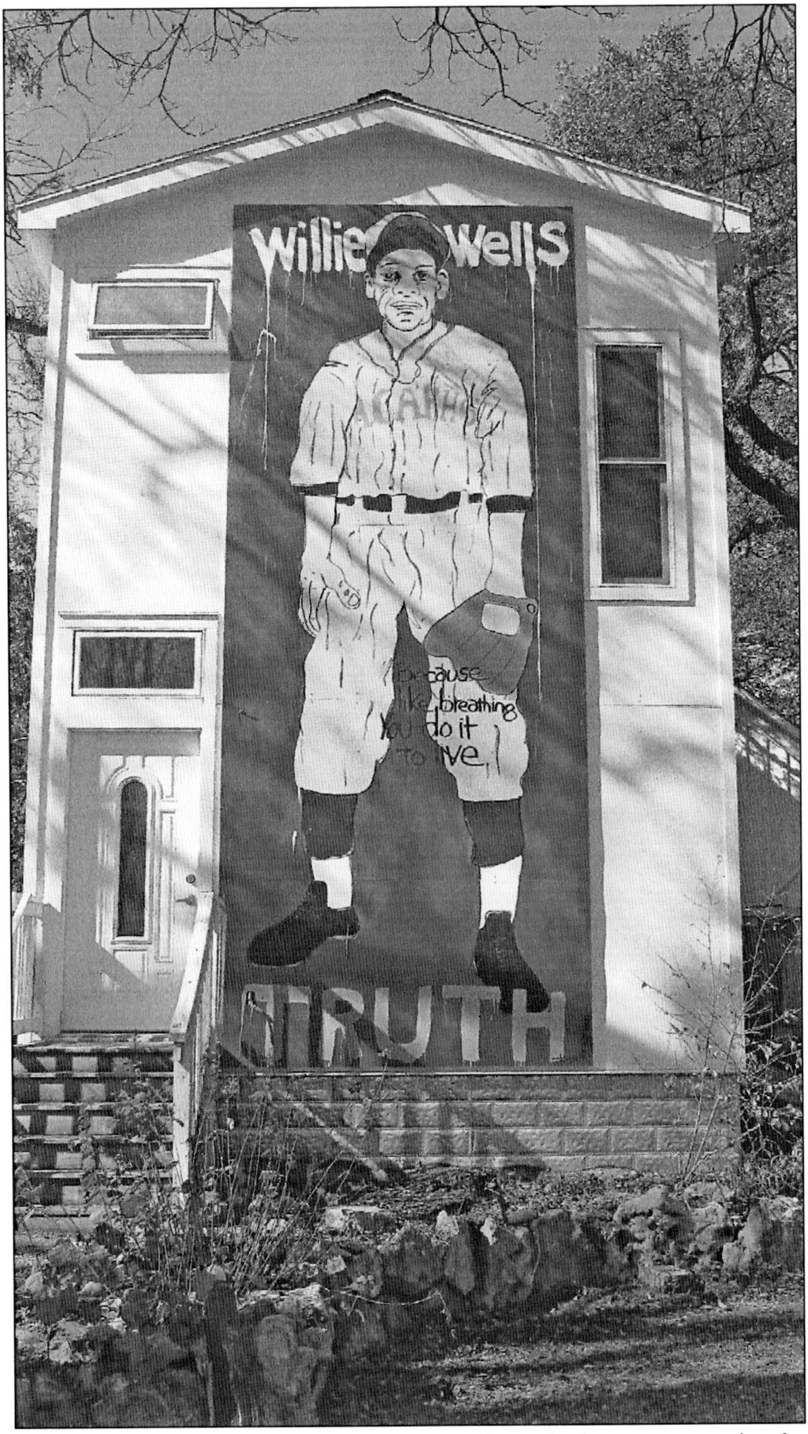

This mural of Mr. Wells in uniform was commissioned on the house next to his former home. Paul Johnson and residents Claire Huie and Rene Pinnell wanted to dedicate a major work of art celebrating Mr. Wells's accomplishments. The mural, which faces the alley behind both houses, reflects Mr. Wells's value to the larger Austin community.

Austin artist Tim Kerr, known for his murals and numerous portraits of historic figures, created the mural to honor and commemorate Willie Wells. This photograph of the artist in a moment of contemplation was taken at the January 7, 2012, dedication of the mural.

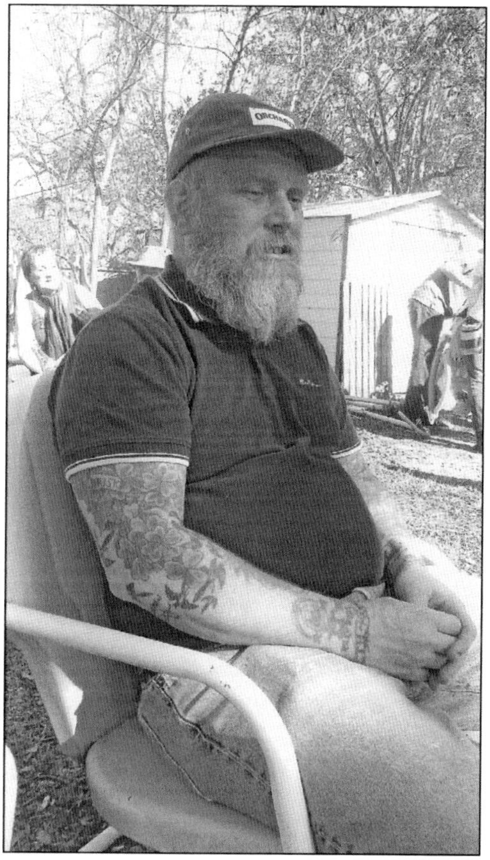

This view is from East Twelfth Street facing downtown. The capitol building can be seen in the distance. The clock, with the mural to its left, forms the entrance to the new neighborhood.

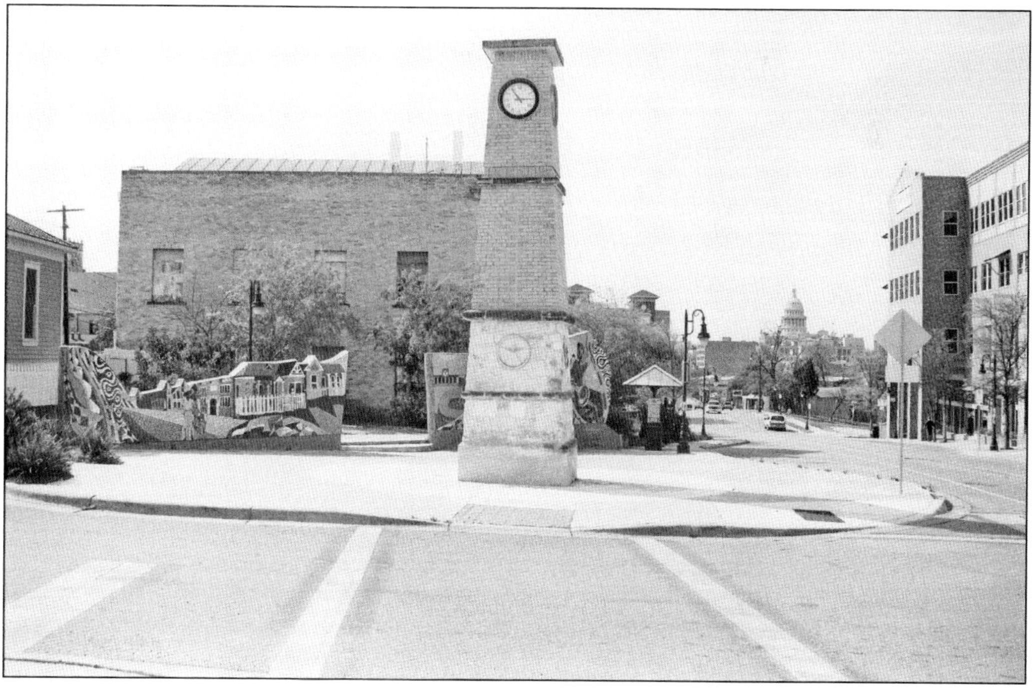

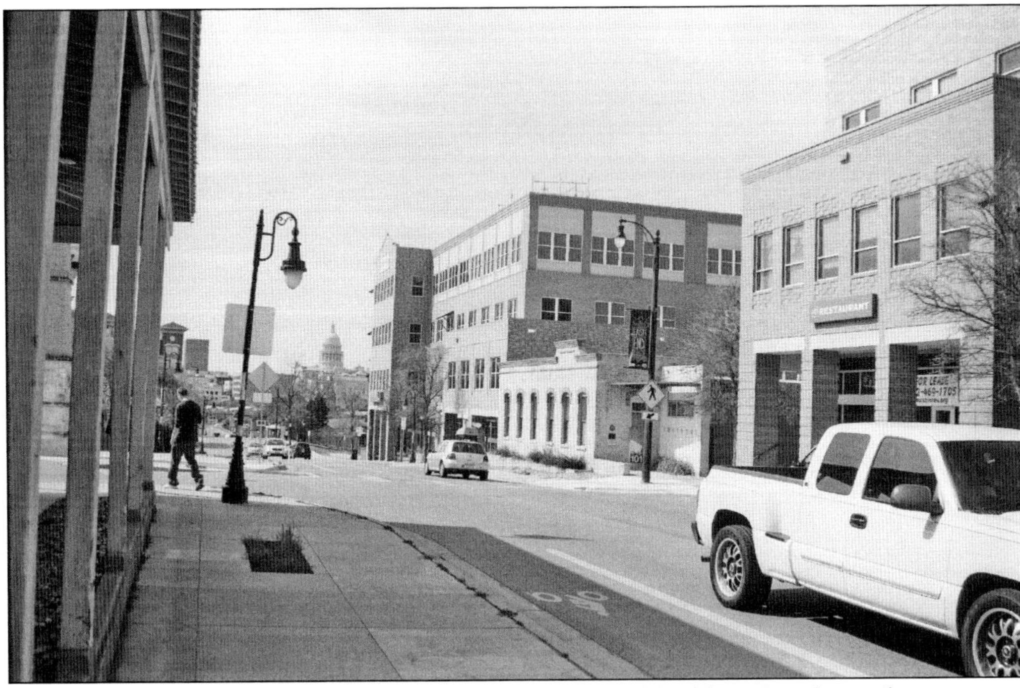

This view on East Twelfth Street is also facing the capitol building, but shows the new retail structures on the north side of the street. Some local African American businesspeople have set up shop in the new buildings.

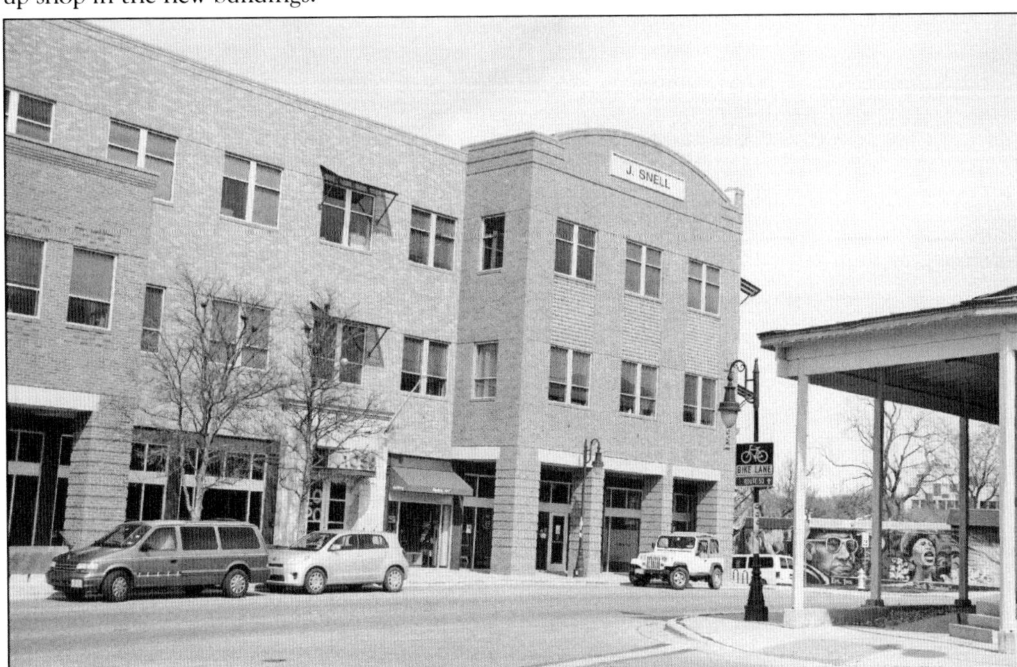

This is a photograph of the north side of East Twelfth Street taken from the south side, showing the new building constructed there. City and business offices are on the upper floors, and local retail is on the street level.

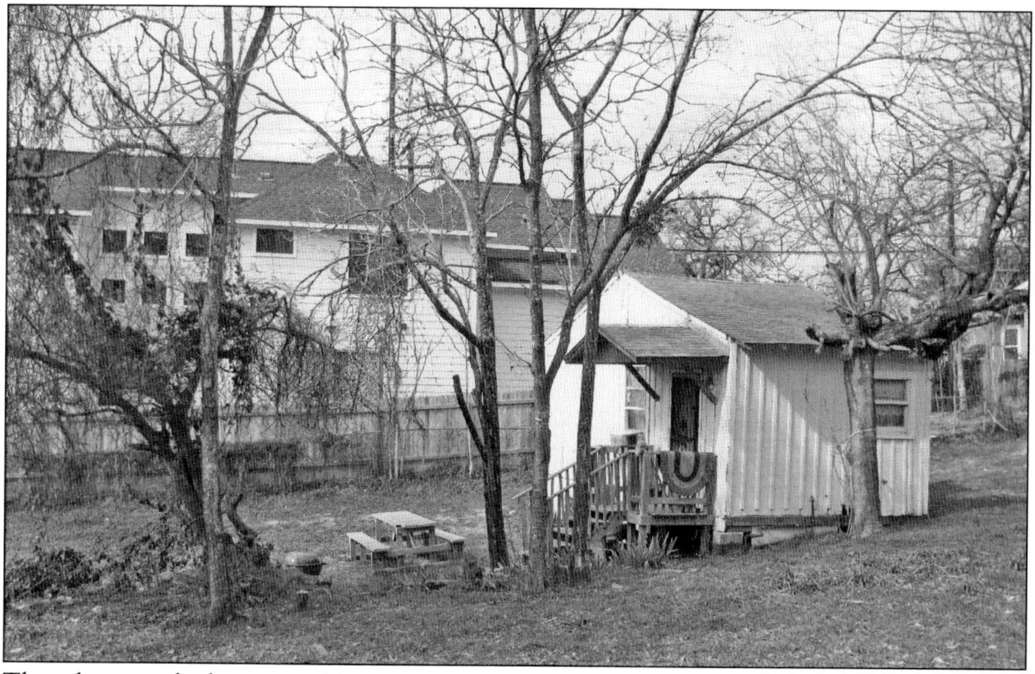

This photograph shows an old, traditional cottage as it would have existed in Rosewood at its inception.

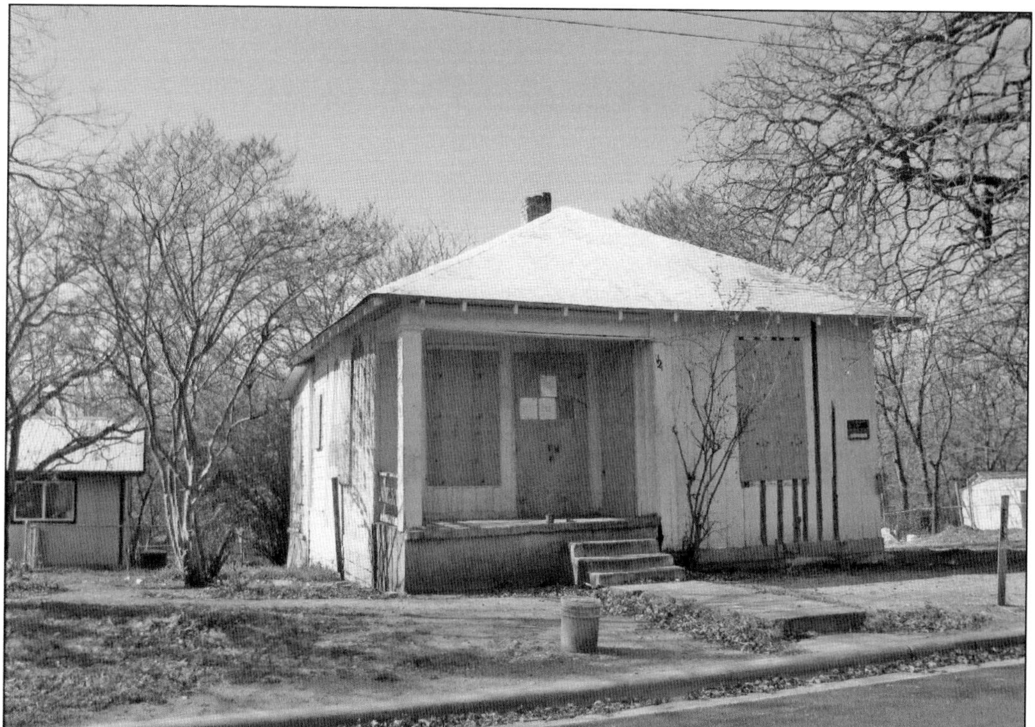

This photograph shows a traditional family home of the type that prevailed throughout Rosewood from the 1940s until the 2000s.

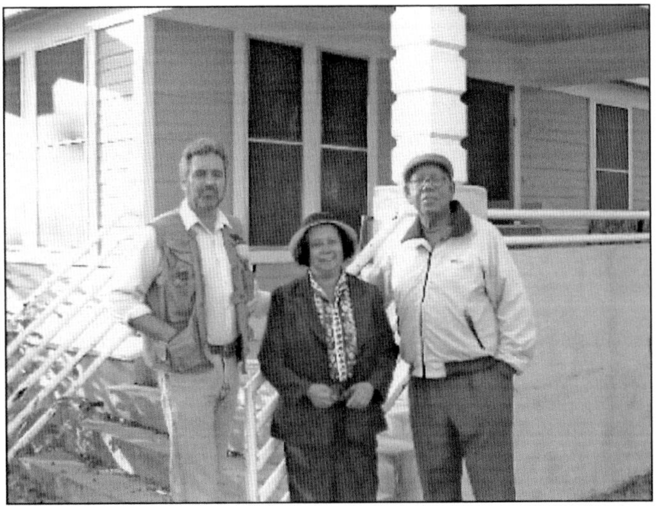

The Blackland Neighborhood, northwest of Rosewood, was encroached upon by the university multiple times. An attempt in 1980 was met with strong neighborhood opposition when the Blackland Neighborhood Association was organized under the leadership of Dr. Bo McCarver (left), Katherine Poole (center), and Charles Smith. The residents formed a nonprofit, Blackland Community Development Corporation (BCDC). (Courtesy of Dr. Bo McCarver.)

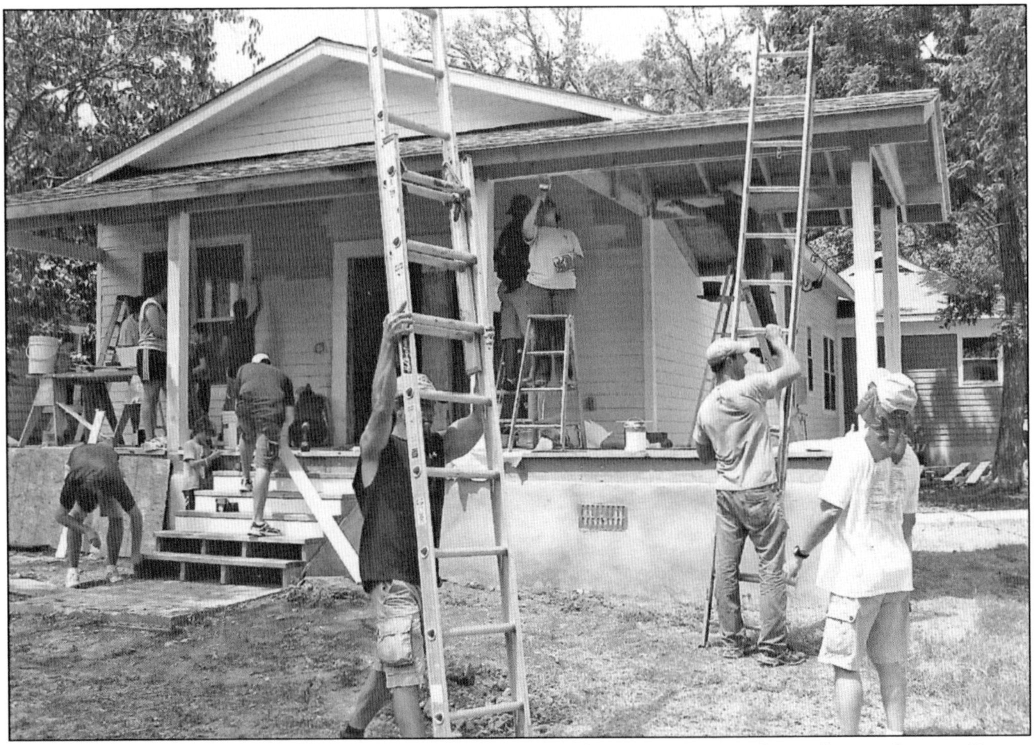

After a 12-year battle in the press, the university agreed to a permanent boundary at Leona Street that has held up, and relations between the residents and the university have improved. The university has donated several houses to the nonprofit, which have been rehabilitated with the help of volunteers and donations. In order to counter intense gentrification, the nonprofit has about 40 units scattered among the 25-block neighborhood. Housing for low-income households is increasingly scarce, so the Blackland CDC has adopted a policy of only renting its units to prevent resale to more affluent families. (Courtesy of Dr. Bo McCarver.)

The City of Austin established the Neighborhood Planning Team process throughout the city starting in 1999. Planning staff combined existing neighborhood associations into what they called "neighborhood planning areas" and tasked the resulting Neighborhood Planning Teams with spelling out a vision for their neighborhood, including approving a future land use map to guide developers and city staff desirous of building new and more dense projects within existing neighborhoods. The planning teams remained active after their plans were improved, and became the groups tasked with reviewing zoning requests prior to city council approval. The Rosewood plan was approved by the Austin City Council in 2000, and the Rosewood Neighborhood Contact Team (RNCT) consists of representatives of the six member neighborhoods and other entities.

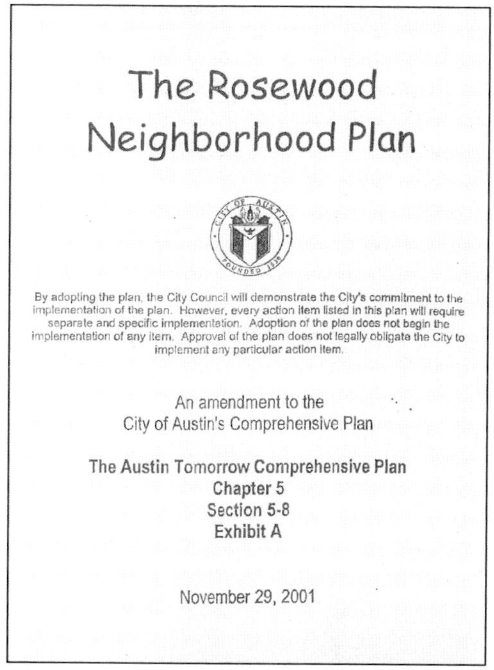

The Rosewood Neighborhood Plan

By adopting the plan, the City Council will demonstrate the City's commitment to the implementation of the plan. However, every action item listed in this plan will require separate and specific implementation. Adoption of the plan does not begin the implementation of any item. Approval of the plan does not legally obligate the City to implement any particular action item.

An amendment to the
City of Austin's Comprehensive Plan

The Austin Tomorrow Comprehensive Plan
Chapter 5
Section 5-8
Exhibit A

November 29, 2001

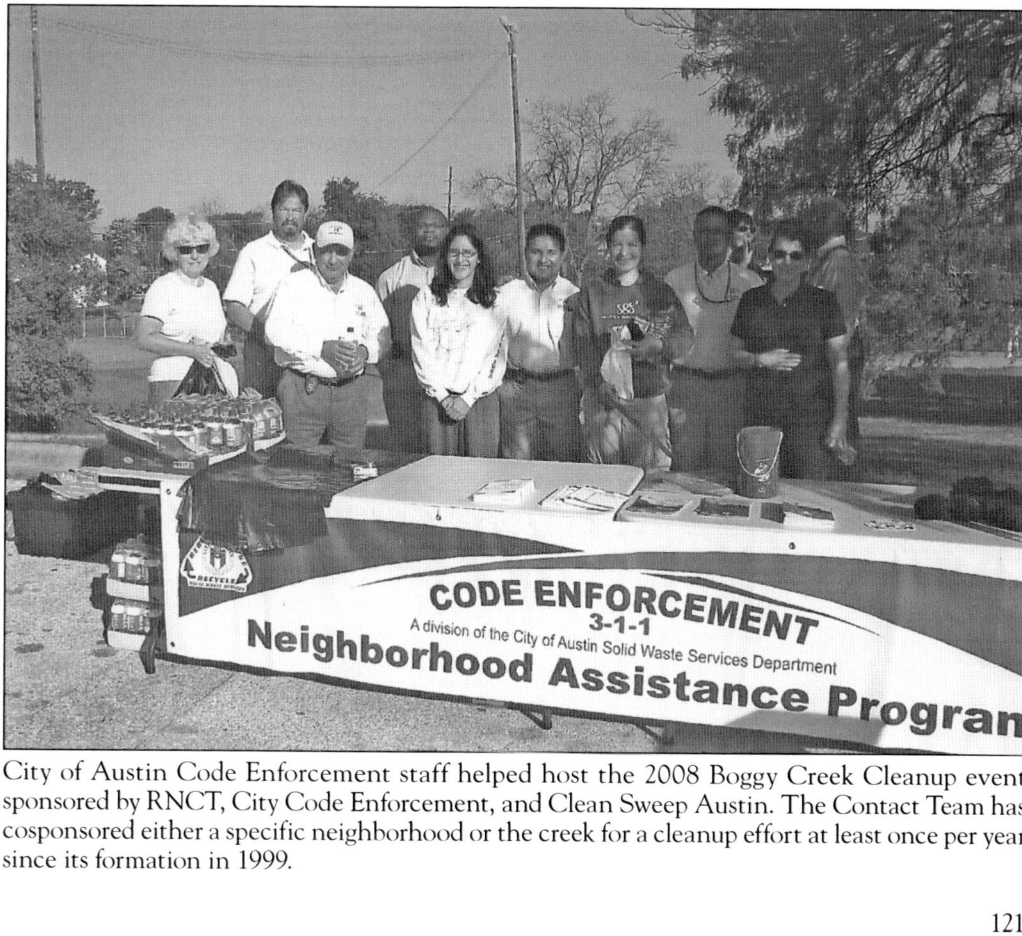

City of Austin Code Enforcement staff helped host the 2008 Boggy Creek Cleanup event sponsored by RNCT, City Code Enforcement, and Clean Sweep Austin. The Contact Team has cosponsored either a specific neighborhood or the creek for a cleanup effort at least once per year since its formation in 1999.

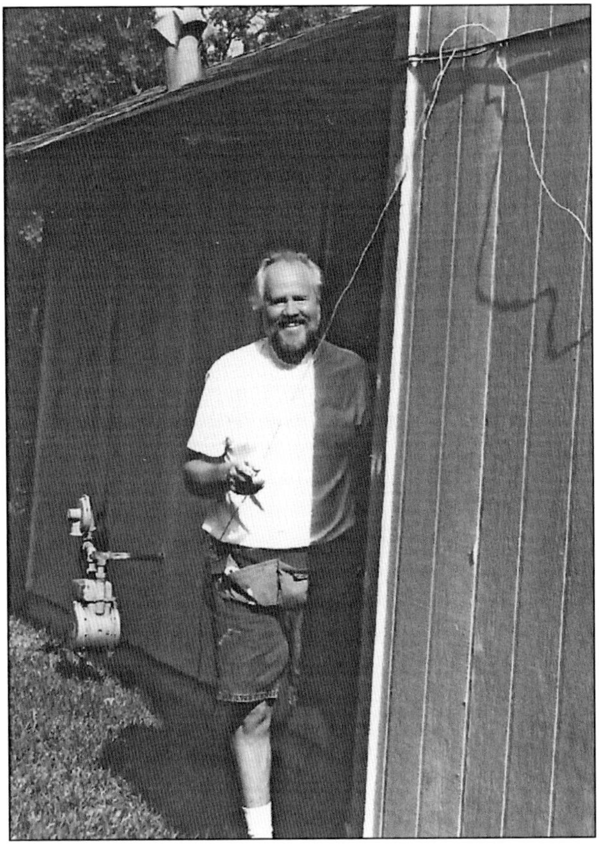

Richard Vogt, a home remodeler from Austin Heights (one of the neighborhoods in the Rosewood planning area) and member of the RNCT, helped repair and paint the home of a disabled neighbor, as shown here, as an RNCT project. Born and raised in Minnesota, Vogt joined the Army to fight in Vietnam at age 19. He was "Richard from Texas," the wise man of Elizabeth Gilbert's memoir *Eat, Pray, Love*, providing colorful homespun wisdom. After Mr. Vogt was a guest on *The Oprah Winfrey Show* and Oprah selected *Eat, Pray, Love* for her book club, it became a national best-seller. Mr. Vogt retired from contracting, and spoke at seminars and participated in spiritual events. He passed away suddenly in 2010.

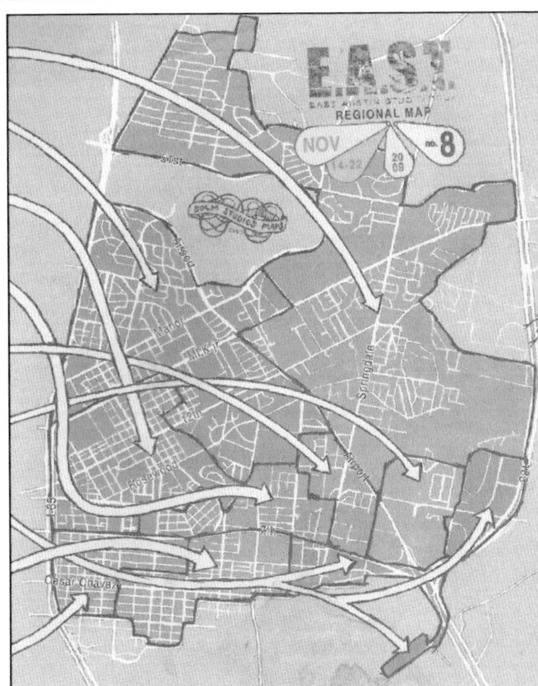

The East Austin Studio Tour (EAST) began in 2001. By the eighth annual event in 2009, people were invited to view the works of over 200 artists at 150 studios and galleries on the East Side, including several in Rosewood. According to EAST, "These remarkable artists comprise a wide range of disciplines, bound only by the common desire to work within a few square miles east of I-35, an area that has thoroughly established itself as the epicenter of visual art in Austin." (Courtesy of East Austin Studio Tour.)

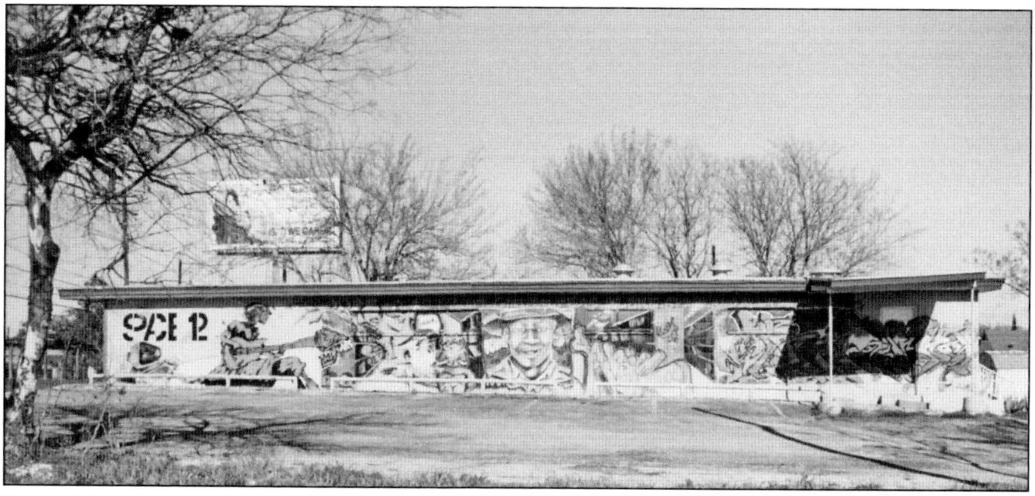

Space 12 is a center run by Austin City Spaces, a private, nonprofit organization that has as its goal to create spaces for community participation through collaborative efforts between local residents, businesses, and city and nonprofit organizations. Space 12 serves as home to The Cipher, Insidebooks Project, Vox Veniae, Mosaic, and recently the Coalition to Save Austin Urban Schools. It serves as a gallery and music venue as well as hosting neighborhood meetings, clothing swaps, and fundraisers.

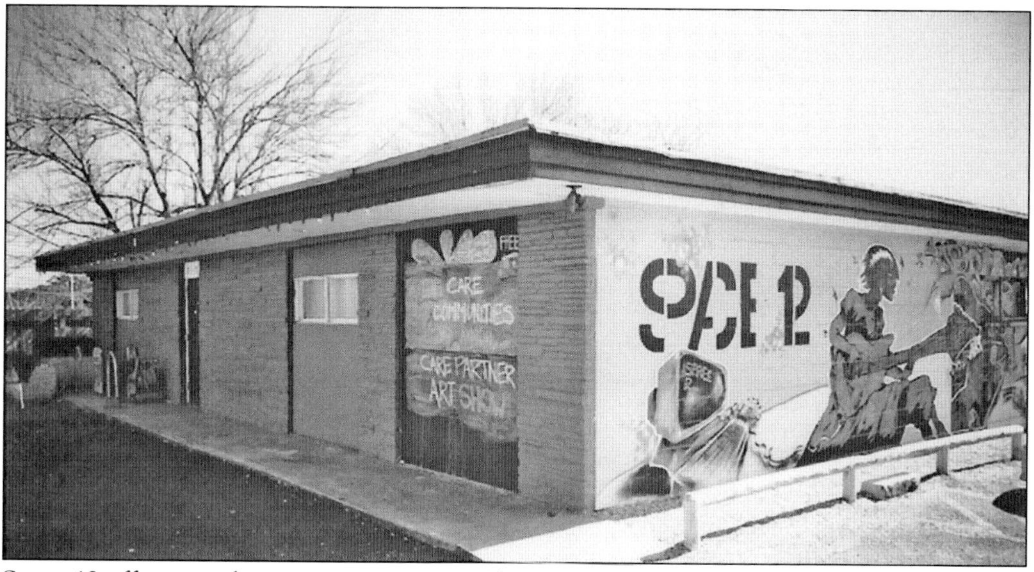

Space 12 offers a stark, positive contrast to Chester's Club, an after-hours club that was in the building for several years and sparked neighborhood protests to local police and the Texas Alcoholic Beverage Commission. Chester's was finally closed in 2007 when the city enacted an ordinance prohibiting such clubs. (Courtesy of Space 12.)

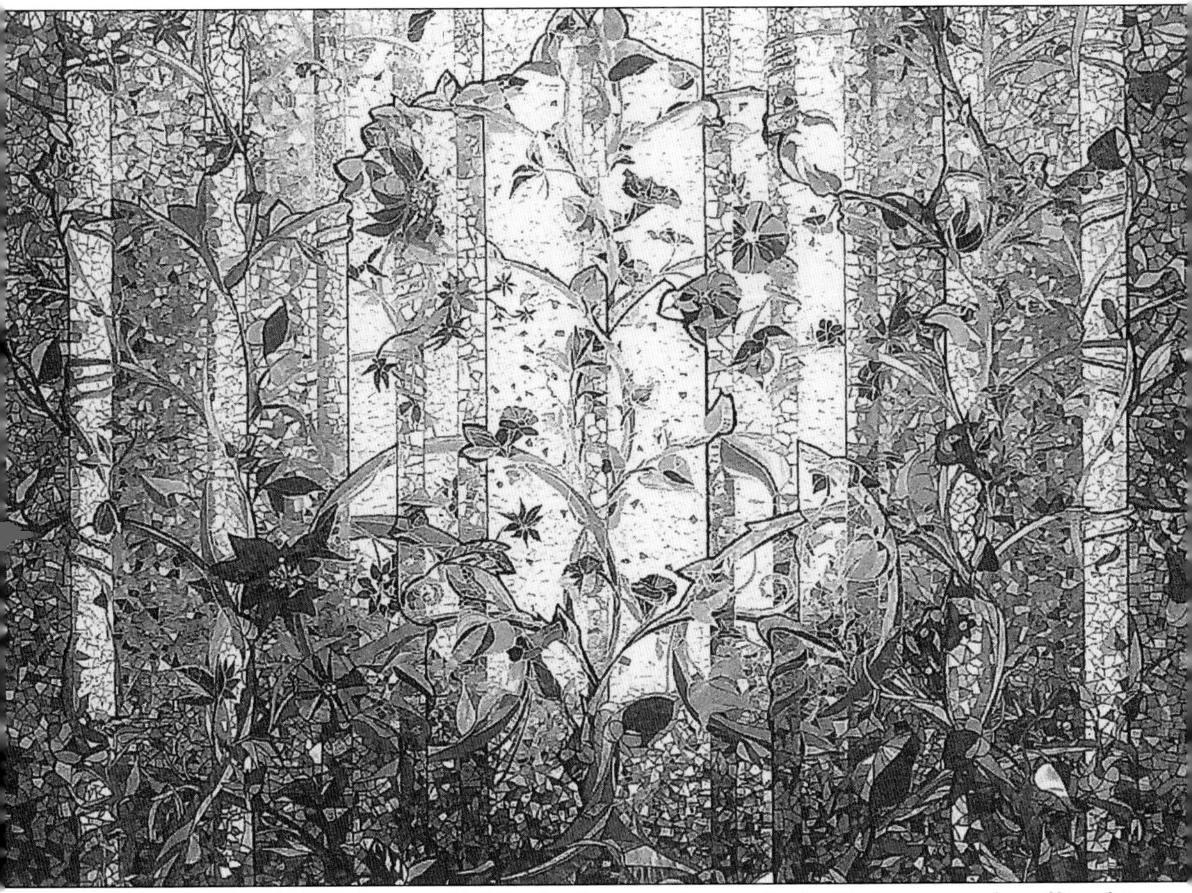

This mural, titled "Robertson Hill," is by Rosewood artist Ryah Christensen, who offers this background: "It is painfully clear that economic ambitions, served by blatant racism, played a leading role in every major Texas historical event, from the brutal War of Independence from Mexico, the relocation of Native Americans to the West, the annexation by the United States, the Civil War, and the struggle through the human rights movements of the 20th century." About the image, she says: "A Red Man, a Brown Man, a Black Man, and a White Man lie buried in the four difficult soils of East Austin—sandy loam, caliche, limestone, and blackland prairie. From their hearts each spring two hardy, willful vines . . . the Morning Glory, the Passion Flower, the Trumpet Creeper, and the Cross vine. Each man's vines entwine with every other man's vines, forming a complicated lattice of twists and knots whose ascendance appear to build a visible, yet surreally permeable wall of bloom, and leaf, and light." (Courtesy of Ryah Christensen.)

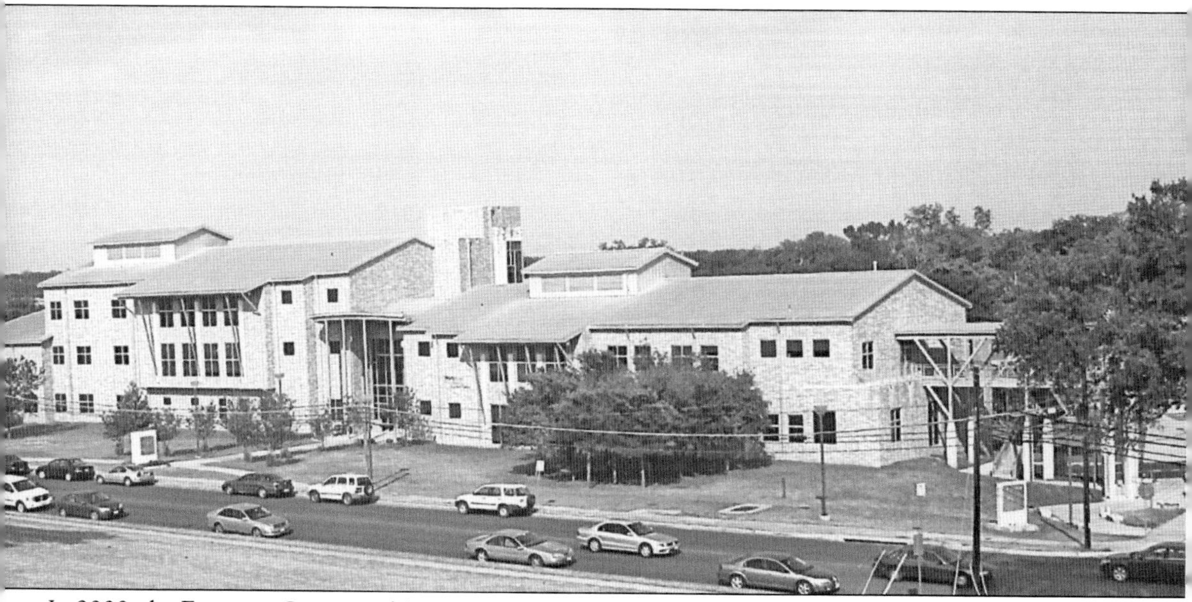

In 2000, the Eastview Campus of Austin Community College (ACC) opened at 3401 Webberville Road, on vacant land that had flooded regularly during the 1940s and 1950s, just east of and adjacent to the Rosewood neighborhood. The property had become an unofficial dump and was an eyesore prior to the construction of the new campus. This new campus replaced the temporary home that ACC had in the old Anderson High School.

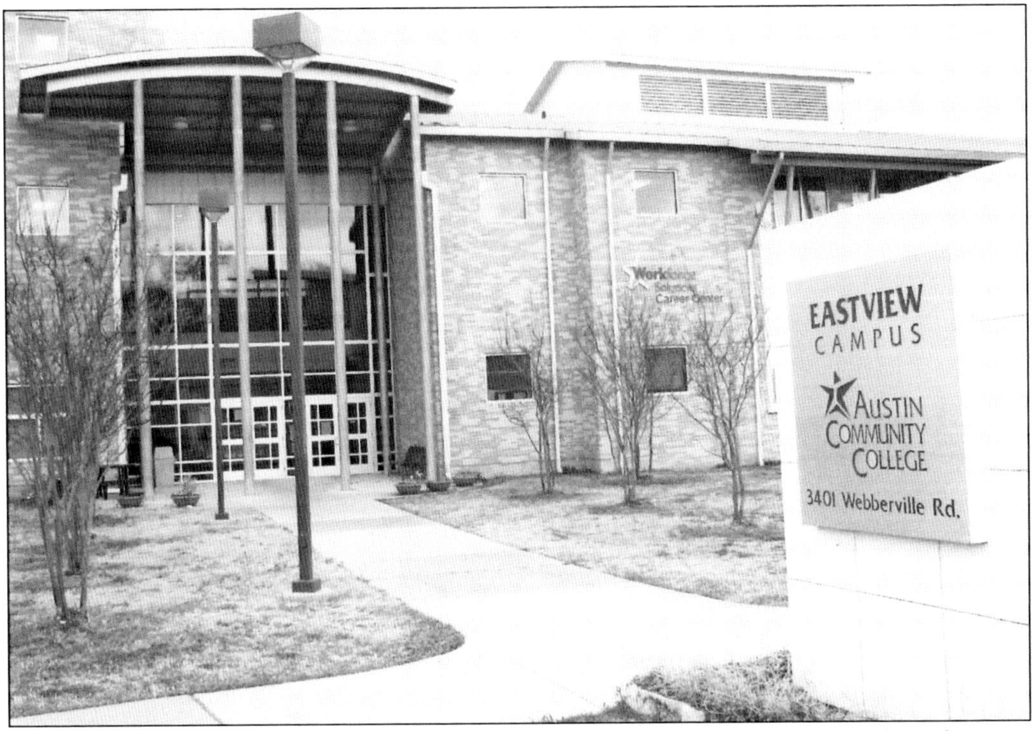

Eastview offers courses that satisfy freshman and sophomore requirements for transfer to four-year institutions as well as a variety of technical certificate and associate degree programs that prepare students for immediate employment. Technical programs offered at Eastview include health sciences, biotechnology, child development, computer studies, criminal justice, and culinary arts. There is also a One-Stop Workforce Center located on the campus, providing career advising and job placement services for ACC students and other interested parties.

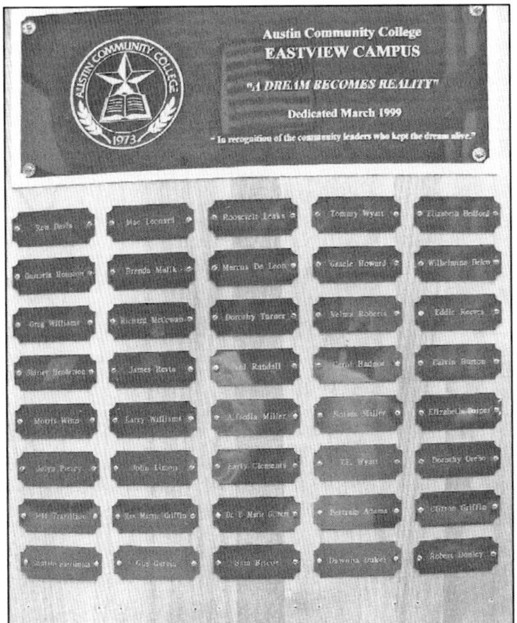

The dedication plaque in the administration building of ACC Eastview includes the names of a number of the people featured in this book, including Rev. Marvin Griffin, Dorothy Turner, Tommy Wyatt, Velma Roberts, Rep. Dawnna Dukes, Rep. Wilhelmina Delco, Elizabeth Snipes, and Jolyn Piercy. Their struggles to continuously improve Rosewood and other East Austin neighborhoods were rewarded in March 1999 with the dedication of ACC Eastview.

Bibliography

1906 Streetcar Boycott, Black in the Past. Directed and edited by K. Anoa Monsho, narrated by Karen Riles. Austin, TX: Austin History Center, Austin Public Library, 2005.

Brewer, J. Mason. *A Pictorial and Historical Souvenir of Negro Life in Austin, Texas 1950–1951*. 1951.

City of Austin Human Relations Department, "Housing Patterns Study of Austin, Texas, 1980."

E.A.S.T. "East Austin Studio Tour." Austin, TX: American Printing and Milling, 2009.

Hardy-Heck-Moore and Myers, Inc. "Survey Report, City of Austin, Texas Historic Resources Survey of East Austin, Texas." Austin: TX, 2000.

Johnson, Lyndon Baines. "Tarnish on the Violet Crown, Extension of Remarks of Hon. Morris Sheppard of Texas in the Senate of the United States, February 3, 1938." Appendix to the Congressional Record. Washington, DC: US Government Printing Office, 1938.

Jones, Carolyn L. *Volma . . . My Journey: One Man's Impact on the Civil Rights Movement in Austin, Texas*. Austin, TX: Eakin Press, 1998.

Koch and Fowler, Consulting Engineers. "A City Plan for Austin." Dallas, 1928.

McCarver, Bo. *The Blackland Miracle*. PhD Dissertation. Austin: University of Texas, 1995.

Perry, Wilhelmina E. and August N. Swain. *The Huston-Tillotson University Legacy: A Historical Treasure*. Austin, TX: Morgan Printing, 2007.

Rameau, Max. *Take Back the Land: Land, Gentrification and the Umoja Village Shantytown*. Miami, FL: Nia Press, 2008.

Thompson, Karen R. and Kathy R. Howell. *Austin, Texas*. Charleston, SC: Arcadia Publishing, 2000.

Tietz, Jeff. "East Austin's Dorothy Turner." *Tejas* Winter 1993-1994: 20–21.

White, Louie. *A Pictorial History of Black Policemen Who Have Served in the Austin Police Department 1871–1982*. Austin, TX: Full Service Printing and Binding, 1982.